The Empire Writes Back

Theory and practice in
post-colonial literatures

BILL ASHCROFT, GARETH GRIFFITHS,
AND HELEN TIFFIN

ROUTLEDGE

London and New York

First published 1989
by Routledge
11 New Fetter Lane, London EC4P 4EE
29 West 35th Street, New York, NY 10001
Reprinted 1991 (twice), 1993 (twice), 1994

© 1989 Bill Ashcroft, Gareth Griffiths, and Helen Tiffin

Typeset by Rowland Phototypesetting Ltd
Bury St Edmunds, Suffolk
Printed in England by Clays Ltd, St Ives plc

British Library Cataloguing in Publication Data

Ashcroft, Bill, *et al.*
The Empire Writes Back
Theory and practice in post-colonial
literatures – (New accents)
1. English literature. Commonwealth writers,
1900 – Critical studies
I. Title   II. Griffiths, Gareth,
III. Tiffin, Helen   IV. Series
820.9 9171241

Library of Congress Cataloguing in Publication Data

Ashcroft, Bill, 1946–
The empire writes back: theory and practice in post-colonial
literatures/by Bill Ashcroft, Gareth Griffiths, and Helen Tiffin.
p.   cm – (New accents)
Bibliography: p. 00
1. English literature – Commonwealth of Nations authors – History
and criticism. 2. English literature – 20th century – History and
criticism. 3. Commonwealth of Nations in literature.
4. Decolonization in
literature 5. Colonies in literature.
I. Griffiths, Gareth, 1943– . II. Tiffin, Helen, III. Title.
IV. Series: New accents (Routledge (Firm))
PR9080.A85   1989
820′.9′9171241 – dc19

ISBN 0-415-01209-0

Contents

General editor's preface

How can we recognise or deal with the new? Any equipment we bring to the task will have been designed to engage with the old: it will look for and identify extensions and developments of what we already know. To some degree the unprecedented will always be unthinkable.

The *New Accents* series has made its own wary negotiation around that paradox, turning it, over the years, into the central concern of a continuing project. We are obliged, of course, to be bold. Change is our proclaimed business, innovation our announced quarry, the accents of the future the language in which we deal. So we have sought, and still seek, to confront and respond to those developments to literary studies that seem crucial aspects of the tidal waves of transformation that continue to sweep across our culture. Areas such as structuralism, post-structuralism, feminism, marxism, semiotics, subculture, deconstruction, dialogism, post-modernism, and the new attention to the nature and modes of language, politics and way of life that these bring, have already been the primary concern of a large number of our volumes. Their 'nuts and bolts' exposition of the issues at stake in new ways of writing texts and new ways of reading them has proved an effective stratagem against perplexity.

But the question of what 'texts' are or may be has also

become more and more complex. It is not just the impact of electronic modes of communication, such as computer networks and data banks, that has forced us to revise our sense of the sort of material to which the process called 'reading' may apply. Satellite television and supersonic travel have eroded the traditional capacities of time and space to confirm prejudice, reinforce ignorance, and conceal significant difference. Ways of life and cultural practices of which we had barely heard can now be set compellingly beside – can even confront – our own. The effect is to make us ponder the culture we have inherited; to see it, perhaps for the first time, as an intricate, continuing construction. And that means that we can also begin to see, and to question, those arrangements of foregrounding and backgrounding, of stressing and repressing, of placing at the centre and of restricting to the periphery, that give our own way of life its distinctive character.

Small wonder if, nowadays, we frequently find ourselves at the boundaries of the precedented and at the limit of the thinkable: peering into an abyss out of which there begin to lurch awkwardly-formed monsters with unaccountable – yet unavoidable – demands on our attention. These may involve unnerving styles of narrative, unsettling notions of 'history', unphilosophical ideas about 'philosophy', even unchildish views of 'comics', to say nothing of a host of barely respectable activities for which we have no reassuring names.

In this situation, straightforward elucidation, careful unpicking, informative bibliographies, can offer positive help, and each *New Accents* volume will continue to include these. But if the project of closely scrutinising the new remains nonetheless a disconcerting one, there are still overwhelming reasons for giving it all the consideration we can muster. The unthinkable, after all, is that which covertly shapes our thoughts.

TERENCE HAWKES

. . . the Empire writes back to the Centre . . .
(Salman Rushdie)

Acknowledgements

For help and generous support we should like to thank our partners, Judy, Carolyn, and Chris.

For generous help in finding material, tracing references, and generally making this book less inadequate than it remains we want to thank many people, but in particular Alan Lawson, David Moody, and Stephen Slemon.

Introduction

More than three-quarters of the people living in the world today
have had their lives shaped by the experience of colonialism. It
is easy to see how important this has been in the political and
economic spheres, but its general influence on the perceptual
frameworks of contemporary peoples is often less evident. Literature offers one of the most important ways in which these new
perceptions are expressed and it is in their writing, and through
other arts such as painting, sculpture, music, and dance that the
day-to-day realities experienced by colonized peoples have been
most powerfully encoded and so profoundly influential.

What are post-colonial literatures?

This book is concerned with writing by those peoples formerly
colonized by Britain, though much of what it deals with is of
interest and relevance to countries colonized by other European
powers, such as France, Portugal, and Spain. The semantic
basis of the term 'post-colonial' might seem to suggest a concern
only with the national culture after the departure of the imperial
power. It has occasionally been employed in some earlier work
in the area to distinguish between the periods before and after
independence ('colonial period' and 'post-colonial period'), for
example, in constructing national literary histories, or in sug-

rative studies between stages in those histories.
aking, though, the term 'colonial' has been used
d before independence and a term indicating a
ting, such as 'modern Canadian writing' or 'recent
in literature' has been employed to distinguish the
perio er independence.

We use the term 'post-colonial', however, to cover all the culture affected by the imperial process from the moment of colonization to the present day. This is because there is a continuity of preoccupations throughout the historical process initiated by European imperial aggression. We also suggest that it is most appropriate as the term for the new cross-cultural criticism which has emerged in recent years and for the discourse through which this is constituted. In this sense this book is concerned with the world as it exists during and after the period of European imperial domination and the effects of this on contemporary literatures.

So the literatures of African countries, Australia, Bangladesh, Canada, Caribbean countries, India, Malaysia, Malta, New Zealand, Pakistan, Singapore, South Pacific Island countries, and Sri Lanka are all post-colonial literatures. The literature of the USA should also be placed in this category. Perhaps because of its current position of power, and the neo-colonizing role it has played, its post-colonial nature has not been generally recognized. But its relationship with the metropolitan centre as it evolved over the last two centuries has been paradigmatic for post-colonial literatures everywhere. What each of these literatures has in common beyond their special and distinctive regional characteristics is that they emerged in their present form out of the experience of colonization and asserted themselves by foregrounding the tension with the imperial power, and by emphasizing their differences from the assumptions of the imperial centre. It is this which makes them distinctively post-colonial.

Post-colonial literatures and English Studies

The study of English has always been a densely political and cultural phenomenon, a practice in which language and literature have both been called into the service of a profound and embracing nationalism. The development of English as a privileged academic subject in nineteenth-century Britain – finally confirmed by its inclusion in the syllabuses of Oxford and Cambridge, and re-affirmed in the 1921 Newbolt Report – came about as part of an attempt to replace the Classics at the heart of the intellectual enterprise of nineteenth-century humanistic studies. From the beginning, proponents of English as a discipline linked its methodology to that of the Classics, with its emphasis on scholarship, philology, and historical study – the fixing of texts in historical time and the perpetual search for the determinants of a single, unified, and agreed meaning.

The historical moment which saw the emergence of 'English' as an academic discipline also produced the nineteenth-century colonial form of imperialism (Batsleer *et al.* 1985: 14, 19–25). Gauri Viswanathan has presented strong arguments for relating the 'institutionalisation and subsequent valorisation of English literary study [to] a shape and an ideological content developed in the colonial context', and specifically as it developed in India, where:

> British colonial administrators, provoked by missionaries on the one hand and fears of native insubordination on the other, discovered an ally in English literature to support them in maintaining control of the natives under the guise of a liberal education.
>
> (Viswanathan 1987: 17)

It can be argued that the study of English and the growth of Empire proceeded from a single ideological climate and that the development of the one is intrinsically bound up with the development of the other, both at the level of simple utility (as propaganda for instance) and at the unconscious level, where it leads to the naturalizing of constructed values (e.g. civilization, humanity, etc.) which, conversely, established 'savagery', 'native', 'primitive', as their antitheses and as the object of a reforming zeal.[1]

A 'privileging norm' was enthroned at the heart of the formation of English Studies as a template for the denial of the value of the 'peripheral', the 'marginal', the 'uncanonized'. Literature was made as central to the cultural enterprise of Empire as the monarchy was to its political formation. So when elements of the periphery and margin threatened the exclusive claims of the centre they were rapidly incorporated. This was a process, in Edward Said's terms, of conscious affiliation proceeding under the guise of filiation (Said 1984), that is, a mimicry of the centre proceeding from a desire not only to be accepted but to be adopted and absorbed. It caused those from the periphery to immerse themselves in the imported culture, denying their origins in an attempt to become 'more English than the English'. We see examples of this in such writers as Henry James and T.S. Eliot.

As post-colonial societies sought to establish their difference from Britain, the response of those who recognized this complicity between language, education, and cultural incorporation was to break the link between language and literary study by dividing 'English' departments in universities into separate schools of Linguistics and of Literature, both of which tended to view their project within a national or international context. Ngugi's essay 'On the abolition of the English department' (Ngugi 1972) is an illuminating account of the particular arguments involved in Africa. John Docker's essay, 'The neocolonial assumption in the university teaching of English' (Tiffin 1978: 26–31), addresses similar problems in the settler colony context, describing a situation in which, in contrast to Kenya, little genuine decolonization is yet in sight. As Docker's critique makes clear, in most post-colonial nations (including the West Indies and India) the nexus of power involving literature, language, and a dominant British culture has strongly resisted attempts to dismantle it. Even after such attempts began to succeed, the canonical nature and unquestioned status of the works of the English literary tradition and the values they incorporated remained potent in the cultural formation and the ideological institutions of education and literature. Nevertheless, the development of the post-colonial literatures has necessitated a questioning of many of the assumptions on which the study of 'English' was based.

Development of post-colonial literatures

Post-colonial literatures developed through several stages which can be seen to correspond to stages both of national or regional consciousness and of the project of asserting difference from the imperial centre. During the imperial period writing in the language of the imperial centre is inevitably, of course, produced by a literate elite whose primary identification is with the colonizing power. Thus the first texts produced in the colonies in the new language are frequently produced by 'representatives' of the imperial power; for example, gentrified settlers (Wentworth's 'Australia'), travellers and sightseers (Froude's *Oceana*, and his *The English in the West Indies*, or the travel diaries of Mary Kingsley), or the Anglo-Indian and West African administrators, soldiers, and 'boxwallahs', and, even more frequently, their memsahibs (volumes of memoirs).

Such texts can never form the basis for an indigenous culture nor can they be integrated in any way with the culture which already exists in the countries invaded. Despite their detailed reportage of landscape, custom, and language, they inevitably privilege the centre, emphasizing the 'home' over the 'native', the 'metropolitan' over the 'provincial' or 'colonial', and so forth. At a deeper level their claim to objectivity simply serves to hide the imperial discourse within which they are created. That this is true of even the consciously literary works which emerge from this moment can be illustrated by the poems and stories of Rudyard Kipling. For example, in the well-known poem 'Christmas in India' the evocative description of a Christmas day in the heat of India is contextualized by invoking its absent English counterpart. Apparently it is only through this absent and enabling signifier that the Indian daily reality can acquire legitimacy as a subject of literary discourse.

The second stage of production within the evolving discourse of the post-colonial is the literature produced 'under imperial licence' by 'natives' or 'outcasts', for instance the large body of poetry and prose produced in the nineteenth century by the English educated Indian upper class, or African 'missionary literature' (e.g. Thomas Mofolo's *Chaka*). The producers signify by the very fact of writing in the language of the dominant culture that they have temporarily or permanently entered a specific and privileged class endowed with the language, education, and leisure necessary to produce such works. The Australian novel *Ralph Rashleigh*, now known to have been written by the convict James Tucker, is a case in point. Tucker, an educated man, wrote *Rashleigh* as a 'special' (a privileged convict) whilst working at the penal settlement at Port Macquarie as storekeeper to the superintendent. Written on government paper with government ink and pens, the novel was clearly produced with the aid and support of the superintendent. Tucker had momentarily gained access to the privilege of literature. Significantly, the moment of privilege did not last and he died in poverty at the age of fifty-eight at Liverpool asylum in Sydney.

It is characteristic of these early post-colonial texts that the potential for subversion in their themes cannot be fully realized. Although they deal with such powerful material as the brutality of the convict system (Tucker's *Rashleigh*), the historical potency of the supplanted and denigrated native cultures (Mofolo's *Chaka*), or the existence of a rich cultural heritage older and more extensive than that of Europe (any of many nineteenth-century Indo-Anglian poets, such as Ram Sharma) they are prevented from fully exploring their anti-imperial potential. Both the available discourse and the material conditions of production for literature in these early post-colonial societies restrain this possibility. The institution of 'Literature' in the colony is under the direct control of the imperial ruling class who alone license the acceptable form and permit the publication and distribution of the resulting work. So, texts of this kind come into being within the constraints of a discourse and the institutional practice of a patronage system which limits and undercuts their assertion of a different perspective. The development of independent literatures depended upon the abrogation of this constraining power and the appropriation of language and writing for new and distinctive usages. Such an appropriation is clearly the most significant feature in the emergence of modern post-colonial literatures (see chs 2 and 3).

Hegemony

Why should post-colonial societies continue to engage with the imperial experience? Since all the post-colonial societies we discuss have achieved political independence, why is the issue of coloniality still relevant at all? This question of why the empire needs to write back to a centre once the imperial structure has been dismantled in political terms is an important one. Britain, like the other dominant colonial powers of the nineteenth century, has been relegated to a relatively minor place in international affairs. In the spheres of politics and economics, and increasingly in the vital new area of the mass media, Britain and the other European imperial powers have been superseded by the emergent powers of the USA and the USSR. Nevertheless, through the literary canon, the body of British texts which all too frequently still acts as a touchstone of taste and value, and through RS-English (Received Standard English), which asserts the English of south-east England as a universal norm, the weight of antiquity continues to dominate cultural production in much of the post-colonial world. This cultural hegemony has been maintained through canonical assumptions about literary activity, and through attitudes to post-colonial literatures which identify them as isolated national off-shoots of English literature, and which therefore relegate them to marginal and subordinate positions. More recently, as the range and strength of these literatures has become undeniable, a process of incorporation has begun in which, employing Eurocentric standards of judgement, the centre has sought to claim those works and writers of which it approves as British.[2] In all these respects the parallel between the situation of post-colonial writing and that of feminist writing is striking (see ch. 5).

Language

One of the main features of imperial oppression is control over language. The imperial education system installs a 'standard' version of the metropolitan language as the norm, and marginalizes all 'variants' as impurities. As a character in Mrs Campbell Praed's nineteenth-century Australian novel *Policy and Passion* puts it, 'To be *colonial* is to talk Australian slang; to be . . . everything that is abominable' (Campbell Praed 1881:154). Language becomes the medium through which a hierarchical structure of power is perpetuated, and the medium through which conceptions of 'truth', 'order', and 'reality' become established. Such power is rejected in the emergence of an effective post-colonial voice. For this reason, the discussion of post-colonial writing which follows is largely a discussion of the process by which the language, with its power, and the writing, with its signification of authority, has been wrested from the dominant European culture.

In order to focus on the complex ways in which the English language has been used in these societies, and to indicate their own sense of difference, we distinguish in this account between the 'standard' British English inherited from the empire and the english which the language has become in post-colonial countries. Though British imperialism resulted in the spread of a language, English, across the globe, the english of Jamaicans is not the english of Canadians, Maoris, or Kenyans. We need to distinguish between what is proposed as a standard code, English (the language of the erstwhile imperial centre), and the linguistic code, english, which has been transformed and subverted into several distinctive varieties throughout the world. For this reason the distinction between English and english will be used throughout our text as an indication of the various ways in which the language has been employed by different linguistic communities in the post-colonial world.[3]

The use of these terms asserts the fact that a continuum exists between the various linguistic practices which constitute english usage in the modern world. Although linguistically the links between English and the various post-colonial englishes in use today can be seen as unbroken, the political reality is that English sets itself apart from all other 'lesser' variants and so demands to be interrogated about its claim to this special status.

In practice the history of this distinction between English and english has been between the claims of a powerful 'centre' and a multitude of intersecting usages designated as 'peripheries'. The language of these 'peripheries' was shaped by an oppressive discourse of power. Yet they have been the site of some of the most exciting and innovative literatures of the modern period and this has, at least in part, been the result of the energies uncovered by the political tension between the idea of a normative code and a variety of regional usages.

Place and displacement

A major feature of post-colonial literatures is the concern with place and displacement. It is here that the special post-colonial

crisis of identity comes into being; the concern with the development or recovery of an effective identifying relationship between
self and place. Indeed, critics such as D. E. S. Maxwell have
made this the defining model of post-coloniality (see ch. 1). A
valid and active sense of self may have been eroded by *dislocation*,
resulting from migration, the experience of enslavement, transportation, or 'voluntary' removal for indentured labour. Or it
may have been destroyed by *cultural denigration*, the conscious
and unconscious oppression of the indigenous personality and
culture by a supposedly superior racial or cultural model. The
dialectic of place and displacement is always a feature of
post-colonial societies whether these have been created by a
process of settlement, intervention, or a mixture of the two.
Beyond their historical and cultural differences, place, displacement, and a pervasive concern with the myths of identity and
authenticity are a feature common to all post-colonial literatures in english.

The alienation of vision and the crisis in self-image which this
displacement produces is as frequently found in the accounts of
Canadian 'free settlers' as of Australian convicts, Fijian–Indian
or Trinidadian–Indian indentured labourers, West Indian
slaves, or forcibly colonized Nigerians or Bengalis. Although
this is pragmatically demonstrable from a wide range of texts, it
is difficult to account for by theories which see this social and
linguistic alienation as resulting only from overtly oppressive
forms of colonization such as slavery or conquest. An adequate
account of this practice must go beyond the usual categories of
social alienation such as master/slave; free/bonded; ruler/
ruled, however important and widespread these may be in
post-colonial cultures. After all, why should the free settler,
formally unconstrained, and theoretically free to continue in the
possession and practice of 'Englishness', also show clear signs
of alienation even within the first generation of settlement,
and manifest a tendency to seek an alternative, differentiated
identity?

The most widely shared discursive practice within which this
alienation can be identified is the construction of 'place'. The
gap which opens between the experience of place and the
language available to describe it forms a classic and all-
pervasive feature of post-colonial texts. This gap occurs for

those whose language seems inadequate to describe a new place, for those whose language is systematically destroyed by enslavement, and for those whose language has been rendered unprivileged by the imposition of the language of a colonizing power. Some admixture of one or other of these models can describe the situation of all post-colonial societies. In each case a condition of alienation is inevitable until the colonizing language has been replaced or appropriated as english.

That imperialism results in a profound linguistic alienation is obviously the case in cultures in which a pre-colonial culture is suppressed by military conquest or enslavement. So, for example, an Indian writer like Raja Rao or a Nigerian writer such as Chinua Achebe have needed to transform the language, to use it in a different way in its new context and so, as Achebe says, quoting James Baldwin, make it 'bear the burden' of their experience (Achebe 1975: 62). Although Rao and Achebe write from their own place and so have not suffered a literal geographical displacement, they have to overcome an imposed gap resulting from the linguistic displacement of the pre-colonial language by English. This process occurs within a more comprehensive discourse of place and displacement in the wider post-colonial context. Such alienation is shared by those whose possession of English is indisputably 'native' (in the sense of being possessed from birth) yet who begin to feel alienated within its practice once its vocabulary, categories, and codes are felt to be inadequate or inappropriate to describe the fauna, the physical and geographical conditions, or the cultural practices they have developed in a new land. The Canadian poet Joseph Howe, for instance, plucks his picture of a moose from some repository of English nursery rhyme romanticism:

> . . . the gay moose in jocund gambol springs,
> Cropping the foliage Nature round him flings.
>
> (Howe 1874:100)

Such absurdities demonstrate the pressing need these native speakers share with those colonized peoples who were directly oppressed to escape from the inadequacies and imperial constraints of English as a social practice. They need, that is, to escape from the implicit body of assumptions to which English was attached, its aesthetic and social values, the formal and historically limited constraints of genre, and the oppressive political and cultural assertion of metropolitan dominance, of centre over margin (Ngugi 1986). This is not to say that the English language is inherently incapable of accounting for post-colonial experience, but that it needs to develop an 'appropriate' usage in order to do so (by becoming a distinct and unique form of english). The energizing feature of this displacement is its capacity to interrogate and subvert the imperial cultural formations.

The pressure to develop such a usage manifests itself early in the development of 'english' literatures. It is therefore arguable that, even before the development of a conscious de-colonizing stance, the experience of a new place, identifiably different in its physical characteristics, constrains, for instance, the new settlers to demand a language which will allow them to express their sense of 'Otherness'. Landscape, flora and fauna, seasons, climatic conditions are formally distinguished from the place of origin as home/colony, Europe/New World, Europe/Antipodes, metropolitan/provincial, and so on, although, of course, at this stage no effective models exist for expressing this sense of Otherness in a positive and creative way.

Post-coloniality and theory

The idea of 'post-colonial literary theory' emerges from the inability of European theory to deal adequately with the complexities and varied cultural provenance of post-colonial writing. European theories themselves emerge from particular cultural traditions which are hidden by false notions of 'the universal'. Theories of style and genre, assumptions about the universal features of language, epistemologies and value systems are all radically questioned by the practices of post-colonial writing. Post-colonial theory has proceeded from the need to address this different practice. Indigenous theories have developed to accommodate the differences within the various cultural traditions as well as the desire to describe in a comparative way the features shared across those traditions.

The political and cultural monocentrism of the colonial enterprise was a natural result of the philosophical traditions of the European world and the systems of representation which this privileged. Nineteenth-century imperial expansion, the culmination of the outward and dominating thrust of Europeans into the world beyond Europe, which began during the early Renaissance, was underpinned in complex ways by these assumptions. In the first instance this produced practices of cultural subservience, characterized by one post-colonial critic as 'cultural cringe' (Phillips 1958). Subsequently, the emergence of identifiable indigenous theories in reaction to this formed an important element in the development of specific national and regional consciousnesses (see ch. 4).

Paradoxically, however, imperial expansion has had a radically destabilizing effect on its own preoccupations and power. In pushing the colonial world to the margins of experience the 'centre' pushed consciousness beyond the point at which monocentrism in all spheres of thought could be accepted without question. In other words the alienating process which initially served to relegate the post-colonial world to the 'margin' turned upon itself and acted to push that world through a kind of mental barrier into a position from which all experience could be viewed as uncentred, pluralistic, and multifarious. Marginality thus became an unprecedented source of creative energy. The impetus towards decentring and pluralism has always been present in the history of European thought and has reached its latest development in post-structuralism. But the situation of marginalized societies and cultures enabled them to come to this position much earlier and more directly (Brydon 1984b). These notions are implicit in post-colonial texts from the imperial period to the present day.

The task of this book is twofold: first, to identify the range and nature of these post-colonial texts, and, second, to describe the various theories which have emerged so far to account for them. So in the first chapter we consider the development of descriptive models of post-colonial writing. Since it is not possible to read post-colonial texts without coming to terms with the ways in which they appropriate and deploy the material of linguistic culture, in the second chapter we outline the process by which language is captured to form a distinctive discursive practice. In the third chapter we demonstrate, through symptomatic readings of texts, how post-colonial writing interacts with the social and material practices of colonialism. One of the major purposes of this book is to explain the nature of existing post-colonial theory and the way in which it interacts with, and dismantles, some of the assumptions of European theory. In the fourth chapter we discuss the issues in the development of indigenous post-colonial theories, and in the fifth we examine the larger implications of post-coloniality for theories of language, for literary theory, and for social and political analysis in general.

Cutting the ground: critical models of post-colonial literatures

As writers and critics became aware of the special character of post-colonial texts, they saw the need to develop an adequate model to account for them. Four major models have emerged to date: first, 'national' or regional models, which emphasize the distinctive features of the particular national or regional culture; second, race-based models which identify certain shared characteristics across various national literatures, such as the common racial inheritance in literatures of the African diaspora addressed by the 'Black writing' model; third, comparative models of varying complexity which seek to account for particular linguistic, historical, and cultural features across two or more post-colonial literatures; fourth, more comprehensive comparative models which argue for features such as hybridity and syncreticity as constitutive elements of all post-colonial literatures (syncretism is the process by which previously distinct linguistic categories, and, by extension, cultural formations, merge into a single new form). These models often operate as assumptions within critical practice rather than specific and discrete schools of thought; in any discussion of post-colonial writing a number of them may be operating at the same time.

National and regional models

The first post-colonial society to develop a 'national' literature was the USA. The emergence of a distinctive American literature in the late eighteenth century raised inevitable questions about the relationship between literature and place, between literature and nationality, and particularly about the suitability of inherited literary forms. Ideas about new kinds of literature were part of the optimistic progression to nationhood because it seemed that this was one of the most potent areas in which to express *difference* from Britain. Writers like Charles Brockden Brown, who attempted to indigenize British forms like the gothic and the sentimental novel, soon realized that with the change in location and culture it was not possible to import form and concept without radical alteration (Fiedler 1960; Ringe 1966).

In many ways the American experience and its attempts to produce a new kind of literature can be seen to be the model for all later post-colonial writing.[1] The first thing it showed was that some of a post-colonial country's most deeply held linguistic and cultural traits depend upon its relationship with the colonizing power, particularly the defining contrast between European metropolis and 'frontier' (see Fussell 1965). Once the American Revolution had forced the question of separate nationality, and the economic and political successes of the emerging nation had begun to be taken for granted, American literature as a distinct collection of texts also began to be accepted. But it was accepted as an offshoot of the 'parent tree'. Such organic metaphors, and others like 'parent–child' and 'stream–tributary' acted to keep the new literature in its place. The plant and parent metaphors stressed age, experience, roots, tradition, and, most importantly, the connection between antiquity and value. They implied the same distinctions as those existing between metropolis and frontier: parents are more experienced, more important, more substantial, less brash than their offspring. Above all they are the *origin* and therefore claim the final authority in questions of taste and value.

But as the extensive literature of the USA developed different characteristics from that of Britain and established its right to be considered independently, the concept of national literary differences 'within' English writing became established. The eventual consequence of this has been that 'newer' literatures from countries such as Nigeria, Australia, and India could also be discussed as discrete national formations rather than as 'branches of the tree'. Their literatures could be considered in relation to the social and political history of each country, and could be read as a source of important images of national identity.

The development of national literatures and criticism is fundamental to the whole enterprise of post-colonial studies. Without such developments at the national level, and without the comparative studies between national traditions to which these lead, no discourse of the post-colonial could have emerged. Nor is it simply a matter of development from one stage to another, since all post-colonial studies continue to depend upon national literatures and criticism. The study of national traditions is the first and most vital stage of the process of rejecting the claims of the centre to exclusivity. It is the beginning of what Nigerian writer Wole Soyinka has characterized as the 'process of self-apprehension' (Soyinka 1976: xi). Recent theories of a general post-colonial discourse question essentialist formulations which may lead to nationalist and racist orthodoxies, but they do not deny the great importance of maintaining each literature's sense of specific difference. It is this sense of difference which constitutes each national literature's mode of self-apprehension and its claim to be a self-constituting entity. However, nationalism, in which some partial truth or cliché is elevated to orthodoxy, is a danger implicit in such national conceptions of literary production. The impetus towards national self-realization in critical assessments of literature all too often fails to stop short of nationalist myth.

Larger geographical models which cross the boundaries of language, nationality, or race to generate the concept of a *regional* literature, such as West Indian or South Pacific literature, may also share some of the limitations of the national model. While the idea of an 'African' literature, for instance, has a powerful appeal to writers and critics in the various African countries, it has only limited application as a descriptive label. African and European critics have produced several regional and national studies which reflect the widespread political, economic, and cultural differences between modern African countries (Gurr and Calder 1974; Lindfors 1975; Taiwo 1976; Ogungbesan 1979).

Clearly some regional groupings are more likely to gain acceptance in the regions themselves than are others, and will derive from a collective identity evident in other ways. This is true of the West Indies. Although the Federation of the West Indies failed, the english-speaking countries there still field a regional cricket team. Both the West Indies and the South Pacific have regional universities with a significant input into literary production and discussion. 'West Indian' literature has almost always been considered regionally, rather than nationally. There have been no major studies of Jamaican or Trinidadian literatures as discrete traditions. A different regional grouping, emphasizing geographical and historical determinants rather than linguistic ones, has also developed to explore 'Caribbean' literature, setting literature in english from the region alongside that written in spanish, french, and other European languages (Allis 1982).

Despite such variants on the national model, most of the english literatures outside Britain have been considered as individual, national enterprises forming and reflecting each country's culture. The inevitable consequence of this is a gradual blurring of the distinction between the national and the nationalist. Nationalism has usually included a healthy repudiation of British and US hegemony observable in publishing, education, and the public sponsorship of writing. Yet all too often nationalist criticism, by failing to alter the terms of the discourse within which it operates, has participated implicitly or even explicitly in a discourse ultimately controlled by the very imperial power its nationalist assertion is designed to exclude. Emphasis may have been transferred to the national literature, but the theoretical assumptions, critical perspectives, and value judgements made have often replicated those of the British establishment.

Comparisons between two or more regions

Theories and models of post-colonial literatures could not emerge until the separate colonies were viewed in a framework centred on their own literary and cultural traditions. Victorian Britain had exulted in the disparateness of its empire, but in representing that empire predominantly as a site of the exotic, of adventure and exploitation, it had defined it as a contrastive element within the British world-view. Differences between colonies were subordinated to their common difference from Britain. Thus the comparative gestures of journals like *Black and White* (1891–1911) which purported to juxtapose different colonies, never escaped from the metropolitan–colonial axis.

Colonial education systems reinforced this axis by providing in-school 'readers' (for example, the Royal Reader Series in the West Indies, or the Queensland Readers in Australia) a normative core of British literature, landscape, and history (Browning's thoughts in exile, Wordsworth's daffodils, Sir Philip Sidney's chivalry) and a sprinkling of colonial adventure which often asserted British values against a hostile physical or human environment (Stanley's explorations, Newbolt's desperate cricketers). It required the aggression of nationalist traditions to break this pattern of inevitable reference to Britain as a standard and to provide space for the consideration of the literary and cultural patterns the colonies shared.

Three principal types of comparison have resulted, forming bases for a genuine post-colonial discourse. These are comparisons between countries of the white diaspora – the USA, Canada, Australia and New Zealand – comparisons between areas of the Black diaspora, and, thirdly, those which bridge these groupings, comparing, say, literatures of the West Indies with that of Australia.

One of the most important early works in the first category is J.P. Matthews' *Tradition in Exile* which offers a comparison between poetry in Canada and Australia in the nineteenth century. *Tradition in Exile* investigated significant similarities and important national and regional differences and though, as the title indicates, it still alluded to the imperial connection, its investigations of developmental parallels occasioned by the transplantation of the english language and traditions into other areas of the world laid the foundations for later studies which would perceive the imperial–colonial relationship as disjunctive rather than continuous. For example, a number of essays in McDougall and Whitlock (1987) which focus on

Canada and Australia; Jones (1976) which considers important literary–political similarities between the USA and Australia, and Kirkby (1982) which argues for the importance of the American, rather than the British, influence on contemporary Australian poetry. W. H. New's recent *Dreams of Speech and Violence* (1987), for instance, suggests, through an exhaustive study of the short story in Canada and New Zealand, that these two post-colonial literatures' relation to Britain is subversive rather than filiastic, counter-discursive rather than a continuing expression of the original imperial discourse.

Other critics like Moore (1969), Ngugi (1972), Griffiths (1978) concentrate on similarities between writing within the Black diaspora, comparing the literatures of African countries with those of the West Indian nations and/or with Black American writing (see p. 29).

Less frequently, comparisons have been drawn between countries or regions across Black and white diasporas – Dorsinville's *Caliban Without Prospero* (1974) which deals with the literatures of Quebec and the Black diaspora (see p. 32), and, more recently, comparisons of Australian convict and West Indian slave literature (Macdonald 1984). Such studies, because they can deal in greater detail with two or three areas, form important bridges for the discourse of post-colonialism which deals with all areas, both Black and white.

The 'Black writing' model

Another grouping which traverses several of the literatures from post-colonial societies is 'Black writing'. This proceeds from the idea of race as a major feature of economic and political discrimination and draws together writers in the African diaspora whatever their nationality – US Blacks, Afro-Caribbeans, and writers from African nations. The African characteristics of the model are important, for although the classification might be extended to include, for instance, Polynesian, Melanesian, or Australian Aboriginal writing (and even writing by whites about Africa or India as an antagonistic term), this extension has never been enthusiastically embraced by critics outside the African diaspora. Even where the idea of Black writing has worked well, in comparing and contrasting Black American writing with that from Africa or the West

Indies (Baker 1976; Barthold 1981), it overlooks the very great cultural differences between literatures which are produced by a Black minority in a rich and powerful white country and those produced by the Black majority population of an independent nation. This is especially so since the latter nations are often still experiencing the residual effects of foreign domination in the political and economic spheres.

Despite these qualifications, race-centred critiques of Black writing and of writing by Europeans about Black societies have been influential within post-colonial discourse. The concept of Négritude developed by the Martinican Aimé Césaire (1945) and the Senegalese poet and politician Leopold Sedar Senghor (Senghor 1977) was the most pronounced assertion of the distinctive qualities of Black culture and identity. But in making this assertion it adopted stereotypes which curiously reflected European prejudice. Black culture, it claimed, was emotional rather than rational; it stressed integration and wholeness over analysis and dissection; it operated by distinctive rhythmic and temporal principles, and so forth. Négritude also claimed a distinctive African view of time–space relationships, ethics, metaphysics, and an aesthetics which separated itself from the supposedly 'universal' values of European taste and style. The danger was that, as a result, it could easily be reincorporated into a European model in which it functioned only as the antithesis of the thesis of white supremacy, a new 'universal' paradigm.

Wole Soyinka makes precisely this point in his analysis of Négritude in *Myth, Literature and the African World*:

> Négritude, having laid its cornerstone on a European intel-
> lectual tradition, however bravely it tried to reverse its
> concepts (leaving its tenets untouched), was a foundling
> deserving to be drawn into, nay, even considered a case for
> benign adoption by European ideological interests.
>
> (Soyinka 1976:134)

As Soyinka perceives it, this is inevitable given that Négritude embraces the essential binary nature of the western philo-sophical tradition.

> Sartre ... classified this colonial movement as springing
> from the intellectual conditioning of the mother culture; he

rightly assumed that any movement founded on an antithesis which responded to the Cartesian 'I think, therefore I am' with 'I feel, therefore I am' must be subject to a dialectical determinism which made all those who 'are' obedient to laws formulated on the European historical experience. How was he to know, if the proponents of the universal vision of Négritude did not, that the African world did not and need not share the history of civilisations trapped in political Manicheisms.

(ibid.:135–6)[2]

In recent years the philosophy of Négritude has been most influential in its derivative form in the Afro-American Black consciousness movement. Senghor's influence in America can be traced to prominent Black intellectuals of the 1920s such as Langston Hughes and Richard Wright; the latter, significantly, spent most of the later part of his life in exile in Paris. The Black Power movements share many of the characteristics of the theory of Négritude in their assertion of the unique and distinctive features of Black thought and emotion.

Modern Afro-American critics continue to assert the existence of a distinctive Black consciousness in their analyses of literature and theory. The collection of essays *Black Literature and Literary Theory* (Gates 1984) illustrates how such concepts as 'soul' or the importance of repetition in Black musical structure can be used to propose a distinctive Black aesthetic. But the fact that these features are *subject* to analysis and that structuralism and discourse analysis are employed in these accounts would suggest how far Black literary theory has come from the broadly polarizing assertions of early Négritudinist criticism, and the extent to which it acknowledges its European critical and epistemological assumptions (e.g. see JanMohammed 1983).

Black writers have been critical of what have appeared to be new hegemonic categories like 'Commonwealth literature', and this has forced critics and writers from colonized white countries to consider their own attitudes to race and to their often ambiguous positions as both colonized and colonizers. Black criticism has been exciting and theoretically adventurous, but it has sometimes run the risk of adopting, in Said's terms, 'a double kind of possessive exclusivism . . . the sense of being an exclusive insider by virtue of experience' (Said 1985:106).

Wider comparative models

Finding a name

One of the first difficulties in developing a wider comparative approach to the literatures has been that of finding an appropriate name to describe them. Some early attempts at a name which indicated the world-wide range of English writing never found general acceptance: for example, Joseph Jones's word 'terranglia', which he employed to describe all writing in english throughout the world (Jones 1965). The term 'Commonwealth literature' which also emerged in the 1960s, although it secured much readier acceptance, nevertheless had geographical and political limitations. It rested purely on the fact of a shared history and the resulting political grouping. In its loosest form it remained a descriptive term for a collection of national literatures united by a past or present membership of the British Commonwealth. But through its relatively widespread acceptance it opened the way for more rigorous conceptions which also postulated a common condition across all former colonies. For a long while these existed, or coexisted, if sometimes uneasily, under the umbrella of 'Commonwealth literature'.

Several attempts have been made to find a politically and theoretically more appropriate name for such literatures than 'Commonwealth literature' (see Tiffin 1983). The limited and pejorative term 'Third World literatures' has been used in some university courses, but the most popular contenders have been 'new literatures in English' and, most recently, 'post-colonial literatures'. Although the first avoids the inclusion of any reference to colonialism, and therefore may be more acceptable to nationalists wishing to de-emphasize the colonial past, it is vague and misleading in other ways, implicitly privileging a European perspective in areas like India or Africa, and providing no theoretical direction or comparative framework. It also has the disadvantage that it compares the literatures to 'old' literature in English, without alluding to the hegemonic power of the British tradition.

The term 'colonial literatures' might focus on what is shared by the writing and therefore suggest the direction in which to proceed theoretically, but the connotations of the term are politically unacceptable to territories which have gained their independence. 'Post-colonial' seems to be the choice which both embraces the historical reality and focuses on that relationship which has provided the most important creative and psychological impetus in the writing. Although it does not specify that the discourse is limited to works in english, it does indicate the rationale of the grouping in a common past and hints at the vision of a more liberated and positive future. In practical terms, the description we adopt – 'post-colonial' – is less restrictive than 'Commonwealth'; it shares with 'new literatures in English' the ability to include, for example, the english literature of the Philippines or of the United States as well as that of 'pakeha' (white) or Maori writing in New Zealand, or that of both Blacks and whites in South Africa.

However, the term 'post-colonial literatures' is finally to be preferred over the others because it points the way towards a possible study of the effects of colonialism in and between writing in english and writing in indigenous languages in such contexts as Africa and India, as well as writing in other language diasporas (French, Spanish, Portuguese). The literature of Ireland might also be investigated in terms of our contemporary knowledge of post-colonialism, thus shedding new light on the British literary tradition. Even so, better terms may still emerge. In his comparative study of the literatures of Quebec and the Black diaspora, Dorsinville, for example, used the term 'post-European'. Although this has not so far been used extensively in critical accounts of the field its political and theoretical implications have much to offer.

Language and place

Several comparative models of post-colonial literature have been developed. An early and influential example, proposed by D.E.S. Maxwell (1965), concentrated on the disjunction between place and language. Place and displacement, as the introduction has suggested, are major concerns of all post-colonial peoples and Maxwell's model for examining their literatures focused on this characteristic, questioning the 'appropriateness' of an imported language to describe the experience of place in post-colonial societies. Maxwell observed the similarity between these societies in their use of a non-indigenous language which was always to some extent 'alien' to that place. He identified two groups; the settler colonies and the invaded colonies. In the case of the settler colonies like the United States, Canada, New Zealand, and Australia, land was occupied by European colonists who dispossessed and over-whelmed the Indigenous populations. They established a transplanted civilization which eventually secured political independence while retaining a non-Indigenous language. Having no ancestral contact with the land, they dealt with their sense of displacement by unquestioningly clinging to a belief in the adequacy of the imported language – where mistranslation could not be overlooked it was the land or the season which was 'wrong'. Yet in all these areas writers have subsequently come, in different ways, to question the appropriateness of imported language to place (see ch. 4).

Maxwell's theory suggests that in the case of invaded societies like those in India or Nigeria, where indigenous peoples were colonized on their own territories, writers were not forced to adapt to a different landscape and climate, but had their own ancient and sophisticated responses to them marginalized by the world-view which was implicated in the acquisition of English. Whether English actually supplanted the writer's mother tongue or simply offered an alternative medium which guaranteed a wider readership, its use caused a disjunction between the apprehension of, and communication about, the world.

For Maxwell, wherever post-colonial writers originated, they shared certain outstanding features which set their work apart from the indigenous literary tradition of England:

> There are two broad categories. In the first, the writer brings his own language – English – to an alien environment and a fresh set of experiences: Australia, Canada, New Zealand. In the other, the writer brings an alien language – English – to his own social and cultural inheritance: India, West Africa. Yet the categories have a fundamental kinship. . . . [The] 'intolerable wrestle with words and meanings' has as its aim to subdue the experience to the language, the exotic life to the imported tongue.
>
> (Maxwell 1965:82–3)

Implicit in Maxwell's analysis of the post-colonial is a particular kind of 'double vision' not available to uncolonized Indigenes. This vision is one in which identity is constituted by difference; intimately bound up in love or hate (or both) with a metropolis which exercises its hegemony over the immediate cultural world of the post-colonial.

There are two major limitations to this model: first, it is not sufficiently comprehensive in that it does not consider the case of the West Indies or of South Africa, which are exceptional in a number of important respects; second, its lack of linguistic subtlety risks encouraging a simplistic and essentialist view of the connection between language and place. To take the first point; in the West Indies, for instance, the Indigenous people (Caribs and Arawaks) were virtually exterminated within a century of the European invasion. So the entire contemporary population has suffered a displacement and an 'exile' – from Africa, India, China, the 'Middle East', and Europe. The West Indian situation combines all the most violent and destructive effects of the colonizing process. Like the populations of the settler colonies all West Indians have been displaced. Yet this displacement includes for those of African descent the violence of enslavement, and for many others (Indian and Chinese) the only slightly less violent disruption of slavery's 'legal' successor, the nineteenth-century system of indentured labour. As in India and African countries the dominant imperial language and culture were privileged over the peoples' traditions.

Settler colonies could at least have the temporary illusion of a filiative relationship with that dominating culture, whilst the colonies of intervention and exploitation had traditional, pre-colonial cultures which continued to coexist with the new imperial forms. In the West Indies though, whilst individual racial groups continued to maintain fragments of pre-colonial cultures brought from their original societies and whilst these continue to be part of the complex reality of contemporary West Indian life (e.g. the many African features in contemporary West Indian culture) the processes of maintaining continuity or of 'decolonizing' the culture are much more obviously problematic. In part this is because the process of disruption brought about by imperialism was not only more violent but also more self-consciously disruptive and divisive. English had a much more tainted historical role in the Caribbean where slaves were deliberately separated from other members of their language group and, to minimize the possibility of rebellion, forced to use the language of the plantation owners. For the slaves, then, this was a language of division imposed to facilitate exploitation.

Maxwell did not include South Africa in his category of settler colonies, but white South African literature has clear affinities with those of Australia, Canada, and New Zealand. Black South African literature, on the other hand, might more fruitfully be compared with that of other African countries. But the contemporary racist politics of South African apartheid creates a political vortex into which much of the literature of the area, both Black and white, is drawn. The common themes of the literatures of settler colonies – exile, the problem of finding and defining 'home', physical and emotional confrontations with the 'new' land and its ancient and established meanings – are still present in literature by white South Africans, but are muted by an immediate involvement in race politics. Pervasive concerns of Nigerian or Kenyan writing, dispossession, cultural fragmentation, colonial and neo-colonial domination, post-colonial corruption and the crisis of identity still emerge in writing by Black South Africans, but again are necessarily less prominent than more specific and immediate matters of race and personal and communal freedom under an intransigent and repressive white regime.

As to the second point, although Maxwell's formulation goes a considerable way towards identifying the scope and unity of post-colonial literatures, it might be seen to encourage an assumption that a language somehow may be inherently in-appropriate for use in another place. This suggests an essential-ism which, taken to its logical extreme, would deny the very possibility of post-colonial literatures in english.

Thematic parallels

Post-colonial critics have found many thematic parallels across the different literatures in english (Matthews 1962; New 1975; Tiffin 1978; Slemon 1988). For example, the theme of the celebration of the struggle towards independence in community and individual emerges in novels as diverse as Rao's *Kanthapura*

(India), Ngugi's *A Grain of Wheat* (Kenya), and Reid's *New Day* (Jamaica); the theme of the dominating influence of a foreign culture on the life of contemporary post-colonial societies is present in works as diverse in origin and style as Achebe's *No Longer at Ease* (Nigeria), Lamming's *In the Castle of My Skin* (Barbados), and the poems of Honi Tuwhare (New Zealand).

Other themes with a powerful metonymic force can also be seen to emerge. For example, the construction or demolition of houses or buildings in post-colonial locations is a recurring and evocative figure for the problematic of post-colonial identity in works from very different societies, as in V.S. Naipaul's *A House For Mr Biswas* (Trinidad), Santha Rama Rao's *Remember the House* (India), Sinclair Ross's *As For Me and My House* (Canada), Peter Carey's *Bliss* (Australia), and Janet Frame's *Living in the Manototo* (New Zealand). Or the theme of the journey of the European interloper through unfamiliar landscape with a native guide is a feature of texts as wide-ranging as Wilson Harris's *Palace of the Peacock* (Guyana), Patrick White's *Voss* (Australia), and Camara Laye's *The Radiance of the King* (Guinea).[3]

Similarities across the different post-colonial literatures are not restricted to thematic parallels. As recent critics have noted they extend to assertions that certain features such as a distinctive use of allegory (Slemon 1986, 1987b), irony (New 1975), magic realism (Dash 1973; Slemon 1988a), and discontinuous narratives are characteristic of post-colonial writing. In W.H. New's *Among Worlds* (1975), a book which 'describes the thematic parallels that mark the literary contemporaneity of each commonwealth culture . . . and the ways in which writers have used their culture's preoccupations to construct separate and multiple worlds', the author makes a very interesting claim for a predominant ironic mode in post-colonial literatures where 'time, place and community . . . give rise to comparable attitudes and constricting dilemmas' (New 1975: 3). The prevalence of irony (and the rise of a species of allegory observable across the various cultures) emphasizes the importance of the language–place disjunction in the construction of post-colonial realities (see ch. 2, pp. 41–2).

New's book also stresses the comparative nature of this experience, finding 'recurrent structural patterns in each literature' which 'offer an approach to the underlying cultural sensibilities'. Significantly, 'the degree to which they overlap provides . . . a guard against easy assertions about national distinctiveness in literature' (New 1975:2–3). One of the recurrent structural patterns New elucidates is that of exile, which had already been explored by Matthews (1962) and later by Gurr (1981). Ngugi (1972) and Griffiths (1978) also deal with exile, focusing on the literatures of Africa, the Caribbean, and the Black diaspora generally.

The existence of these shared themes and recurrent structural and formal patterns is no accident. They speak for the shared psychic and historical conditions across the differences distinguishing one post-colonial society from another. For instance, the theme of exile is in some sense present in all such writing since it is one manifestation of the ubiquitous concern with place and displacement in these societies, as well as with the complex material circumstances implicit in the transportation of language from its place of origin and its imposed and imposing relationship on and with the new environment. As a result, accounts of comparative features in post-colonial writing need to address the larger issues of how these literatures bear the imprint of the material forces of politics, economics, and culture which act upon them within the imperial framework, and of how this is bound up with the re-placing of the imposed language in the new geographical and cultural context.

Colonizer and colonized

Another major post-colonial approach, derived from the works of political theorists like Frantz Fanon (1959, 1961, 1967) and Albert Memmi (1965), locates its principal characteristic in the notion of the imperial–colonial dialectic itself. In this model the act of writing texts of any kind in post-colonial areas is subject to the political, imaginative, and social control involved in the relationship between colonizer and colonized.

This relationship posits important questions; for example, that of the possibility of 'decolonizing' the culture. Some of the most vigorous debates in post-colonial societies have centred on exactly what such 'decolonization' implies and how it should be achieved. Some critics have stressed the need vigorously to recuperate pre-colonial languages and cultures. For the most resolute of these critics, colonization is only a passing historical feature which can be left behind entirely when 'full independence' of culture and political organization is achieved (Ngugi 1986). Others have argued that not only is this impossible but that cultural syncreticity is a valuable as well as an inescapable and characteristic feature of all post-colonial societies and indeed is the source of their peculiar strength (Williams 1969).

In African countries and in India, that is in post-colonial countries where viable alternatives to english continue to exist, an appeal for a return to writing exclusively, or mainly in the pre-colonial languages has been a recurring feature of calls for decolonization. Politically attractive as this is, it has been seen as problematic by those who insist on the syncretic nature of post-colonial societies. Syncreticist critics argue that even a novel in Bengali or Gikuyu is inevitably a cross-cultural hybrid, and that decolonizing projects must recognize this. Not to do so is to confuse decolonization with the reconstitution of pre-colonial reality. Nevertheless, especially in India where the bulk of literature is written in indigenous Indian languages, the relationship between writing in those languages and the much less extensive writing in english has made such a project a powerful element in post-colonial self-assertion, and the same may increasingly become true in African countries. In settler colonies, where decolonizing projects underlay the drive to establish national cultures, the problem of language at first seemed a less radical one. The fact that the language seemed to sit uncomfortably with the local 'reality' was perceived to be a minor irritant that would be solved in time, and, in any case, there was no other available language (though movements like the Jindyworobak in Australia which turned to Aboriginal language and culture for an 'authentic' inspiration in creating a 'native' voice suggested directions such a search might take). Nevertheless, as later critics have perceived, this position, too, glossed over major problems of language and 'authenticity'.

This debate between theories of pre-colonial cultural re-cuperation and theories which suggest that post-colonial syncreticity is both inevitable and fruitful emerges in a number of places. For example, it emerged in Africa, in the famous debate between the Nigerian writer Wole Soyinka and the so-called 'troika' of Chinweizu, Jemie, and Madubuike (Soyinka 1975; Chinweizu *et al.* 1983), which raised important questions about national or group exclusivism and the impossibility of avoiding syncreticism (particularly in the fusion of cultures which is implied in the use of english). These questions are also implicit in Caribbean writing in the perspectives exemplified by Edward Brathwaite's early writing on the one hand and Derek Walcott's and Wilson Harris's on the other (Ismond 1971). Brathwaite and Chinweizu regard a return to African roots as crucial to contemporary West Indian and Nigerian identity: Soyinka and Harris espouse a cultural syncretism which, while not denying ancestral affiliations, sees Afro-Caribbean destiny as inescapably enmeshed in a contemporary, multi-cultural reality. These clashes have succeeded in isolating some of the most important theoretical problems in post-colonial criticism.

From a different perspective, it is in this area of the relationship between colonizer and colonized that the input from European structuralist, post-structuralist, and Marxist criticism has been significant. A stress on the pre-eminence of textuality has particular application to the imperial–colonial literary encounter, and structuralists like Tzvetan Todorov and post-structuralists like Edward Said have been important in elucidating the dialectical encounters between Europe and the Other (Todorov 1974; Said 1978, 1985). Clearly, too, Marxist analyses (for example those of Althusser, Pêcheux, and Jameson) which stress the importance of ideology in forming the ideas of the colonial subject have had a strong impact on post-colonial cultural and literary interpretation. Critics like Homi Bhabha (1983, 1985), Abdul JanMohamed (1983, 1985), and Gayatri Spivak (1985a, 1987) have adapted different aspects of these contemporary Euro-American theories to an analysis of the colonial encounter.

Feminist perspectives are of increasing importance in post-colonial criticism and indeed the strategies of recent feminist and recent post-colonial theory overlap and inform each other. Jean Rhys, Doris Lessing, Toni Morrison, Paule Marshall, and Margaret Atwood have all drawn an analogy between the relationships of men and women and those of the imperial power and the colony, while critics like Gayatri Spivak (1985b, 1987) have articulated the relationship between feminism, post-structuralism, and the discourse of post-coloniality.

'Dominated' and 'dominating'

A comparative approach closely related to that based on the tension between colonizer and colonized is that of Max Dorsinville (1974, 1983), which emphasizes the relationship between dominated and dominating societies. Dorsinville explores this distinction in his studies of the social and literary relations of oppressor and oppressed communities in French Africa, Quebec, Black America, and the Caribbean. Clearly, by dispensing with the special historical relationship produced by colonialism and stressing the importance of the politics of domination this model can embrace a much wider hierarchy of oppression. While Dorsinville is not specifically concerned with post-colonial societies, his approach can easily be adapted to cover them.

Cultural change both within societies and between societies can be neatly accounted for by this hierarchy. In this respect, Dorsinville's model can be used to extend Maxwell's (see pp. 24–7). For example, one might explain changes in theme, emphasis, and design in the literature of the USA from the nineteenth century to the twentieth on the basis of a relative change in international importance as the USA moves from a dominated to a dominating position, giving its literature greater affinities with those of Europe in terms of its power to produce 'canonical' texts and to influence other literatures.

Dorsinville's model also accounts for the productions of literary and cultural minorities within one country or area, and accounts for conflicting postures of the dominant society which might itself be subtly dominated by another power. In Australia, for instance, Aboriginal writing provides an excellent example of a dominated literature, while that of white Australia has characteristics of a dominating one in relation to it. Yet white Australian literature is dominated in its turn by a relationship with Britain and English literature. A study of the contradictions which emerge in such situations, and of the reflection of changes through time of imperial–colonial status within, say, the American or British traditions, would be a fascinating one.

A model such as Dorsinville's also makes less problematical the situation of Irish, Welsh, and Scottish literatures in relation to the English 'mainstream'. While it is possible to argue that these societies were the first victims of English expansion, their subsequent complicity in the British imperial enterprise makes it difficult for colonized peoples outside Britain to accept their identity as post-colonial. Dorsinville's dominated–dominating model forcefully stresses linguistic and cultural imposition, and enables an interpretation of British literary history as a process of hierarchical interchange in internal and external group relationships.

A characteristic of dominated literatures is an inevitable tendency towards subversion, and a study of the subversive strategies employed by post-colonial writers would reveal both the configurations of domination and the imaginative and creative responses to this condition. Directly and indirectly, in Salman Rushdie's phrase, the 'Empire writes back' to the imperial 'centre', not only through nationalist assertion, proclaiming itself central and self-determining, but even more radically by questioning the bases of European and British metaphysics, challenging the world-view that can polarize centre and periphery in the first place. In this way, concepts of polarity, of 'governor and governed, ruler and ruled' (Harris 1960) are challenged as an essential way of ordering reality. Writers such as J.M. Coetzee, Wilson Harris, V.S. Naipaul, George Lamming, Patrick White, Chinua Achebe, Margaret Atwood, and Jean Rhys have all rewritten particular works from the English 'canon' with a view to restructuring European 'realities' in post-colonial terms, not simply by reversing the hierarchical order, but by interrogating the philosophical assumptions on which that order was based (Brydon 1984b; Gardiner 1987; Slemon 1987b; Tiffin, 1987).

Models of hybridity and syncreticity

While post-colonial literary theory has drawn on European theoretical systems it has done so cautiously and eclectically. Alterity implies alteration, and no European theory is likely to be appropriate in different cultural circumstances without itself undergoing radical rethinking – an 'appropriation' by a different discourse.

Theories proposed by critics like Homi Bhabha and writers like Wilson Harris or Edward Brathwaite proceed from a consideration of the nature of post-colonial societies and the types of hybridization their various cultures have produced. In much European thinking, history, ancestry, and the past form a powerful reference point for epistemology. In post-colonial thought, however, as the Australian poet Les Murray has said, 'time broadens into space' (Murray 1969). Works like Joseph Furphy's *Such is Life* (1903), Salman Rushdie's *Midnight's Children* (1981), G.V. Desani's *All About H. Hatterr* (1948), the novels of Wilson Harris, and many others, all deliberately set out to disrupt European notions of 'history' and the ordering of time. Novels like Patrick White's *Voss* (1957), or poem sequences like Francis Webb's 'Eyre All Alone' (1961) or *Leichhardt In Theatre* (1952) run European history aground in a new and overwhelming space which annihilates time and imperial purpose. Received history is tampered with, rewritten, and realigned from the point of view of the victims of its destructive progress. The same is true of Raja Rao's *Kanthapura* (1938), V. S. Reid's *New Day* (1949), and Rudy Weibe's *The Temptations of Big Bear* (1973). In all these texts the perspective changes to that of the 'Other'.

Homi Bhabha has noted the collusion between narrative mode, history, and realist mimetic readings of texts. Taking V.S. Naipaul's *A House for Mr Biswas* as his example, Bhabha demonstrates the dangers of the way in which readings of post-colonial works as socially and historically mimetic foster their reabsorption into an English tradition, domesticating their radicalism by ignoring the important colonial disruptions to the 'English' surface of the text (Bhabha 1984a). Similarly, the St Lucian poet, Derek Walcott, in his essay, 'The muse of history', takes issue with what he regards as the West Indian writer's obsession with the destructions of the historical past, and makes a plea for an escape from a prison of perpetual recriminations into the possibilities of a 'historyless' world, where a fresh but not innocent 'Adamic' naming of place provides the writer with inexhaustible material and the potential of a new, but not naive, vision (Walcott 1974b).

The West Indian poet and historian E.K. Brathwaite proposes a model which, while stressing the importance of the need to privilege the African connection over the European, also stresses the multi-cultural, syncretic nature of the West Indian reality. Similarly, for the Guyanese novelist and critic, Wilson Harris, cultures must be liberated from the destructive dialectic of history, and imagination is the key to this. Harris sees imaginative escape as the ancient and only refuge of oppressed peoples, but the imagination also offers possibilities of escape from the politics of dominance and subservience. One of his most important images for this process is provided by the folk character of Anancy, the spider man, from Akan folklore. Anancy can and does take many forms in his transplanted West Indian setting, but for Harris he provides the key to an imaginative recrossing of the notorious 'Middle Passage' through which the slaves originally crossed from Africa to the Caribbean (Harris 1970a: 8ff; see also Brathwaite 1973:165–7). The trickster character of the spider man, like the limbo 'gateway' of the Middle Passage, offers a narrow psychic space through which radical transformation may occur. Mixing past, present, future, and imperial and colonial cultures within his own fiction, Harris deliberately strives after a new language and a new way of seeing the world. This view rejects the apparently inescapable polarities of language and deploys the destructive energies of European culture in the service of a future community in which division and categorization are no longer the bases of perception.

In *The Womb of Space* (1983) Harris demonstrates the ways in which this philosophy can be used in the radical reading of texts, for, like Jameson, he is able to draw out the creative multi-cultural impulses inevitably present below the apparently antagonistic surface structures of the text.[4] Hence, Harris argues that although, on the surface, post-colonial texts may deal with divisions of race and culture which are apparently obdurately determined, each text contains the seeds of 'community' which, as they germinate and grow in the mind of the reader, crack asunder the apparently inescapable dialectic of history.

In Harris's formulation, hybridity in the present is constantly struggling to free itself from a past which stressed ancestry, and which valued the 'pure' over its threatening opposite, the 'composite'. It replaces a temporal lineality with a spatial plurality. The complication of time meeting space in literary theory and historiography, with its attendant clash of the 'pure' and the 'hybrid', is well illustrated by the contradictions that have arisen in the Canadian situation. In Canada, where the model of the 'mosaic' has been an important cultural determinant, Canadian literary theory has, in breaking away from European domination, generally retained a nationalist stance, arguing for the mosaic as characteristically Canadian in contrast to the 'melting-pot' of the USA. But the internal perception of a mosaic has not generated corresponding theories of literary hybridity to replace the nationalist approach. Canadian literature, perceived internally as a mosaic, remains generally monolithic in its assertion of Canadian difference from the canonical British or the more recently threatening neo-colonialism of American culture.[5] Alternatively, it has striven for outside recognition by retreating from the dynamics of difference into the neo-universalist internationalist stance. Where its acute perception of cultural complexity might have generated a climate in which cross-national or cross-cultural comparative studies would be privileged, little work of this kind seems to have been done.

Post-colonial literary theory, then, has begun to deal with the problems of transmuting time into space, with the present struggling out of the past, and, like much recent post-colonial literature, it attempts to construct a future. The post-colonial world is one in which destructive cultural encounter is changing to an acceptance of difference on equal terms. Both literary theorists and cultural historians are beginning to recognize cross-culturality as the potential termination point of an apparently endless human history of conquest and annihilation justified by the myth of group 'purity', and as the basis on which the post-colonial world can be creatively stabilized. Nationalist and Black criticisms have demystified the imperial processes of domination and continuing hegemony, but they have not in the end offered a way out of the historical and philosophical impasse. Unlike these models, the recent approaches have recognized that the strength of post-colonial theory may well lie in its inherently comparative methodology and the hybridized and syncretic view of the modern world which this implies. This view provides a framework of 'difference on equal terms' within which multi-cultural theories, both within and between societies, may continue to be fruitfully explored.

The various models by which texts and traditions in post-colonial literatures are discussed intersect at a number of points. However, place is extremely important in all the models, and epistemologies have developed which privilege space over time as the most important ordering concept of reality. In the same way the poles of governor–governed, ruler–ruled, etc. are inverted and the concept of dominance as the principal regulator of human societies is recognized but challenged. Likewise, language localizes and attracts value away from a British 'norm' eventually displacing the hegemonic centrality of the idea of 'norm' itself. Finally, the 'double vision' imposed by the historical distinction between metropolis and colony ensures that in all post-colonial cultures, monolithic perceptions are less likely.

2

Re-placing language: textual strategies in post-colonial writing

Abrogation and appropriation

The crucial function of language as a medium of power demands that post-colonial writing define itself by seizing the language of the centre and re-placing it in a discourse fully adapted to the colonized place. There are two distinct processes by which it does this. The first, the abrogation or denial of the privilege of 'English' involves a rejection of the metropolitan power over the means of communication. The second, the appropriation and reconstitution of the language of the centre, the process of capturing and remoulding the language to new usages, marks a separation from the site of colonial privilege.

Abrogation is a refusal of the categories of the imperial culture, its aesthetic, its illusory standard of normative or 'correct' usage, and its assumption of a traditional and fixed meaning 'inscribed' in the words. It is a vital moment in the de-colonizing of the language and the writing of 'english', but without the process of appropriation the moment of abrogation may not extend beyond a reversal of the assumptions of privilege, the 'normal', and correct inscription, all of which can be simply taken over and maintained by the new usage.

Appropriation is the process by which the language is taken and made to 'bear the burden' of one's own cultural experience, or, as Raja Rao puts it, to 'convey in a language that is not one's own the spirit that is one's own.' (Rao 1938:vii).[1] Language is adopted as a tool and utilized in various ways to express widely differing cultural experiences. These differences may exist in cultures which appear to be quite similar. For in one sense all post-colonial literatures are cross-cultural because they negotiate a gap between 'worlds', a gap in which the simultaneous processes of abrogation and appropriation continually strive to define and determine their practice. This literature is therefore always written out of the tension between the abrogation of the received English which speaks from the centre, and the act of appropriation which brings it under the influence of a vernacular tongue, the complex of speech habits which characterize the local language, or even the evolving and distinguishing local english of a monolingual society trying to establish its link with place (see New 1978).

Language in post-colonial societies

There are three main types of linguistic groups within post-colonial discourse: monoglossic, diglossic and polyglossic. Monoglossic groups are those single-language societies using english as a native tongue, which correspond generally to settled colonies, although, despite the term, they are by no means uniform or standard in speech. Monoglossic groups may show linguistic peculiarities as significant as those in more complex linguistic communities. Diglossic societies are those in which bilingualism has become an enduring societal arrangement, for example, in India, Africa, the South Pacific, for the Indigenous populations of settled colonies, and in Canada, where Québecois culture has created an officially bilingual society.[2] In diglossic societies english has generally been adopted as the language of government and commerce, and the literary use of english demonstrates some of the more pronounced forms of language variance. Polyglossic or 'poly-dialectical' communities occur principally in the Caribbean, where a multitude of dialects interweave to form a generally comprehensible linguistic continuum.[3] The world language called english is a continuum of 'intersections' in which the speaking habits in various communities have intervened to reconstruct the language. This 'reconstruction' occurs in two ways: on the one hand, regional english varieties may introduce words which become familiar to all english-speakers, and on the other, the varieties themselves produce national and regional peculiarities which distinguish them from other forms of english.

The resulting versatility of english has often been regarded as an inherent quality of English itself. In *The Swan and the Eagle* C.D. Narasimhaiah claims that the variability of the contributing sources of English make it ideal for the complexity of Indian culture:

> that it is not the language of any region is precisely its strength, and its extraordinarily cosmopolitan character – its Celtic imaginativeness, the Scottish vigour, the Saxon concreteness, the Welsh music and the American brazenness – suits the intellectual temper of modern India and a composite culture like ours. English is not a pure language but a fascinating combination of tongues welded into a fresh unity.
>
> (Narasimhaiah 1969: 8)

These are compelling metaphors but we should be careful about ascribing such qualities to a language as though they were inherent properties. These features are true of a language because they are potentialities of its use, potentialities which have been realized in its adaptation to different cultural requirements. Because language is such a versatile tool, English is continually changing and 'growing' (becoming an 'english') because it realizes potentials which are then accorded to it as properties. Thus english is no different from any other language in its potential versatility. It merely appears more versatile because it has been used by a greater variety of people. This, of course, supports Narasimhaiah's main point, that english has been historically subject to a large variety of uses and has therefore become an efficient tool for conveying cultural complexity, as well as functioning as an inter-regional language. The application of a language to different uses is therefore a continuous process. And these uses themselves become the language.

Language and abrogation

In the early period of post-colonial writing many writers were forced into the search for an alternative authenticity which seemed to be escaping them, since the concept of authenticity itself was endorsed by a centre to which they did not belong and yet was continually contradicted by the everyday experience of marginality. The eventual consequence of this experience was that notions of centrality and the 'authentic' were themselves necessarily questioned, challenged, and finally abrogated.

This is not to say that post-colonial critics have always avoided an essentialist view of language or of some 'authentic' cultural experience. The process of decolonization, which sometimes becomes a search for an essential cultural purity, does not necessarily harness the theoretical subversiveness offered by post-colonial literatures. Nevertheless, writers as diverse as Janet Frame (1962), Dennis Lee (1974), Robert Kroetsch (1974), and Wole Soyinka (1976) have argued that not only is the notion of authentic experience as false as its validating concept of the 'centre', but that the inauthentic and marginal is in fact the 'real'. Thus the conditions of post-colonial experience encouraged the dismantling of notions of essence and authenticity somewhat earlier than the recent expressions of the same perception in contemporary European post-structuralist theory.

This privileging of the 'margins' in post-colonial writing produces a particularly practical orientation to questions of theory. Language is a material practice and as such is determined by a complex weave of social conditions and experience. So, for example, because the traversal of the text by these conditions becomes so clear and so crucial in post-colonial literature, the idea of art existing for its own sake or of literature appealing to some transcendent human experience are both rejected.

As the contemporary accounts discussed above are beginning to assert, the syncretic and hybridized nature of post-colonial experience refutes the privileged position of a standard code in the language and any monocentric view of human experience. At the same time, however, it also refutes the notions that often attract post-colonial critics: that cultural practices can return to some 'pure' and unsullied cultural condition, and that such practices themselves, such as the use of vernacular terms or grammatical forms in english literature, can embody such an authenticity. Therefore, syncretic views of the post-colonial distance themselves from the universalist view of the function of language as representation, and from a culturally essentialist stance which might reject the use of english because of its assumed inauthenticity in the 'non-English' place (a danger which haunts theories such as Maxwell's – see ch. 1, pp. 26–7).

The fallacy of both the representationist and culturally determinist views of language may be demonstrated by a brief example. In *The Voice* (1964) Gabriel Okara attempts to develop a 'culturally relevant' use of english by adapting Ijaw syntax and lexical parameters to english. This exercise specifically demonstrates the importance of the *situation* of the word in the discourse by giving rise to lexical items which have various meanings depending on how they are employed in the text. A significant example of this is the use of the terms 'inside' and 'insides', which are employed in a variety of ways in the novel:

> 'Listen. Asking the bottom of things in this town will take you no place. Hook this up with your little finger. Put it in your inside's box and lock it up.'
> 'Your teaching words do not enter my inside.' (36)

> 'You must leave this town. It will pain our *insides* too much to see you suffer.' (48)

> But Okolo looking at them said in his *inside* that his spoken words would only break against them as an egg would against a stone. (48)

> 'These happening things make my *inside* bitter, perhaps more bitter than yours.' (48)

> 'How can I change my *inside*?' he said.' (49)

> 'I see in my *insides* that your spoken words are true and straight. But you see it in your *inside* that we have no power to do anything. The spirit is powerful. So it is they who get the spirit that are powerful and the people believe with their *insides* whatever they are told. The world is no longer straight

. . . So turn this over in your *inside* and do as we do so that you will have a sweet *inside* like us.' (49)

In these passages, it would be possible to gloss these uses of 'inside(s)' as 'emotions or feelings', 'self-referentiality', 'outlook on life', 'personality', 'intellectual perception', 'understanding', 'intellectuality', 'heart' and 'mind'. But to do so would be to interpret Okara's words and contain them rather than allow their meaning to be determined by their place in the discourse. The term 'sweet inside' is dense with metaphoric possibility, connoting all the characteristics of a harmonious and congenial spirit. We may make some very clear deductions from these passages about the holistic nature of self in Ijaw culture, of the notion of the 'inside' as that which responds to everything which is 'other' or 'outside' (and, on further reading, of the notion of the 'inside' and 'outside' as coextensive). But it would be erroneous to believe that this sense of self is a contingent component in the communication of the meaning of the term 'insides' when used in the novel. This is because the word does not have some 'essential' meaning which is unique to Ijaw and experientially inaccessible to members of another culture; the meaning of the word is that composite of uses which emerges in any reading. 'Inside' is not a metaphor for 'the Ijaw sense of self', when used in these ways in the novel. It is a metaphor for 'self', and may give rise to the possibility of many meanings: 'mind', 'will', 'spirit', or 'emotion', according to the ways in which it functions in the text.

Given this deployment of the word in its situation, the 'meaning' of the term 'inside(s)' becomes virtually limitless, and many more senses of the term could be compiled from this one novel: 'Our father's insides always contained things straight' (50); 'everybody's inside is now filled with cars and money' (50); 'he remained talking with his inside until sundown' (51); 'My inside has become hard' (53); 'You are indeed a child in your inside' (55). Clearly, the notion of a referent for the term 'insides' apart from its application in the context of discourse ceases to have any meaning. The 'objective' and 'universal' state represented by the word does not exist. Such a metaphoric use of language may or may not be indicative of language use in Okara's native Ijaw, but this is immaterial to the function of the word in the english text and to its ability to mean in the same way as it does in Ijaw.

This shows the creative potential of intersecting languages when the syntactic and grammatical rules of one language are overlaid on another, and of the way in which cross-cultural literature reveals how meanings work. In a consumption of the text which is divorced from any knowledge of what is being represented, the field of intersection, the literary work, is the field within which the word announces its purpose. Similarly, in whatever way the prolixity of the word 'insides' is linked to the Ijaw perception of the world, this function cannot be limited to the understanding of the Ijaw consciousness. The 'world' as it exists 'in' language is an unfolding reality which owes its relationship to language to the fact that language interprets the world in practice, not to some imputed referentiality.

Language exists, therefore, neither before the fact nor after the fact but in the fact. Language constitutes reality in an obvious way: it provides some terms and not others with which to talk about the world. Because particular languages provide a limited lexicon they may also be said (metaphorically) to 'use' the speaker, rather than vice versa. But the worlds constituted in this way do not become fixed composites in the speaker's mind, a set of images which differs, by definition, from the set in the mind of the speaker of a different language. Worlds exist by means of languages, their horizons extending as far as the processes of neologism, innovation, tropes, and imaginative usage generally will allow the horizons of the language itself to be extended. Therefore the english language becomes a tool with which a 'world' can be textually constructed. The most interesting feature of its use in post-colonial literature may be the way in which it also constructs difference, separation, and absence from the metropolitan norm. But the ground on which such construction is based is an abrogation of the essentialist assumptions of that norm and a dismantling of its imperialist centralism.

A post-colonial linguistic theory: the Creole continuum

One example of the way in which the decentring impetus of post-colonial discourse abrogates the centre and leads to new theories is the extension of the concept of the Creole continuum in the polyglossic communities of the Caribbean. Jean D'Costa, the Jamaican children's author, says of Caribbean writers:

> The [Caribbean] writer operates within a polydialectical continuum with a creole base. His medium, written language, belongs to the sphere of standardised language which exerts a pressure within his own language community while embracing the wide audience of international standard English.

> (D'Costa 1983: 252)

The polydialectical culture of the Caribbean reveals that the complex of 'lects', or distinguishable forms of language use, which overlap in a speaking community, can have a central function in the development of a local variety of english. In fact, the view of language which polydialectical cultures generate dismantles many received views of the structure of language.

Such a theory focuses on the variations generated in the habits of speakers rather than on the putative grammatical 'standard', and can be observed in the working of the Creole continuum. The concept of a Creole continuum is now widely accepted as an explanation of the linguistic culture of the Caribbean. Its general nature has been understood since Reinecke and Tokimasa (1934) and its specific application to the Caribbean (in particular, Jamaica) has been discussed over the past three decades (Le Page and DeCamp 1960; Alleyne 1963; Bailey 1966; Le Page 1969; DeCamp 1971; Bickerton 1973; D'Costa 1983, 1984). The theory states that the Creole complex of the region is not simply an aggregation of discrete dialect forms but an overlapping of ways of speaking between which individual speakers may move with considerable ease. These overlapping 'lects', or specific modes of language use, not only contain forms from the major languages 'between' which they come into being, but forms which are also functionally peculiar to themselves (Bickerton 1973: 642). Thus they meet the paradoxical requirements of being identifiable as stages on a continuum without being wholly discrete as language behaviours.

The theory of the Creole continuum is an outstanding example of a post-colonial approach to linguistics because it reaffirms the notion of language as a practice and reintroduces the 'marginal' complexities of speakers' practice as the subject of linguistics.[4] This undermines the traditional project of post-Saussurian linguistics. As Chomsky states: 'Linguistic theory is concerned primarily with an ideal speaker–listener, in a completely homogeneous speech community' (Chomsky 1965: 3). Orthodox linguistic theory deals exclusively in terms of static models of discrete languages, and data not readily incorporated in such models is consigned to the 'wastebasket of performance' (Labov 1969: 759). The Creole continuum reminds us that a language is a human behaviour and consists in what people do rather than in theoretical models. In a similar way, post-colonial literature reasserts that just as performance is language, so what is written in english, and the rich plethora of constructions and neologisms introduced by such writing, continually reconstitutes that which can be called 'English Literature', but is now more properly conceived as 'english literatures'.

For the writer working within the Creole continuum the consequences are considerable. Since it is a continuum the writer will usually have access to a broad spectrum of the linguistic culture, and must negotiate a series of decisions concerning its adequate representation in writing. This involves an adjustment of word use and spelling to give an accessible rendering of dialect forms. For example, take the Barbadian writer George Lamming in *The Emigrants*:

> Some people say them have no hope for people who doan' know exactly w'at them want or who them is, but that is a lot of rass-clot talk. The interpretation me give hist'ry is people the world over always searchin' an' feelin' . . . An' when them dead an' gone, hist'ry write things 'bout them that them themself would not have know or understand.
>
> (Lamming 1954: 68)

Writers in this continuum employ highly developed strategies of code-switching and vernacular transcription, which achieve the dual result of abrogating the Standard English and appropriating an english as a culturally significant discourse. A multilingual continuum such as the one in which Caribbean writers work requires a different way of theorizing about language; one which will take into account all the arbitrary and marginal variations. This 'different' way is really a process of greater consistency. If all human speech is rule-governed, then theory must take all speech behaviour into account rather than consigning some examples to the 'too hard' basket.

The result is 'a metatheory which takes linguistic variation as the substance rather than the periphery of language study' (Bickerton 1973: 643). Such a metatheory is extremely important because it demonstrates the way in which a post-colonial orientation can confront received theoretical norms. Where traditional theory posits the ideal speaker in order to deal with a language which is grammatically consistent, a 'standard' language which can be approached with the use of consistent and coherent structures, polydialectical theory reveals that the performance of speakers, with all the variations that must be taken into account, is the true subject of linguistics.

The theory of the Creole continuum, undermining, as it does, the static models of language formation, overturns 'concentric' notions of language which regard 'Standard' English as a 'core'. Creole need no longer be seen as a peripheral variation of English. Those rules which develop as approximations of English rules are by no means random or unprincipled, and the concept of what actually constitutes 'English' consequently opens itself to the possibility of radical transformation. It is indisputable that english literature extends itself to include all texts written in language communicable to an english-speaker. Elements of a very wide range of different lects contribute to this, and the only criterion for their membership of english literature is whether they are used or not.

A number of conclusions may be made from observation of the Creole continuum which hold true for all language use: that the language is constituted of several overlapping lects or distinguishable forms of language use; that the variants or 'edges' of language are the substance of linguistic theory; that the characteristics of language are located in actual practice rather than structural abstraction. Because these conclusions affirm the plurality of practice, the linguistic theory of the Creole continuum offers a paradigmatic demonstration of the abrogating impetus in post-colonial literary theory.

Language and subversion

Some Caribbean theorists propose a distinctly political basis to the operation of the linguistic continuum. In Cliff Lashley's view the 'official pre-emption of native conceptual space' by the imperial English culture resulted in the subversive practice of Jamaican adaptive code-switching, in which 'the Jamaican capacity to encode and decode any native linguistic accultural sign by either of the two semiological systems is advantageous' (Lashley 1984: 2). Lashley insists that any Jamaican literary theory must be linked to the dynamics of the 'essentially political relationship' between the two poles of the Creole continuum, a continuum which he sees as disguising or at least obfuscating the radical political opposition represented by the poles. Lashley and other critics prefer to see a relationship of subversion being invoked here and, indeed, not a subversion of language alone, but of the entire system of cultural assumptions on which the texts of the English canon are based and the whole discourse of metropolitan control within which they were able to be imposed. Such subversion, they argue, has been characteristic of much West Indian literature and culture. These subversive strategies not only have historical and social antecedents, but provide the only possible means of linguistic assertion where there is no alternative language in which to reject the language (and hence the vision) of the colonizers.

These concerns have not been limited to literary theory. The problem inherent in using a language while trying to reject the particular way of structuring the world it seems to offer also forms the basis of the deliberate Creole restructuring undertaken by the populist political and religious Rastafarian movement of Jamaica. The Rastafarians attempt to 'deconstruct' what they see as the power structures of English grammar, structures in themselves metonymic of the hegemonic controls exercised by the British on Black peoples throughout Caribbean and African history – controls no less present today, though they may take different forms. While the language remains as it is, however, there is no hope of genuine 'freedom', and consequently the Rastafarians have adopted various strategies by which language might be 'liberated' from within. Although the basis of Rasta speech is Jamaican Creole, it is deliberately altered in a number of ways. In Jamaican Creole the first person singular is usually expressed by the pronoun 'me': 'Me see me 'oman in street.' The plural form substitutes 'we' for 'me'. To the Rastafarians, however, both 'me' and 'we' as objects of the sentence are always dominated or 'governed' by the subject, in the way in which white Europeans governed the slaves. On the purely verbal level too, 'me' conjures the subservient attitude into which Blacks were forced for their own survival under the plantation system. Consequently, the Rastas insist on the use of 'I' for the personal pronoun in all positions:

> The pronoun 'I' has a special importance to Rastas and is expressly opposed to the servile 'me'. Whether in the singular ('I') or the plural ('I and I' or briefly: 'I-n-I') or the reflexive ('I-sel', 'I-n-I self') the use of this pronoun identifies the Rasta as an individual . . . Even the possessive 'my' and the objective 'me' are replaced by 'I'.
>
> (Owens 1976: 65, 66)

As Owens goes on to note, once the 'I' has been liberated from its English function in this fashion, it is 'available' for use in other grammatical positions where it and its homonym 'high', can continually recall for the Rasta his/her own personhood and its value in constant association with Jah (the Rastafarian term for Godhead) (66).

Wilson Harris also uses language in a way which specifically and deliberately disturbs its attendant assumptions, particularly its binary structuration. This pattern of binary structuration in European and many other languages, Harris asserts, lies at the root of the ceaseless pattern of conquest and domination that has formed the fabric of human history. Consequently Harris takes direct issue with language in all his works and effects a radical disruption of its binary bases. Take, for example, this passage from the novel *Ascent To Omai*:

> The judge shuffled his sketches and cards. There stood Victor within schooldoor marked prospects and futures: alternatives.
>
> Shuffled his sketches again. There – thought the judge – stands primary mask and clown, scholar: life-mask, death-mask. Born during World War I in a British Colony on the

coastlands of South America. Steeped in the three R's. One foot in two M's (mathematics and mythology), the other in a single L (Latin) – residual functions of Pythagoras and Homer, Caesar and Hannibal.

Shuffled his sketches again. One hand on an expurgated series, English history and literature. The other on limbo pavement – East Indian/African folk tales, stories of pork-nocker/sailor/welder/El Dorado, charcoal limbs, artists' wall in the marketplace.

There he was – Sailor/Victor – washed ashore upon ancient pavement as if, for him, the new world on which he had been drawn was still unborn – hallucinated womb of the gods. Yet unborn as it was, the birth of memory presided there to confirm violence or death – death by drowning, misadventure, war, suicide, knife, tarantula – as another substitute, another portrait of innermost conviction, innermost sacrifice in the name of conqueror/conquered whose light could still be garnered into extrapolative design-vicar of freedom.

(Harris 1970b: 124–5)

In examples like this the word is

'liberated', hollowed out, emptied, through a dialectical process of paired contradictions . . . Images crumble, shift, dissolve and coalesce in strange combinations or, to use Harris's own term, 'paradoxical juxtapositions', reflecting a universe in the process of becoming . . .

Harris's works constitute a programme for the dismantling of myth, a dismantling of history and society, of the object and even the word.

(Shaw 1985: 125, 127)

West Indian groups and individuals have always been intensely involved in the 'struggle over the word' in making the only language available 'native' to Caribbean person and place.

However, not all Caribbean theorists reject the language of the master or strive to effect such radical subversion of its codes. As an alternative strategy Derek Walcott advocates appropriation and celebration, arguing that to the Caribbean writer falls the enviable task, (unavailable to Europe and Europeans) of 'giving things their names'. In Walcott's view it is a common

Caribbean error to 'see history as language' (Walcott 1974b: 3), specifically in terms of the history of slavery and the language of the master. Instead, he proposes an Adamic celebration of language, invoking the poet's excitement in establishing 'original relations' with his 'new' universe, the newness qualified of course by the prior experiences of the old. 'A political philosophy rooted in elation would have to accept belief in a second Adam, the re-creation of the entire order, from religion to the simplest domestic rituals' (5). But here too, it is 'the bitter memory' (6) of the old which supplies the energy in the new, and ultimately the creative dynamic Walcott advocates is not so very far removed from Harris's philosophic position, with his insistence on the 'mutual erosion' of the relationship between the dominated and dominating cultures as the source of the peculiar energy of the Caribbean experience. Nor, although he would probably strenuously deny it, is it so very different in effect from the Rasta language project.

The metonymic function of language variance

Predictably, it is in the practice of post-colonial writing, rather than the development of linguistic theories, that the abrogation of authenticity and essence most often takes place. Whether written from monoglossic, diglossic, or polyglossic cultures, post-colonial writing abrogates the privileged centrality of 'English' by using language to signify difference while employing a sameness which allows it to be understood. It does this by employing language variance, the 'part' of a wider cultural whole, which assists in the work of language seizure whilst being neither transmuted nor overwhelmed by its adopted vehicle.

The introduction of language variance in this way could be seen to propose a metaphoric entry for the culture into the 'English' text. Metaphor has always, in the western tradition, had the privilege of revealing unexpected truth. As Aristotle put it: 'Midway between the unintelligible and the commonplace, it is metaphor which most produces knowledge' (Aristotle, Rhetoric, III, 1410). The importance of the metaphor/metonymy distinction was first suggested by Roman Jakobson in his article 'Two types of language and two types of aphasic disturbances' (Jakobson and Halle, 1956: 78). Jakobson refers

to the importance of metaphor in the literary schools of romanticism and symbolism, and posits the predominance of metonymy in the so-called 'realist' school. This has greatly exercised
many structuralist and poststructuralist critics (scc Ruegg
1979). Paul de Man summarizes the preference for metaphor
over metonymy by aligning analogy with necessity and contiguity with chance: The inference of identity and totality that is
constitutive of metaphor is lacking in the purely relational
metonymic contact (de Man 1979: 14). The importance of the
metaphor/metonymy distinction to post-colonial texts is also
raised by Homi Bhabha (1984a). His point is that the perception of the figures of the text as metaphors imposes a universalist
reading because metaphor makes no concessions to the cultural
specificity of texts. For Bhabha it is preferable to read the tropes
of the text as metonymy, which symptomatizes the text, reading
through its features the social, cultural, and political forces
which traverse it.

However, while the tropes of the post-colonial text may be
fruitfully read as metonymy, language variance itself in such a
text is far more profoundly metonymic of cultural difference.
The variance itself becomes the metonym, the part which
stands for the whole. That 'overlap' of language which occurs
when texture, sound, rhythm, and words are carried over from
the mother tongue to the adopted literary form, or when the
appropriated english is adapted to a new situation, is something
which the writer may take as evidence of his ethnographic or
differentiating function – an insertion of the 'truth' of culture
into the text (sometimes conceived as an insertion of its essential
cultural 'purity'). Technical devices used by writers who come
from an oral society (one with no tradition of writing), for
instance, can be mistaken for 'power words', 'power syntax',
and 'power rhythms' which reproduce the culture by some
process of embodiment. Such language use seems to be keeping
faith with the local culture and transporting it into the new
medium. Thus the untranslated words, the sounds and the
textures of the language can be held to have the power and
presence of the culture they signify – to be metaphoric in their
'inference of identity and totality'.

It is commonly held that in this way words somehow embody
the culture from which they derive. Thus a word that is

'characteristically' Australian or Caribbean may be held to be predicated on certain untransferable cultural experiences (D'Costa 1984). The idea that language somehow 'embodies' culture in this way is a seductive one for post-colonial readers. Superficially, it seems to be demonstrable from the texts, where words such as '*obi*' (hut), '*kurta*' (shirt), etc. embedded in the English text seem to 'carry' the oppressed culture, just as the english which surrounds them may be seen to be 'tainted' by its colonial origins. Such an essentialist view of language has an appeal within an abrogative stance, and has been invoked by some post-colonial writers engaged in 'decolonizing' projects. But it is a false and dangerous argument. It is false because it confuses usage with property in its view of meaning, and it is ultimately contradictory, since, if it is asserted that words do have some essential cultural essence not subject to changing usage, then post-colonial literatures in english, predicated upon this very changing usage, could not have come into being. Language would be imprisoned in origins and not, as is the demonstrable case, be readily available for appropriation and liberation by a whole range of new and distinctive enterprises.

However, such uses of language as untranslated words do have an important function in inscribing difference. They signify a certain cultural experience which they cannot hope to reproduce but whose difference is validated by the new situation. In this sense they are directly metonymic of that cultural difference which is imputed by the linguistic variation. In fact they are a specific form of metonymic figure: the synecdoche. The technique of such writing demonstrates how the dynamics of language change are consciously incorporated into the text. Where a source culture has certain functional effects on language use in the english text, the employment of specific techniques formalizes the cross-cultural character of the linguistic medium.

The use of english inserts itself as a political discourse in post-colonial writing, and the use of english variants of all kinds captures that metonymic moment between the culture affirmed on the one hand as 'indigenous' or 'national', and that characterized on the other as 'imperialist', 'metropolitan', etc. Thus in the play *The Cord* by the Malaysian writer K.S. Maniam the english variant establishes itself in clear contradistinction to the 'Standard' within the dialogue itself.

> *Muthiah*: What are you saying? Speaking English?
> *Ratnam*: The language you still think is full of pride. The language that makes you a stiffwhite corpse like this!
> *Muthiah*: But you're nothing. I'm still the boss here.
> *Ratnam*: Everything happens naturally. Now the language is spoke like I can speak it . . . I can speak real life English now.
> *Muthiah*: You can do that all day to avoid work!
> *Ratnam*: You nothing but stick. You nothing but stink. Look all clean, inside all thing dirty. Outside everything. Inside nothing. Taking-making. Walking-talking. Why you insulting all time? Why you sit on me like monkey with wet backside?

(Ooi 1984: 95)

There are two principles operating in this passage which are central to all post-colonial writing: first, there is a repetition of the general idea of the interdependence of language and identity – you are the way you speak. This general idea includes the more specific Malaysian and Singaporean debate about whether 'standard' English or local variants should be spoken in the region. The language of power, the language of the metropolitan centre, is that of Muthiah, while the 'real life English' (english), the language variant of cultural fidelity, is the one spoken by Ratnam: second, there is the more distinctive act of the post-colonial text, which is to inscribe difference and absence as a corollary of that identity. The articulation of two quite opposed possibilities of speaking and therefore of political and cultural identification outlines a cultural space between them which is left unfilled, and which, indeed, locates a major signifying difference in the post-colonial text. The 'cultural space' is the direct consequence of the metonymic function of language variance. It is the 'absence' which occupies the gap between the contiguous inter/faces of the 'official' language of the text and the cultural difference brought to it. Thus the alterity in that metonymic juncture establishes a silence beyond which the cultural Otherness of the text cannot be traversed by the colonial language. By means of this gap of silence the text resists incorporation into 'English literature' or some universal literary mode, not because there is any inherent hindrance to someone from a different culture understanding what the text means, but because this constructed gap consolidates its difference. The local culture, through the inclusion of such variance, abuts, rather than encloses, the putative metropolitan specificity of the english text. Consequently the gap of silence enfolds that space between the simultaneous abrogation of language as normative standard and the appropriation of language as cultural mode in the post-colonial text.

The idea that absence and difference are constructed in Maniam's text is supported by Ooi Boo Eng's observation that 'Ratnam's pidgin English reads to me like Maniam's inventive blending together of approximations of pidgin and Malaysian English, the whole sounding more pidgin than Malaysian English (good Malaysian English, which is closer to standard English)' (Ooi 1984: 96). The 'absence' is a construction just as the language variant is itself a construction, rather than the reflection of any particular Malaysian practice. This is also true, for instance, of the usage of idiom in Raja Rao's novel *Kanthapura* which does not always conform to actual usage in the Kannada language (Kantak 1972). The illusion, continually undermined by post-colonial literature, is that literary discourse constitutes a process of mimetic representation (see also Bhabha 1984a). In fact, the signs of identity and of difference are always a matter of invention and construction.

A brilliant demonstration of this occurs in Naipaul's *The Mystic Masseur* (1957) where Ganesh's future wife puts up a sign (44) in which an obsession with punctuation directly signifies the gaps constructed between language and lived experience:

NOTICE!
NOTICE, IS. HEREBY; PROVIDED: THAT, SEATS!
ARE, PROVIDED. FOR; FEMALE: SHOP, ASSISTANTS!

Signs and signwriting are, of course, very important in Naipaul's work because they directly signify the iconic and constitutive function of language. In this case the punctuation is not merely idiosyncratic but directly synecdochic of the gaps, caesuras, and silences which exist between the language, which is the signifier of power, and the experience it is called upon to 'represent'. These gaps are effectively elaborated later in the novel when Ganesh and Beharry decide to practise speaking 'proper English', a task which becomes far too ludicrous to sustain.

Although language variance seems most prominent when english writing borrows from a different language, the construction of Otherness is just as important in the monoglossic texts of the USA, english-speaking Canada, Australia, and New Zealand. English is adopted as the national language, so its local development into vernacular form is one of both evolution and adaptation. In this process of 'becoming', english, by asserting its opposition to the centre and constantly interrogating the dominance of the 'standard', establishes itself as a contrastive or counter-discourse (Terdiman 1985; see ch. 5, pp. 168–9 below). At the same time, that is, as an english 'emerges' from English it establishes itself as distinct and separate. A considerable range of linguistic variance is generated, even though such variance is always attacked from the centre by the dismissive terms 'colloquialism' or 'idiom'.

In a story by the Australian writer Henry Lawson, 'A bluff that failed', Australian 'identity' is established not only in the vernacular discourse but also in a posited difference from New Zealand society:

> Maoriland scenery is grand mostly and the rivers are beautiful – They are clear and run all summer. The scenery don't seem to brood and haunt you like our bush. It's a different sort of loneliness altogether – sort of sociable new-mate kind of loneliness – and not that exactly. I can't describe it. But there was something wanting and I soon fixed on it. You see, they don't understand travelling and mateship round there – they're not used to it. A swagman is a tramp with them – same as in the old coastal district of N.S.W. . . . But that was on another track, afterwards where they were all Scotch and Scandies (Norwegians), and I had a pound or two and a programme then.

> (Kiernan 1982: 167)

The strategy of glossing, which may seem coy to the local reader, nevertheless signifies the self-conscious processes of language variation in which the text is engaged. The *theme* of difference which the passage asserts is directly signified in the language variance employed. We can detect a process here which mirrors the function of the metonymic strategies of the cross-cultural text. Just as that text inserts language variance as a signifying difference, the installation of an absence, so monoglossic texts can employ vernacular as a linguistic variant to signify the insertion of the outsider into the discourse. In the same way then, the vernacular appropriates the language for the task of constituting new experience and new place.

The following passage from Mark Twain's *Huckleberry Finn* demonstrates how subtly yet completely this difference can be announced:

> We slept most all day, and started out at night, a little ways behind a monstrous long raft that was as long going by as a procession. She had four long sweeps at each end, so we judged she carried as many as thirty men, likely. She had five big wigwams aboard, wide apart, and an open camp fire in the middle, and a tall flag-pole at each end. There was a power of style about her. It *amounted* to something being a raftsman on such a craft as that.
>
> (Twain 1885: 86)

Although language does not embody culture, and therefore proposes no inherent obstacles to the communication of meaning, the notion of difference, of an indecipherable juncture between cultural realities, is often just as diligently *constructed* in the text as that of identity. Even in the monoglossic Twain text such difference is constructed by lexis, orthography, grammar and syntax. The synecdochic function of such strategies, to form a bridge between the 'centre' and 'margin', simultaneously defines their unbridgeable separation.

Allusion and difference

Allusion can perform the same function of registering cultural distance in the post-colonial text, according to the extent to which the text itself provides the necessary context for the allusion. An example of this occurs in Ngugi wa Thiongo's novel

A Grain Of Wheat in which Gikonyo sings the following song to his future wife Mumbi:

> 'Haven't you heard the new song?'
> 'Which? Sing it'
> You know it too. I believe it is Kihika who introduced it here. I only remember the words of the chorus:

> > Gikuyu na Mumbi
> > Gikuyu na Mumbi
> > Gikuyu na Mumbi
> > Nikihui ngwatiro

> It was Mumbi who now broke the solemnity. She was laughing quietly.
> 'What is it?'
> 'Oh, Carpenter, Carpenter. So you know why I came?'
> 'I don't!' he said, puzzled.
> 'But you sing to *me* and *Gikuyu* telling us it is burnt at the *handle*.'

> > > (Ngugi 1967: 92)

This simple chorus is dense with cultural signifiers. Gikuyu was the first man of the Kikuyu tribe, the man from whom all the Kikuyu were descended, and Mumbi was his wife, the first woman. 'Nikihui' literally means that something is 'ready' or 'cooked'. Ngwatiro is literally a 'handle'. But when used together the term means that 'someone is in trouble' because the handle is too hot. The song as invented by Kihika means that the relationship between man and woman spells 'trouble'. The relationship is 'too hot to handle' and as a chorus it has both sexual and political overtones. But Mumbi laughs because it foretells her reason for visiting Gikonyo: her panga handle has actually been burnt in the fire and needs repair.

This example reconfirms that absence which lies at the point of interface between the two cultures. Here it is demonstrated by Ngugi's refusal to gloss the song directly and the consequent exchange between the man and woman. This does not mean that the song cannot be understood once the whole context is grasped, but rather that the process of allusion installs linguistic distance itself as a subject of the text. The maintenance of this 'gap' in the cross-cultural text is of profound importance to its ethnographic function. The danger in 'transcultural dialogues', such as those represented by some traditional anthropological texts, is that a new set of presuppositions, resulting from the interchange of cultures, is taken as the cultural reality of the Other. The described culture is therefore very much a product of the particular ethnographic encounter – the text creates the reality of the Other in the guise of describing it. Although the post-colonial text can operate as ethnography, its use of language incorporates the warning that the site of the shared discourse – the literary text – is not the site of a shared mental experience, and should not be seen as such.

Language variance, with its synecdochic function, is thus a feature of all post-colonial texts. The writer 'function' meets the reader 'function' in the writing itself which dwells at the intersection of a vast array of cultural conditions. Such writing neither represents culture nor gives rise to a world-view, but sets the scene of a constitution of meaning. The strategies which such writing employs to maintain distance and otherness while appropriating the language are therefore a constant demonstration of the dynamic possibilities available to writing within the tension of 'centre' and 'margin'.

Strategies of appropriation in post-colonial writing

Post-colonial texts may signify difference in their representations of place, in nomenclature, and through the deployment of themes. But it is in the language that the curious tension of cultural 'revelation' and cultural 'silence' is most evident. Significantly, most of these strategies, in which difference is constructed and english appropriated, are shared by all the post-colonial societies, be they monoglossic, diglossic, or polyglossic.

One way to demonstrate an appropriated english is to contrast it with another still tied to the imperial centre. This contrast very often stands as a direct indication of the extent to which post-colonial writers have succeeded in constituting their sense of a different place. For instance, when the Australian colonial poet Henry Kendall writes a poem about the seasons, 'September in Australia', it is severely constrained by the language of British late romanticism within which it is realized:

> Grey Winter hath gone, like a wearisome guest,
>   And behold, for repayment,
> September comes in with the wind of the West
>   And the Spring in her raiment!
> The ways of the forest have been filled of the flowers,
>   Whilst the forest discovers
> Wild wings, with the halo of hyaline hours,
>   And a music of lovers.
>
> (Kendall 1870: 79)

Kendall is not writing (indeed, cannot write) about any place conceivable outside the discourse in which he is located, even though the very point of the poem is to attempt to distance Australian seasons from those of the northern hemisphere. In Les Murray's 'A New England farm, August 1914', however, where the language has been fully appropriated, place is not only constituted 'beyond' an English literary tradition, but is constituted in terms of resonant historical experience, the First World War which is so important to Australian myths of cultural identity;

> August is the new year's hinge:
> Time out of mind we've stacked the raddled autumn
> Cornstalks on the river bank for burning,
> Watching the birds come dodging through the smoke
> To feast on beetles. Time out of mind
> We've retraced last year's furrows with the plough:
> How can this August fail us?
>
> Why do the young men saddle horses?
> Why do the women grieve together?
>
> (Murray 1965: 22)

A modern writer, such as Murray, stands in an interpretative space quite unlike that of an earlier author, like Kendall, who is still writing within the metropolitan discourse imposed during the imperial period (even though he was passionate about being recognized as an Australian poet). A writer like Murray is the archetypal ethnographer whose cultural location 'creates' two audiences and faces two directions, wishing to reconstitute experience through an act of writing which uses the tools of one culture or society and yet seeks to remain faithful to the experience of another. In the foreword to his novel *Kanthapura* Raja Rao explains the particular tasks faced by the writer in conveying cultural specificity in a different language:

> The telling has not been easy. One has to convey in a language that is not one's own the spirit that is one's own. One has to convey the various shades and omissions of a certain thought-movement that looks maltreated in an alien language. I use the word 'alien', yet English is not really an alien language to us. It is the language of our intellectual make-up – like Sanskrit or Persian was before – but not of our emotional make-up. We are all instinctively bilingual, many of us writing in our own language and English. We cannot write like the English. We should not. We cannot write only as Indians.
>
> (Rao 1938: vii)

Such writing is, in effect, an ethnography of the writer's own culture. The post-colonial writer, whose gaze is turned in two directions, stands already in that position which will come to be occupied by an interpretation, for he/she is not the object of an interpretation, but the first interpreter. Editorial intrusions, such as the footnote, the glossary, and the explanatory preface, where these are made by the author, are a good example of this. Situated outside the text, they represent a reading rather than a writing, primordial sorties into that interpretative territory in which the Other (as reader) stands.

Glossing

Parenthetic translations of individual words, for example, 'he took him into his *obi* (hut)', are the most obvious and most common authorial intrusion in cross-cultural texts. Although not limited to cross-cultural texts such glosses foreground the continual reality of cultural distance. But the simple ostensive matching of '*obi*' and 'hut' reveals the general inadequacy of such an exercise. Juxtaposing the words in this way suggests the view that the meaning of a word is its referent. But it becomes clear in reading that the Igbo word '*obi*' is one of the buildings which makes up the family's communal compound. If simple ostensive reference does not work even for simple objects, it is even more difficult to find a referent for more abstract terms. Glossing is far less prevalent than it was twenty or thirty years ago, but it is useful for showing how simple referential bridges establish themselves as the most primitive form of metonymy. The implicit gap between *obi* [ ] (hut) in fact disputes the putative referentiality of the words and establishes *obi* as a cultural sign. The retention of the Igbo word perpetuates the metonymic function of the cross-cultural text by allowing the word to stand for the latent presence of Ibo culture. The requisite sense of difference is implicitly recorded in the gap [ ] between the word and its referent, a 'referent' which (ironically) accords the english word the status of the 'real'. This absence, or gap, is not negative but positive in its effect. It presents the difference through which an identity (created or recovered) can be expressed.

The problem with glossing in the cross-cultural text is that, at its worst, it may lead to a considerably stilted movement of plot as the story is forced to drag an explanatory machinery behind it. Yet in one sense virtually everything that happens or everything that is said can be ethnographic. A casual conversation can reveal a complex social structure, as in the following passage from the Papua New Guinea writer Vincent Eri's *Crocodile*:

> Death had claimed another victim. The crying that Hoiri had heard earlier had increased in volume. The victim was an old man. . . . He had been married once but his liquid brought forth no sons and daughters . . .
>
> 'You see how important it is to get married and have children,' Suaea warned. 'When one is young one has many friends. But when the skin shrivels up and the mind becomes forgetful, it is one's own children, children from one's own liquid who will bother to wipe away the mucus or do the menial tasks. . . . See what has happened to old Ivurisa. He had no children on whom he could rely . . . so he took the short way of ending all his troubles.'
>
> (Eri 1970: 24)

What might seem to be a merely gratuitous observation in the novel is in fact just one part of a picture being painstakingly compiled throughout most of the book. For this is part of the point. It is a novel about cultural fragmentation, a fragmentation caused by the influx of Australians during the Second World War and the profound historical change this meant for the people of Papua New Guinea. The story is a subtly constructed view of the culture which will be contrasted, in retrospect, with the changing values and attitudes with which Hoiri comes in contact. In this sense, the novel, like so much of post-colonial literature (whether monolingual, polydialectical, or diglossic), is 'about' a void, a psychological abyss between cultures. Ethnographic detail serves not as local colour, but as the central feature of a structuring which gives this essay into the void some specific reference point. Canadian author Dennis Lee notes that this gap is both the site and the challenge of the post-colonial writer (Lee 1974). For Lee, the exploration of this gap, its acceptance, and its installation as the legitimate subject-matter of the post-colonial, rather than a sign of failure and inauthenticity, is the crucial act of appropriation (see ch. 5, pp. 141–3).

While glossing may be less obvious in the literatures of settler cultures than in African, Indian, and South Pacific writing, it nevertheless has the same function. This is demonstrated by the beginning of Henry Lawson's story 'Brighten's sister-in-law':

> Jim was born on the Gulgong, New South Wales. We used to say 'on' the Gulgong – and old diggers still talked of being 'on th' Gulgong' – though the goldfield there had been worked out for years, and the place was a dusty little pastoral town in the scrubs. Gulgong was about the last of the great alluvial 'rushes' of the 'roaring days' – and dreary and dismal enough it looked when I was there. The expression 'on' came from being on the 'diggings' or goldfield – the workings or the goldfield was all underneath, of course, so we lived (or starved) *on* them – not in nor at 'em.

> (Roderick 1972: 555).

The term 'on' is glossed at some length as a way of inserting a mildly ethnographic discourse into what has immediately taken on the patterns of vernacular speech ('We used to say . . .'). But at the same time, 'rushes' and 'roaring days' are marked off without gloss, their difference signified by punctuation, but the difference of their cultural provenance, the 'gap of silence', also signified by the omission of glossing. While their place or use in the text establishes their meaning, their function in the text is highly ambivalent. They work ethnographically, by their very presence, but at the same time their major purpose is to signify difference. As the text continues, the differences are increasingly internalized:

> We lived in an old weather-board shanty that had been a sly-grog-shop, and the Lord knows what else! in the palmy days of Gulgong; and I did a bit of digging ('fossicking', rather), a bit of shearing, a bit of fencing, a bit of Bush-carpentering, tank-sinking, – anything, just to keep the billy boiling.

> (ibid.)

Doing anything 'just to keep the billy boiling' is a characteristic vernacular metaphor, but one which is left to do its own work of cultural placement. 'Shanty', 'sly-grog', even 'weather-board' or 'Bush' are local uses which are left unglossed and do their work in context, conveying the syntax of colloquial speech.[5]

Untranslated words

The technique of selective lexical fidelity which leaves some words untranslated in the text is a more widely used device for conveying the sense of cultural distinctiveness. Such a device not only acts to signify the difference between cultures, but also illustrates the importance of discourse in interpreting cultural concepts. Australian writer Randolph Stow's novel *Visitants*, set in Papua New Guinea, uses Biga-Kiriwini words throughout the english text. The use here of untranslated words is a clear signifier of the fact that the language which actually informs the novel is an/Other language. The text constantly draws attention to cultural differences between the groups of people involved – expatriates and islanders:

> 'These taubadas,' Naibusi said, 'when will they come?'
> 'Soon. Before night.'
> 'They will bring food perhaps? Dimdim food?'
> 'Perhaps.'
> 'They might eat chicken,' Naibusi said, wondering. 'I do not know. The dimdim yams are finished.'

'E,' said Misa Makadoneli, 'green bananas then. They are the same as potatoes. And *lokwai*.'

'They will eat *lokwai*?' said Naibusi. 'Perhaps it is not their custom.'

'My grief for them,' Misa Makadoneli said . . . 'see what there is in the cookhouse.'

(Stow 1979: 9)

Like Ngugi's refusal to gloss the song about Gikonyo and Mumbi, this not only registers a sense of cultural distinctiveness but forces the reader into an active engagement with the horizons of the culture in which these terms have meaning. The reader gets some idea about the meaning of these words from the subsequent conversation, but further understanding will require the reader's own expansion of the cultural situation beyond the text. What is significant about the use of untranslated terms such as *lokwai* is that they constitute a specific sign of a post-colonial discourse rather than a specific Papua New Guinean usage: the term *'lokwai'* in Biga-Kiriwini speech is one among many, but placed in the english text it signifies difference.

Such usage may seem to be no different from other novels in which much that is recondite and inaccessible must become the subject of deeper examination. But in the post-colonial text the absence of translation has a particular kind of interpretative function. Cultural difference is not inherent in the text but is inserted by such strategies. The post-colonial text, by developing specific ways of both constituting cultural distance and at the same time bridging it, indicates that it is the 'gap' rather than the experience (or at least the *concept* of a gap between experiences) which is created by language. The absence of explanation is, therefore, first a sign of distinctiveness, though it merely makes explicit that alterity which is implicit in the gloss. More importantly, it is an endorsement of the facility of the discourse situation, a recognition that the message event, the 'scene of the Word', has full authority in the process of cultural and linguistic intersection.

The use of the Hindi word *'hubshi'* rather than 'Negro' in V.S. Naipaul's story 'One out of many' (1971: 23–62), prepares the reader for a gradual discovery of the peculiar significance of the word, indicating as it does the singular aversion, the ritual uncleanness, and religious horror which the Indian protagonist attaches to the touch of the Negro maid, who eventually seduces him. In Naipaul's case the word is used to indicate the protagonist's culture rather than the writer's, and in this sense is a self-consciously detached use of language difference. With this word '*hubshi*' we do not have a different signified for the signifier 'Negro', as we might in a translation; we have a different sign altogether. It is a metonym of the Indian cultural experience which lies beyond the word but of which it is a part. Similar usage, such as '*osu*' in Achebe's *No Longer at Ease* (1963: 46) which literally means a 'cult slave of a god' and which in modern usage indicates a hereditary 'untouchable' in Ibo society, or the Igbo word '*chi*' which refers to an individual's god or fate, or spiritual alter ego, generate nuances which are only accessible through an observation of their use.

The gradual discarding of glossing in the post-colonial text has, more than anything, released language from the myth of cultural authenticity, and demonstrated the fundamental importance of the situating context in according meaning. While the untranslated word remains metonymic and thus emphasizes the (posited) experiential gap which lies at the heart of any cross-cultural text, it also demonstrates quite clearly that the use of the word, even in an english-language context, confers the meaning, rather than any culturally hermetic referentiality. Ultimately, the choice of leaving words untranslated in post-colonial texts is a political act, because while translation is not inadmissable in itself, glossing gives the translated word, and thus the 'receptor' culture, the higher status.

Interlanguage

The use of untranslated words as interface signs seems a successful way to foreground cultural distinctions, so it would appear even more profitable to attempt to generate an 'inter-culture' by the fusion of the linguistic structures of two languages. Amos Tutuola published his first novel in 1952 with a language which seemed to do just this:

> I was a palm-wine drinkard since I was a boy of ten years of age. I had no other work more than to drink palm-wine in my

life. In those days we did not know other money except COWRIES, so that everything was very cheap, and my father was the richest man in town.

(Tutuola 1952: 7)

Tutuola's work has been the centre of controversy since it was published. It was simultaneously read by English critics as a delightful post-Joycean exercise in neologism, whilst being rejected by many African critics as simply an inaccurate plagiarization of traditional oral tales, though in fact the relationship between Tutuola and traditional and modern Yoruba writing was more complex than this accusation suggested (Afolayan 1971). Important as the entire controversy over Tutuola's work has been in the articulation of different critical positions in Africa, viewed in a wider context the work may suggest totally different issues.

For example, Tutuola's style may fruitfully be described by the term 'interlanguage', a term coined by Nemser (1971) and Selinker (1972) to characterize the genuine and discrete linguistic system employed by learners of a second language. The concept of an interlanguage reveals that the utterances of a second-language learner are not deviant forms or mistakes, but rather are part of a separate but genuine linguistic system. Such a system, along with its concomitant features of inscription, characterizes Tutuola's process of appropriation of english. Nemser identifies the learner-language as an 'approximate system' which is cohesive and distinct from both source language and target language. It is by definition transient and gradually restructured from initial through advanced learning. But we can contend that if arrested in writing at any stage, such an interlanguage may become the focus of an evocative and culturally significant idiom. Selinker finds the evidence for interlanguage in fossilizations, which are phonological, morphological, and syntactic forms in the speech of the speaker of a second language which do not conform to target language norms even after years of instruction.

It is important to discard the notion of these forms as 'mistakes', since they operate according to a separate linguistic logic. Bearing no relation to either source or target language norms, they are potentially the basis of a potent metaphoric mode in cross-cultural writing. It may well be that Tutuola, in the early years of the post-war African novel, located the most primal form of language variance. If this is so, Tutuola's work may not be the mere linguistic aberration it has sometimes been dismissed as, but an important and early example of a diglossic formation in post-colonial literature. In this sense Tutuola's 'interlanguage' may be seen as paradigmatic of all cross-cultural writing, since the development of a creative language is not a striving for competence in the dominant tongue, but a striving towards appropriation, in which the cultural distinctiveness can be simultaneously overridden–overwritten.

Syntactic fusion

Tutuola's novels uncovered a widely held assumption that alien world-views might come closer if their linguistic structures were somehow meshed. This was more obviously and self-consciously the project of Gabriel Okara's attempt in *The Voice* to marry the syntax of his tribal language, Ijaw, to the lexical forms of English (see pp. 42–4).

But syntactic fusion is much more common in post-colonial writing as a less overt feature of the linguistic material. A multilingual society like Papua New Guinea, for example, provides a rich source for syntactic variation. The following passage from a story (an excerpt from an unpublished novel) by John Kasaipwalova, called 'Bomanus kalabus o sori o!', demonstrates two sources of linguistic influence:

> The afternoon passed very quickly, and soon four o'clock brought more people into the bar until it was full with men, beers, smoke and happiness. My head was already starting to turn and turn, but I didn't care as much as I was feeling very happy and wanted to sing. The waiters by now had become like Uni Transport trucks speeding everywhere to take away our empty bottles and bring new ones to our table. They liked our group very much because each time they came we gave them each one bottle also, but because their boss might angry them for nothing, they would bend their bodies to the floor pretending to pick up rubbish and while our legs hid them from sight they quickly emptied the beers into their open throats. By five o'clock our waiter friends couldn't walk

straight, and their smart speeding started to appear like they were dancing to our singing.

That was when their boss saw them. He gave a very loud yell and followed with bloody swearings. But our waiter friends didn't take any notice. Our beer presents had already full up their heads and our happy singings had grabbed their hearts. . . . Man, man, *em gutpela pasin moa ya! maski boss!* Everybody was having a good time, and the only thing that spoiled the happiness was that there was not the woman in the bar to make it more happier.

(Beier 1980: 69–70)

This passage manages to adhere very subtly to the rhythms of the vernacular voice. But the syntactic influence comes from both Melanesian *tok pisin* and the syntactic tendencies in Papua New Guinean vernacular languages. Some locutions borrow directly from *tok pisin*: the use of nouns as verbs, 'their boss might *angry* them for nothing'; '*full* with men'; '*full up* their heads'; a metonymic use of adjectives, '*bloody* swearings'; the use of conjunctions, 'we gave them each one bottle *also*'; the use of double comparatives, 'more happier'. But in addition to this, the use of plurals, 'swearings', 'singings', is the result of a much more complex influence, stemming from the habit in Papua New Guinean cultures to talk about all things in the plural as a statement of communal involvement. The linguistic adaptation signifies both the difference and the *tension* of difference, for it is out of this tension that much of the political energy of the cross-cultural text is generated. This same tension is also emphasized in the passage above by the inclusion of direct pidgin transcription.

The literature of the Caribbean continuum provides the widest range of possibilities of syntactic variation. The following passage from St Lucian poet and playwright Derek Walcott's poem 'The schooner *Flight*' is a subtle demonstration of the way in which poetry can hover in the tension between the vernacular and the standard by alternating one with the other:

Man, I brisk in the galley first thing next dawn,
brewing li'l coffee; fog coil from the sea
like the kettle steaming when I put it down
slow, slow, 'cause I couldn't believe what I see:

> where the horizon was one silver haze,
> the fog swirl and swell into sails, so close
> that I saw it was sails, my hair grip my skull,
> it was horrors, but it was beautiful.
>
> (Walcott 1979: 10)

The adaptation of vernacular syntax to standard orthography makes the rhythm and texture of vernacular speech more accessible.

The Trinidadian writer Samuel Selvon's novel *Moses Ascending* ironically portrays the process of appropriation as one of 're-invasion' of the centre. There is a tension established between the narrator's aspiration to the values of the upper-middle-class white society – his 'incorporation' in the centre – and the demonstration in the language of the novel of the opposite process, an appropriating syntactical fusion which invades the home of Received Standard English with a Caribbean dialect-influenced patois:

> It is true that racial violence going to erupt, but not for that reason. What going to happen is one of these days the white man going to realize that the black man have it cushy, being as he got the whole day to do what he like, hustle pussy or visit the museums and the historical buildings, what remain open to facilitate him (yet another boon) and close-up the moment that he, the white man, left work.
>
> (Selvon 1975: 15)

Disentangling the interweaving ironies of this novel is a fascinating process, but the entanglement itself is focused in the language, which constantly dismantles the aspirations and values of Moses himself.

The Jamaican novelist Vic Reid's *New Day* demonstrates a construction of vernacular rhythm which is a consummate example of the possibilities available to writing in appropriated english:

> MAS'R, is a heady night, this. Memory is pricking at me mind, and restlessness is a-ride me soul. I scent many things in the night-wind; night-wind is a-talk of days what pass and gone.
> But the night-wind blows down from the mountains, touching only the high places as it comes; so then, 'member, I

can remember only those places which stand high on the road
we ha' travelled.

Such a way my people are a-sing, though! You know they
will sing all night tonight so till east wind brings the morning?
Torch-light and long-time hymns, and memory a-knock at
my mind. *Aie*, and there is tomorrow what I must ha' faith in.

(Reid 1949: 169)

This technique is neither 'standard' nor direct transcription,
and attacks on it for failing fully to be either miss the point. ('It
falls between two stools of art speech and vernacular', writes
R.J. Owens, 'and is neither successfully' quoted in Morris 1973,
Introduction to Reid's *New Day*). Its purpose is not verisimili-
tude, but rhythmic fidelity, for the poetic mode in any speech is
a constituted dimension. This form of syntactic fusion is more
than purely linguistic, for it includes the ranges of allusion, the
nature of the imagery, and the metaphoric orientation of the
language of an oppressed people deeply immersed in biblical
discourse.

One very specific form of syntactic fusion is the development
of neologisms in the post-colonial text. Successful neologisms in
the english text emphasize the fact that words do not embody
cultural essence, for where the creation of new lexical forms in
english may be generated by the linguistic structures of the
mother tongue, their success lies in their function within the text
rather than their linguistic provenance. The compound 'purity-
heart', for example, as used by the Bengali poet Sri Chinmoy
(1978: 279), is a fusion of the senses of 'pure-heart' and 'heart of
purity' and is linked to the fact that in Bengali, the grammar of
compound nouns cannot be distinguished from that of phrases
(see Bennett 1982). But its value lies in its success as a
metaphor, and it can no more embody the cultures it is uniting
than a metaphor can 'embody' its tenor and vehicle.

In all english variants the characteristic identity of the
linguistic culture is continually being constructed by the
invention of 'neologisms' which are invariably dismissed as
'colloquial' or 'idiomatic', mere ephemera revolving round a
'Standard' English. But as we saw above, what makes a characteristically Indian, Australian, or Trinidadian english is not the
embodiment of some kind of cultural essence, but the use of

language in a particular place and time. Neologisms become an important sign of the coextensivity between language and cultural space, and are an important feature of the development of english variants. Colloquial neologisms are a particularly important example of the metonymic function of all post-colonial literature.

Code-switching and vernacular transcription

Perhaps the most common method of inscribing alterity by the process of appropriation is the technique of switching between two or more codes, particularly in the literatures of the Caribbean continuum. The techniques employed by the polydialectical writer include variable orthography to make dialect more accessible, double glossing and code-switching to act as an interweaving interpretative mode, and the selection of certain words which remain untranslated in the text. All these are common ways of installing cultural distinctiveness in the writing. But probably the most distinctive feature of the Caribbean novel is the narrator who 'reports' in standard English, but moves along the continuum in the dialogue of the characters:

> 'The moment you start reading to me you does make me feel sleepy. I know some people does feel sleepy the moment they see a bed.'
> 'They is people with clean mind. But listen, girl. A *man may turn over half a library to make one book*. It ain't me who make that up, you know.'
> 'How I know you ain't fooling me, just as how you did fool Pa?'
> 'But why for I go want to fool you, girl?'
> 'I ain't the stupid little girl you did married, you know.'
> And when he brought the book and revealed the quotation on the printed page, Leela fell silent in pure wonder. For however much she complained and however much she reviled him, she never ceased to marvel at this husband of hers who read pages of print, chapters of print, why, whole big books; this husband who, awake in bed at nights, spoke, as though it were nothing, of one day writing a book of his own and having it *printed!*

(Naipaul 1957: 85)

Naipaul's novel *The Mystic Masseur* is not only a typical example of the interspersion of Standard English and Trinidadian dialect, but a masterful demonstration of the ability of writing to accord power, as a sign of that power invested in the colonial centre which controls the language (see ch. 3).

As the following passage from de Lisser's *Jane's Career* (de Lisser 1913) demonstrates, the writer in the polydialectical continuum may move easily from one code to another:

> 'So this is the way you use me yard!' was her greeting to both the young women. 'You bring you' dirty friends into me place up to twelve o'clock at night and keep me up and disgrace me house. Now, don't tell me any lie! . . .
>
> Sarah knew that Mrs Mason may have heard but could not possibly have seen them, since only by coming out into the yard could she have done that. She therefore guessed that the lady was setting a trap for her . . .
>
> 'Y'u know, Miss Mason,' she protested, 'y'u shouldn't do that. It's not becausen I are poor that you should teck such an exvantage of me to use me in dat way; for y'u never catch me tellin' you any lie yet, ma'am' . . .
>
> (de Lisser 1913: 53)

For a particularly rich use of this strategy to satirize middle-class pretensions see also Merle Hodge's *Crick Crack Monkey* (Hodge 1970).

An interesting feature of some monoglossic literatures is the importance of the transcription of dialect forms or radical variants informed in one way or another by a mother tongue or by the exigencies of transplantation. The Australian novelist Joseph Furphy, writing at the turn of the century, demonstrates a brilliant use of the strategy of code-switching. In his novel *Such Is Life* (1903), the function of variant transcription is still metonymic, but the aggregation of so many variants in his novel operates to give the sense of the language itself in the process of change. Where many of the early poets, such as Henry Kendall, write in an unabrogated language, and nationalists such as Lawson tend to write in a fully appropriated language (albeit self-consciously at times), Furphy's employment of language variance represents a stage of 'becoming' which exists between the two (interestingly, the stage in which the book is set: the later nineteenth century rather than the time of writing, which was early twentieth century). Of course, Furphy's strategy is possibly not primarily linguistic – his plethora of language variants reveals a deeply complex and syncretic society in the process of gathering to itself a vast array of cultural influence. Thus at a very early stage it interrogates the emerging culturally monist myths of national identity in terms of a language use which foregrounds the hybridized nature of any post-colonial society.

Furphy's characters include the patrician bullock-driver Willoughby, who is here discussing some national heroes with another bullocky, Mosey:

> 'Now, Mosey,' said Willoughby, courteously but tenaciously, 'will you permit me to enumerate a few gentlemen – gentlemen, remember – who have exhibited in a marked degree the qualities of the pioneer. Let us begin with those men of whom you Victorians are so justly proud – Burke and Wills. Then you have –'
>
> 'Hold on, hold on,' interrupted Mosey. 'Don't go no furder, for Gossake. Yer knocking yerself bad, an' you know it. Wills was a pore harmless weed, so he kin pass; but look 'ere – there ain't a drover, nor yet a bullock driver, nor yet a stock-keeper, from 'ere to 'ell that couldn't 'a' bossed that expegition straight through to the Gulf, an' back agen an' never turned a hair – with sich a season as Burke had.'
>
> (Furphy 1903: 32–3)

There is a social contest being engaged here for which the language variance is synecdochic. The very concept of national heroes is embedded in a particular kind of discourse of power for which Willoughby's language is itself a sign. It is a discourse of the monumental, the patriarchal, and the political which converts itself very easily into an officially sanctioned nationalism. But Furphy densely packs his novel with language variants which directly propose a cultural syncreticity which continually undermines such a monist and official nationalism; the Irish brogue of Rory O'Halloran:

> 'Blessin's on ye Tammas! Would it be faysible at all at all fur ye till stap to the morrow mornin', an' ride out wi' me the day?' (98)

and the Chinese inflections of the boundary-rider:

> 'Me tellee Missa Smyte you lescue . . . All li; you name Collin;
> you b'long-a Gullamen Clown; all li; you killee me bimeby;
> all li.' (191)

and many others. This linguistic multiplicity outlines both the
complexity of the society and the complexity of a language in the
process of formation. Variance in this novel is a signifier of a
radical Otherness, not just as a construct which continually
reinserts the gap of silence, but as a process which relentlessly
foregrounds variance and marginality as the norm.

In settler cultures, even more than in most post-colonial
societies, abrogation will almost certainly not be total within the
speaking community. Both english and English, with their
attendant social, cultural, and political allegiances, will exist
side by side as 'vernacular' and 'standard'. In the literature this
division works on behalf of the literary text in english to signify
difference, but it also indicates the very complex dynamic of
appropriation in these cultures. Since the notion of a historical
moment of language change is only ever a heuristic device the
'standard' code and the appropriated usage continue to exist
side by side within the permanently bifurcated situation of a
settler culture. The continued opposition of the two discourses
underlies many of the 'psychological' characteristics of such
societies; their obsession with nationalism, their unresolved
passion for 'identity', and the conflict of both these impulses
with the residual links to European culture. Code-switching is
thus only one strategy of that widespread, though often un-
detected, linguistic variance in monoglossic literatures, which
belies the apparent uniformity of the language. Literatures of
the settler cultures reveal some of the most subtle examples of
those processes by which post-European cultures make english
'bear the burden' of an experience for which the terms of the
inherited language do not seem appropriate. But such strategies
involve much more than the development of a new tool. They
enable the construction of a distinctive social world.

Some of the clearer examples of switching between codes
occurs in texts which directly transcribe pidgin and Creole
forms. The most significant feature of their use in the literature
is that they become a common mode of discourse between

classes. But class in the post-colonial text is a category occasioned by more than an economic structure; it is a discourse
traversed by potent racial and cultural signifiers. This class
distinction is the hidden dichotomy in the exchange between
Willoughby and Mosey in Furphy's novel. But in texts which
use pidgin the dichotomy is not so hidden. The pidgin forms
which have been inherited from British occupation ostensibly
perform the same function as they performed in colonial times:
to provide a serviceable bridge between speakers of different
languages in everyday life. But in the literature (written by
English-speakers who are *ipso facto* members of a higher class)
pidgin and Creole do not indicate the communication between
people of different regions (because the varieties of standard
English perform this function for members of the educated
class) so much as a communication between classes. In this way
the post-colonial text evinces the inheritance of the political as
well as the linguistic reality of pidgin and Creole as it functioned
in colonial times. Pidgin was inevitably used in the context of
master–servant relationships during the period of European
colonization. So the social and economic hierarchies produced
by colonialism have been retained in post-colonial society
through the medium of language. Of course, pidgin remains a
dominant mode of discourse among all non-English-speakers
wherever it exists, but its role in most literature, except that of
the polydialectical communities of the Caribbean, is both to
install class difference and to signify its presence.

> Amamu sat in the living room, not exactly sober, and not
> exactly drunk. Yaro came in reeking of his own sweat and
> muddy. He had been arranging his flower pots. His master
> had called him thrice.
> Yes sah, masa.
> You no finish for outside?
> No sah.
> Finish quick and come clean for inside. We get party
> tonight. Big people dey come. Clean for all de glass, plate,
> fork, spoon, knife everything. You hear?
> Yes sah. Yaro shuffled off on silent feet. Amamu stretched
> himself in the armchair, covering his face with yesterday's
> *Daily Graphic*.
>
> (Awoonor 1971: 123)

The *Daily Graphic* with which Amamu covers his face is, in a sense, the principal sign of his mastery. The English-language newspaper is the purveyor of those mysteries which will always be inaccessible to the 'uneducated', for education, class status, and an ability to speak 'standard English' will usually be synonymous.[6] Dialect is yet another demonstration of the place and political function of the concept of 'correct' or 'Standard' English in all english-speaking societies.

Strategies of appropriation, then, seize the language, re-place it in a specific cultural location, and yet maintain the integrity of that Otherness, which historically has been employed to keep the post-colonial at the margins of power, of 'authenticity', and even of reality itself. These strategies of writing have increasingly been allied to strategies of reading – the recognition that 'theory' is no more necessarily European than english is necessarily English. But they are specific features of texts which constantly address themselves to the task of dismantling those assumptions which have historically constituted 'English literature'.

3
Re-placing the text: the liberation of post-colonial writing

The appropriation of the english language is the first of a range of appropriations which establish a discourse announcing its difference from Europe. These include the adaptation or evolution of metropolitan practices: for example, genres such as 'the ballad' or 'the novel' or even epistemologies, ideological systems, or institutions such as literary theory. But the appropriation which has had the most profound significance in post-colonial discourse is that of writing itself. It is through an appropriation of the power invested in writing that this discourse can take hold of the marginality imposed on it and make hybridity and syncreticity the source of literary and cultural redefinition. In writing out of the condition of 'Otherness' post-colonial texts assert the complex of intersecting 'peripheries' as the actual substance of experience. But the struggle which this assertion entails – the 're-placement' of the post-colonial text – is focused in their attempt to control the processes of writing.

The imperial moment: control of the means of communication

A major work of discourse analysis which bears directly on the function and power of writing in the colonial situation is *The*

Conquest of America by Tzvetan Todorov (Todorov 1974). The revolutionary insight of this book is its location of the key feature of colonial oppression in the control over the *means of communication* rather than the control over life and property or even language itself.

Cortez's successful campaign against the Aztecs of Central America is explained by the Spaniard's seizure and domination from the beginning of the means of communication. The problem for Aztec oral culture, based as it was on a ritual and cyclic interpretation of reality, was that there was simply no place in its scheme of things for the unpredicted arrival of Cortez. Todorov's contention is that, as a result, when Aztec and Spanish culture met they constituted nothing less than two entirely incommensurable forms of communication. Aztec communication is between man and the world, because knowledge always proceeds from a reality which is already fixed, ordered, and given. On the other hand European communication (although this is not automatic and inevitable, as we see from Columbus's lack of rapport with the Indians) is between man and man. The principle which Todorov sees as central, the control of the means of communication, is the empowering factor in any colonial enterprise. The intrusion of the colonizer is not always attended by the confusion which gripped the Aztecs, but control is always manifested by the imposed authority of a system of *writing*, whether writing already exists in the colonized culture or not.

Montezuma's problem was that no basis existed for an adequate understanding of the information he received about the *conquistadores* because no place existed for them in Aztec reality – the Other was always that which could be foreseen. The only explanation was that they were gods, in which case opposition would be futile. This reaction to the radical incursion of the Other is paradigmatic for the incursion of the written word into the oral world. When he receives information from spies about Cortez, 'Montezuma lowered his head, and without answering a word, placed his hand upon his mouth'. Faced with the inexplicable, the only recourse of the oral system is silence. But silence envelops the written word which proceeds 'from silence to possibility . . . What Cortez wants from the first is not to capture but to comprehend; it is signs which chiefly interest him, not their referents.' To this end his first and most significant action is to find an interpreter.

The role of the first interpreter in the colonial contact is a profoundly ambiguous one. The ambivalent interpretative role and the significance of the interpretative site forms one of the major foci of the processes of abrogation and appropriation. The interpreter always emerges from the dominated discourse. The role entails radically divided objectives: it functions to acquire the power of the new language and culture in order to preserve the old, even whilst it assists the invaders in their overwhelming of that culture. In that divided moment the interpreter discovers the impossibility of living completely through either discourse. The intersection of these two discourses on which the interpreter balances constitutes a site both exhilarating and disturbing. The role of the interpreter is like that of the post-colonial writer, caught in the conflict between destruction and creativity. As the Nigerian Chinua Achebe puts it:

> We lived at the cross-roads of cultures. We still do today, but when I was a boy, one could see and sense the peculiar quality and atmosphere of it more clearly . . . But still the cross-roads does have a certain dangerous potency; dangerous because a man might perish there wrestling with multiple-headed spirits, but also he might be lucky and return to his people with the boon of prophetic vision.
>
> (Achebe 1975: 67)

This transitional moment is the most difficult to describe. A clear example of this is the absence of the 'proposed' second volume of Achebe's trilogy which would have dealt with the adulthood of his father Nwoya/Isaac. Achebe can write about his role as a teacher in African culture but appears to have been unable to confront his role as interpreter/post-colonial writer (see Griffiths 1987b). However, the act of interpretation has great creative potential, as illustrated by the way in which the trope of the interpreter has been explored in other post-colonial texts; for example, in Wole Soyinka's *The Interpreters* or Randolph Stow's *Visitants*.

But in Todorov's account, it is in the production of discourse and symbols that Cortez reveals his dominance over the means of communication. His every action is designed to control what others can *know* about him, for instance, he takes care to bury horses killed in battles to maintain the impression that they are supernatural. Thus Cortez controls the parameters of the discourse in which he and Montezuma are situated. The issue here is not the domination of one language over another but of one form of communication over another, and specifically of writing over orality.

The 'intersection' of language which occurs in the literatures of formerly oral societies does not take place simply between two different languages but between two different ways of conceiving the practice and substance of language. One characteristic of the world-views of oral cultures is the assumption that words, uttered under appropriate circumstances have the power to bring into being the events or states they stand for, to embody rather than represent reality. This conviction that the word can create its object leads to a sense that language possesses power over truth and reality.

The introduction of writing into these societies leads to the development of a different kind of consciousness which might be characterized as 'historical'. Thus literacy and writing, as JanMohammed notes, by recording particular facts and so making available in time a dense and specific past, 'will not allow memory, the major mode of temporal mediation in oral cultures, to eliminate facts that are not consonant with or useful for contemporary needs'. Literacy, he argues, 'also destroys the immediacy of personal experience and the deeper socialisation of the world and consequently the totalising nature of oral cultures'. Thus literacy leads to the development of historic consciousness. It allows scrutiny of a fixed past. It enables distinctions to be made between truth and error and so permits the development of 'a more conscious, critical, and comparative attitude to the accepted world picture'. (Though, of course, we need to note that history as an institution is itself under the control of determinate cultural and ideological forces which may seek to propose the specific practice of history as neutral and objective.) Literacy, then, eventually produces 'a sense of change, of the human past as an objective reality available to causal analysis, and of history as a broad attempt to determine reality in every (diachronic) area of human concern. This in

turn permits a distinction between "history" and "myth"'
(JanMohammed 1983: 280). JanMohammed is careful to note
that this does not imply that oral societies do not have a history,
nor that their tendency to generate 'mythic' rather than 'historical' accounts of the world implies that they are unable to reason
logically or causally. However, he argues that the logic and
causality of oral cultures are more 'magical' whilst those of
literate cultures are more 'empirical' (ibid.: 300). In this respect
his argument is in line with the ideas implicit in Todorov about
the vulnerability of oral societies to the intrusion of literacy
controlled as it is by the imperial power.

The presence or absence of writing is possibly the most
important element in the colonial situation. Writing does not
merely introduce a communicative instrument, but also involves an entirely different and intrusive (invasive) orientation
to knowledge and interpretation. In many post-colonial
societies, it was not the English language which had the greatest
effect, but writing itself. In this respect, although oral culture is
by no means the universal model of post-colonial societies, the
invasion of the ordered, cyclic, and 'paradigmatic' oral world by
the unpredictable and 'syntagmatic' world of the written word
stands as a useful model for the beginnings of post-colonial
discourse. The seizing of the means of communication and the
liberation of post-colonial writing by the appropriation of the
written word become crucial features of the process of self-
assertion and of the ability to reconstruct the world as an
unfolding historical process.

The Spanish conquest of Central America was the model for
all colonialist enterprises to follow. Imperial conquest has
always destroyed the land and often regarded the human
occupants as disposable, almost as if they were a species of
exotic fauna. But the conquerors themselves, the present con-
trollers of the means of communication, those who have subju-
gated or annihilated the original occupants could not feel at
home in the *place* colonized. Out of this sense of displacement
emerges the discourse of place which informs the post-colonial
condition. This *Unheimlichkeit* (Heidegger 1927) or 'not-at-
homeness' motivates the reconstruction of the social and imaginative world in post-colonial writing. Such *Unheimlichkeit* is
experienced not only by the residents of the settler colonies but

by all people situated at the ambi/valent site of interpretation itself.

It is not always possible to separate theory and practice in post-colonial literature. As the works of Wilson Harris, Wole Soyinka, and Edward Brathwaite demonstrate, creative writers have often offered the most perceptive and influential account of the post-colonial condition. Accordingly, the analysis and exegesis of a specific text may be one of the most crucial ways of determining the major theoretical and critical issues at stake. Such analyses are not directed towards totalizing 'interpretations' but towards symptomatic readings which reveal the discursive formations and ideological forces which traverse the text. As a result, readings of individual texts may enable us to isolate and identify significant theoretical shifts in the development of post-colonial writing.

The symptomatic readings of texts which follow serve to illustrate three important features of all post-colonial writing. The silencing and marginalizing of the post-colonial voice by the imperial centre; the abrogation of this imperial centre within the text; and the active appropriation of the language and culture of that centre. These features and the transitions between them are expressed in various ways in the different texts, sometimes through formal subversions and sometimes through contestation at the thematic level. In all cases, however, the notions of power inherent in the model of centre and margin are appropriated and so dismantled.

Colonialism and silence: Lewis Nkosi's *Mating Birds*

South Africa is a society in which control of the means of communication is still held by the colonial authority of the racist state. In this sense, it is a society caught between two phases, manifesting the dynamic of colonial domination but producing both white and Black writers whose engagement with the processes of abrogation and appropriation is part of a continuing struggle for survival. South African writing clearly demonstrates the fact that the political impetus of the post-colonial begins well before the moment of independence.

Of the many perceptions generated from this situation, one of the most significant is the way in which control of the means of communication by the state gags the voice of the individual. This silence is literally and dramatically revealed in the censorship exercised by the government over newspapers, journals, and much creative writing. It has two aspects: there is the literal silencing which will not permit the freedom necessary to appropriate language, and there is the further silence which necessarily precedes the act of appropriation. Even those post-colonial writers with the literal freedom to speak find themselves languageless, gagged by the imposition of English on their world. Paradoxically, in order to develop a voice they must first fall silent (see Stow 1962; Lee 1974). Because the control of the means of communication is so pronounced in South Africa, it provides one of the clearest and most extreme examples of how the political condition of colonized people is bound up with language. This is not to say that there is no speech possible within that double (literal and metaphorical) 'silencing', but that such 'speech' can only demonstrate that neither the language nor the means of communication have been fully appropriated. In effect, all writing in South Africa is by definition a form of protest or a form of acquiescence. Which it is depends on how it situates itself within the political realities of the daily struggle against apartheid. Clearly all Black writing and, to some extent, that white writing which opposes apartheid, such as the work of André Brink, Breyten Breytenbach, J.M. Coetzee, etc., functions as protest. But, since all writing in South Africa has obvious and immediate political consequences, it must *explicitly* engage in resistance to the oppressive regime in order fully to avoid acquiescence.

Lewis Nkosi's novel *Mating Birds* (1986) is a fine example of the post-colonial perception of the relation between knowledge and control. While situating itself within the discourse of resistance and abrogation, it provides a penetrating example of the silence into which the colonized consciousness is driven by the cultural conditions of South Africa and by the state control over the means of communication. The novel ostensibly describes the ordeal of a Black South African gaoled and executed for the rape of a white woman. The book finds the narrator in gaol awaiting execution and relates the series of circumstances leading up to the attempted 'rape' which reveal a profound impotence as well as a profound lack of communication between individuals who remain metonymic of the distance between cultures in South Africa.

Significantly, the prejudice concerning the danger of knowledge is articulated by the prison commandant. His fear is well founded. As in all post-colonial societies the word leads to knowledge, which provokes questioning, which generates change. The corpus of post-colonial literature is replete with examples of the fear that the dominated will gain knowledge and hence, power. The prison commandant is quite certain that

> the natives, left to their tribal environment, were all right, their morals were even superior to those of some whites, but given a smattering of education, they became spoiled and thought of themselves as the equal of white men. He concluded by citing as an example the rapid increase of incidents of assault on white women. This, Van Rooyen said, was the necessary and tragic consequence of the ill-conceived projects of social uplift, which the liberals fondly hoped would transform the natives into something like white men.
>
> (Nkosi 1986: 82)

Equality with the white man 'spoils' the natural state of the indigenous people. Learning, with its necessary initiation into the mystic processes of writing, is an assumption of the power to dominate. Ironically, this assumption is shared by the colonizer and the colonized and lies firmly behind the efforts of the mother to send the boy to the white school:

> No doubt, she was convinced that an encounter, however brief, with books, would confer upon her offspring awesome powers of the occult, an almost miraculous ability to manipulate the universe at will. 'A real devil Ndi is going to be with a pen, you wait and see.' (85)

The 'book' and the 'pen' are the keys to power, for 'knowledge' in the South African context means 'writing' and hence the control over communication. But in *Mating Birds* the outcome is ambiguous. Ndi is 'a real devil', since the pen and the phallus become interchangeable symbols which have deep and obvious significance in this reverse metaphor of cultural rape. The girl in this story is an obvious metonym for white society and values, but the relationship between her and Ndi which leads up to the rape is even more a figure of the relation between the literate white and oral Black societies.

She is first discovered on the beach lying provocatively within feet of the boundary which separates the white and non-white sections of the beach. After the first encounter, Ndi goes to the beach day after day obsessed with the vision of possible attainment. But the most significant feature of this developing relationship between the seductive woman and the obsessed Black man is that it is conducted entirely in *silence*. Looking across the barrier represented by the white/non-white line drawn down the beach, Ndi surrenders his own world of speech and enters the world of non-verbal signs. Day after day communication proceeds through the signs of eye and body, signs which are dominated by the iconic sign which symbolizes the emptiness in which this communication is conducted – BATHING AREA – FOR WHITES ONLY. Signs are at once an index of Ndi's attempt to cross the barrier, and its prevention. The communication by signs continues even to the point at which the two people engage in a simultaneous orgasm, conducted entirely in silence and separated by the gulf of the barrier indicated by the beach sign itself. The grounding of this relationship in silence is crucial in the metaphoric architecture of the story. It occurs in a space committed neither to speech nor writing, but which deludes the Black man into a vision of dominance. One day he follows the woman to her home where she disrobes in front of her open door in apparent invitation. At the moment of ultimate sexual union her sudden screams attract a passerby and Ndi is overpowered; the approach to power (the penetration into the world of written signs embodied in the white woman) has revealed itself as illusory.

Significantly, the writer makes no attempt to explain the motives of the woman. The gulf of silence – the absence which is indicated in the man's surrender of speech and his entry into the linguistic vacuum of the situation iconized by the divided beach – stands as the signifying difference of the post-colonial text. It captures that profound silence between cultures which finally cannot be traversed by understanding. The line drawn down the beach signifies the plane of meeting between the two cultures, and at this line no meeting takes place, only silence.

Only by denying the authenticity of the line and taking control of the means of communication can the post-colonial text overcome this silence.

Ndi is forced into silence by the culture which controls the signs in both a literal and a linguistic sense. This world of written signs is the province of writing, not of speech, and Ndi's attempt to enter it is doomed to failure because the culture which controls the means of communication also controls the means of [af]filiation. The interrelation between the desire to enter the literate world and the rape of the woman is significant. Both the phallus and the pen are instruments of domination. Sexual union with the tantalizing but unattainable woman is the metaphoric equivalent of the Black child's attempt to enter the world of white society (and therefore of power) through the wielding of the pen. Though not conferring the awesome powers of the occult, as his mother would believe, the pen would seem to confer the powers of the culture which controls the written word. But the issue is not so simple. What confers power, as Cortez knew, is not the possession of the means of communication, but their control. In the silent encounter between the Black man and white woman, control is maintained by those who erect the sign: BATHING AREA – FOR WHITES ONLY. Although the two separated individuals seem to communicate quite successfully with the language of the body, even to the point of reaching simultaneous orgasm without touching, this is merely the illusion of communication, as Ndi discovers to his cost. Silence has deceived him.

Although *Mating Birds* demonstrates the catastrophic meeting of the oral and literate worlds, this is only a specific instance of the broader post-colonial experience. What characterizes this experience in any cultural setting is not simply the history of colonial oppression or the intersection of languages, but the struggle for control of the word. And this is a struggle which, ironically, the older and stronger metropolitan order cannot finally win because writing, once seized, retains the seeds of self-regeneration and the power to create and recreate the world. By inscribing meaning, writing releases it to a dense proliferation of possibilities, and the myth of centrality embodied in the concept of a 'standard language' is forever overturned. It is at this moment that English becomes *english*.

Colonialism and 'authenticity': V.S. Naipaul's
The Mimic Men

One of the most persistent prejudices underlying the production of the texts of the metropolitan canon is that only certain categories of experience are capable of being rendered as 'literature'. This privileging of particular types of experience denies access to the world for the writer subject to a dominating colonial culture. It works in a complicated and reciprocal way, both denying value to the post-colonial experience itself, as 'unworthy' of literature, and preventing post-colonial texts from engaging with that experience. The result is that the post-colonial writer is consigned to a world of mimicry and imitation, since he is forced to write about material which lies at one remove from the significant experiences of the post-colonial world.

The Trinidadian writer V.S. Naipaul examines the dilemma of the post-colonial writer in many of his works, but particularly in *The Mimic Men* (1967). Since Naipaul has a pessimistic view of the possibility of escape from this situation, he views the mimicry implicit in the post-colonial condition and, hence, its literary text, as permanently disabling, because of the disorder and inauthenticity imposed by the centre on the margins of empire. The distinction is between the authentic experience of the 'real' world and the inauthentic experience of the unvalidated periphery. The polarity is repeated in the book in an aggregation of opposites: order and disorder, authenticity and inauthenticity, reality and unreality, power and impotence, even being and nothingness. Clearly, the dominance of the centre and its imprimatur on experience must be abrogated before the experience of the 'periphery' can be fully validated.

The novel's identification of the union of language and power also identifies a geographic structure of power. In imperial terms this can be seen as a geometric structure in which the centre, the metropolitan source of standard language, stands as the focus of order, while the periphery, which utilizes the variants, the 'edges' of language, remains a tissue of disorder. Such geometric opposites are articulated clearly by the narrator, Kripal ('Cripple') Singh in *The Mimic Men*; a novel which incorporates an extreme version of the opposition between centre and margin. The book contrasts the metropolitan centre, which is the location not only of the power which comes from the control of language but also of order itself, with the periphery of the colonial world, in which only the illusion of power exists and in which disorder always predominates:

> I have read that it was a saying of an ancient Greek that the first requisite for happiness was to be born in a famous city . . .
>
> To be born on an island like Isabella, an obscure New World transplantation, second-hand and barbarous, was to be born to disorder. From an early age, almost from my first lesson at school about the weight of the king's crown, I had sensed this. Now I was to discover that disorder has its own logic and permanence.
>
> (Naipaul 1967: 141–2)

The child's first lesson about the weight of the king's crown is a richly evocative image of dependence and Otherness. Such physical and metaphoric weight – the weight of the crown and the weight of the empire – demands and legitimizes power. Such weight represents order as well as power, since order is the essence of imperial authority. On the other hand the disorder of the peripheral corresponds to a fundamental lack of power:

> We lack order. Above all, we lack power, and we do not understand that we lack power. We mistake words and the acclamation of words for power; as soon as our bluff is called we are lost. (10–11)

In mistaking words for power, the inhabitants of the margins fail to understand that the nexus between language and power lies in the ability to control the means of communication.

To the colonial politician, no matter what rhetoric may win him votes, both the language and the economic structure of the society he vainly hopes to change are controlled from outside. Language is power because words construct reality. The assumption by the powerless is that words are the signifiers of a pre-given reality, a reality and a truth which is only located at the centre. The colonial 'mimicry' is thus a mimicry of the 'original' the 'true' which exists at the source of power:

> There, in Liège, in a traffic jam, on the snow slopes of the Laurentians, was the true, pure world. We, here on our island, handling books printed in this world, and using its goods, had been abandoned and forgotten. We pretended to be real, to be learning, to be preparing ourselves for life, we mimic men of the New World. (175)

The peripheral lacks order because it lacks the power of representation. Since the truth lies elsewhere, language can only mimic the representation of the truth. This has its own profoundly ontological ramifications for the inhabitant of the margins:

> Coming to London, the great city, seeking order, seeking the flowering, the extension of myself that ought to have come in a city of such miraculous light, I had tried to hasten a process which had seemed elusive. I had tried to give myself a personality. (32)

Such a recourse to the city by the colonials in order to find an identity has too many historical antecedents to be merely idiosyncratic. The writer has detected the very tension which keeps the centre at the centre. But the perception that being itself is located at the centre, and that nothingness (by implication) is the only possibility for the margins, operates as a driving force in Naipaul's own work. This geometry of colonialism operates through the constant imposition of the feeling of disorder, placelessness, and unreality.

Although Naipaul has one of the clearest visions of the nexus of power operating in the imperial–colonial world, he is paradoxically drawn to that centre even though he sees it constructing the 'periphery' as an area of nothingness. Yet he is simultaneously able to see that the 'reality', the 'truth', and 'order' of the centre is also an illusion. For those who lose the game of politics at the margins, and nearly everybody loses,

> there is only one course: flight. Flight to the greater disorder, the final emptiness: London and the home counties. (11)

The idea of the centre as permanent and unrefractory is endlessly deferred. The centre of order is the ultimate disorder.

This perception is both the ultimate rebellion and the ultimate unveiling performed by post-colonial literature. There is no centre of reality just as there is no pre-given unmediated reality. If language constructs the world then the margins are the centre and may reconstruct it according to a different pattern of conventions, expectations, and experiences.

Naipaul's position is a deeply ambiguous one in that his writing does not always carry the conviction of this perception. The result is a curious ambivalence when the novel considers the authenticity of the margins. Yet such an ambivalence is by no means disabling, for it provides the tension out of which emerges a rich and incisive reconstruction of post-colonial experience.

Abrogating 'authenticity': Michael Anthony's 'Sandra Street'

One of the major acts of abrogation in post-colonial literature is a rejection of the process by which 'authenticity' is granted to the categories of experience authorized by the centre at the expense of those relegated to the margins of Empire. The short story 'Sandra Street' by the Trinidadian writer Michael Anthony (Anthony 1973), which focuses on the process of learning to write, directly confronts the dilemma of authenticity which faces those both teaching and learning 'writing' in a post-colonial culture.

The text appears to operate unselfconsciously within the existing categories of autobiographical 'tale', realistic tone, and unfolding linear narrative, without overtly or deliberately rejecting the structures of 'literature' offered by the dominant culture through the educational system, curriculum, and text book. But it questions these in an indirect way by demonstrating the manner in which a dominant discourse circumscribes the expression of self and place in the post-colonial world. The overt 'work' of the text is abrogation, an abrogation of the formations which constitute certain experiences as 'authentic'. But the text itself as activity demonstrates the act of appropriation by which such formations are subverted and the 'marginal' is liberated as an appropriate(d) subject. The text as a whole is a sign of this appropriation.

The story tells of the relationship between a teacher (Mr Blades) and a pupil (Steve, the narrator) whom Mr Blades is teaching to write English 'composition' (narrative essays) in a class whose competitiveness, divisiveness, and insecurity mirrors the conditions of the society in which it exists. Deceptively simple on the surface, the text nevertheless subverts the 'normal rules' of narrative. For example, the story refuses to establish a single centring consciousness for more than three paragraphs. Mr Blades, the teacher, is the subject of the opening. The subject of paragraphs two and three is the anonymous 'boy', who, we are later to learn, is the author of the composition which Mr Blades singles out for praise, and which describes Sandra Street as 'dull and uninteresting', 'not . . . a part of our town at all'. A third subject emerges in paragraph three, the 'I' who is placed only by a geographical and, significantly, communal tag ('the few of us from Sandra Street') which contrasts him with the 'boy'.

The emergence of the 'I', who is not named as the centring consciousness until half-way through the story, thus functions as a sign of the *process* the text replicates. This process involves the emergence of the possibility of conceiving oneself as a *subject*. This is achieved not within the story as narrated sequence, but in its existence and its condition as completed product. It is this which signals the fact that the 'I' of the story has become the author of a text. The features and events of the text need to be read metonymically rather than metaphorically for the full significance of the text as symptom to be so reproduced.

Within the text, Sandra Street itself is described in a number of ways. It is the home street of the 'I', it is where the school is situated, and it is on the edge of town. But the significant description is a negative one. The 'boy' of paragraph two (who is named later as Kenneth) declares in his composition that Sandra Street lacks the 'gay attractions [of] the other side of town, some of which, he said, Sandra Street could never hope to have'. Kenneth, like the bulk of the class, comes, of course, from this 'other side'. Mr Blades, the teacher, we are told 'also came from the other side of the town'.

The perception of the 'I' figure is contained within the framework of 'the other side of town', in so far as the conceptual possibilities available to him for placing and distinguishing

Sandra Street, exist only in terms of the categories of 'the other side'. As the 'I' reflects,

> the boy's composition was very *truthful*. Sandra Street *was so different from the other streets beyond.* Indeed it came from the very quiet fringes and ran straight to the forests. (Anthony 1973:10, emphasis added)

The potential for alternative values in the last sentence is suppressed by the discourse, which must express value in some relationship, positive or negative, to those of 'the other side' and it is to the negative expression of these values that the 'I' turns in his own 'composition':

> During the day all would be very quiet except perhaps for the voice of one neighbour calling to another, and if some evenings brought excitement to the schoolyard, these did very little to disturb the calmness of Sandra Street.
>
> Nor did the steel-band gently humming from the other side of the town. I had to remember the steel band because although I liked to hear it I had to put into my composition that it was very bad. We had no steel bands in Sandra Street, and I thought I could say that this was because we were decent, cultured folk, and did not like the horrible noises of steel bands. (10–11)

The use of the image of the 'steel band' as characteristic of both the 'I's' and the boy (Kenneth's) worlds (worlds ostensibly in opposition) is a timely reminder, too, that all this experience is contained within a disabling cultural framework in which 'metropolitan' imperial values are still the source of legitimization.

Thus the story is not a simple allegory of colony and metropolis. The world of 'the other side' of town does not stand for the metropolitan centre in some kind of detached and self-conscious symbolic patterning. In fact, the assignment of value is only a feature of the process being examined, not its purpose. Thus to oppose the 'gay' and 'quiet' worlds of the 'I' narrator or the boy (Kenneth) is not to express some comparison of intrinsic value, but rather the process by which a discourse which privileges certain experiences over others is transmitted via an educational system. Any way of life within a post-colonial society, like the ways of life of both 'sides' of town, is forced to generate images of itself only in terms of its success or lack of success in being something 'Other'.

Thus, the relationship between Sandra Street and the Other underlies any definition of value. This is revealed, in the quotation above, by the use of the conditional tense – 'I thought I *could* say . . .' – in other words, I was (or might be) empowered to say a certain thing *as correct* because it would be acceptable within a particular hierarchy of value. A structure of privileging distinctions has been imported into this discourse as the means by which any experience is to be understood. This enforces the dividing and denigrating conditionality of the imperial mode even within the expression of the individual post-colonial experience.

Mr Blades' function in the text as the transmitter of this discourse is highly problematical, since his role as 'teacher' instantly privileges his viewpoint. So the 'I' seeks to learn how he can please him and become a person (Steve) in his eyes, attempting to present his experience within this discourse of empowering code masquerading as 'objective' description and 'observation'.

> 'Did you notice the cedar grove at the top?' he went on. 'You spoke of the steel band at the other side of town. Did you speak of the river? Did you notice the hills?' (14)

and again

> 'There is something like observation, Steve', he said. '*Observation*. You live in Sandra Street, yet Kenneth writes a composition on your own place better than you.'

Steve's anguished inner response to this, which he can't say aloud,

> I felt like crying out; 'I wanted to show it to you' (14)

is only comprehensible within the limitations implicit in Mr Blades' demands. Steve cannot 'show it' because the discourse only permits it to be shown in terms of its relationship to an enabling other, which is privileged as norm. Thus Mr Blades 'prefers' Kenneth's composition. But clearly, his reasons for doing so are themselves highly problematical, as the following quotation makes clear:

[The 'He' here is the boy, Kenneth; the speaker is the 'I' of the text, Steve; and the respondent the teacher Mr Blades]

'He said Sandra Street was soppy,' I cried.
'Of course he said it was soppy. It was to his purpose. He comes from the other side of town. What's he got to write on – gaudy houses with gates like prisons around them? High walls cramping the imagination? The milling crowd with faces impersonal as stone, hurrying on buses, hurrying off trams? Could he write about that?' (14)

In fact, of course, he could. Just as Steve's reality is denigrated by a discourse which must privilege the 'objective', a detachment which serves to occlude the privileging norm implicit in such a discourse, so Kenneth's reality is denigrated by the implicit norm in the teacher's discourse, one in which the subject-matter of 'literature', conceived as a category above its historical production, is similarly privileged.

This kind of literary production values fields over streets, isolation over crowds, 'subtle' colour over the 'gaudy', individuals over 'milling crowds'. Mr Blades' objective concept of 'literature' reveals itself to be a product of a specific conditioning (romantic, nineteenth century, English) privileged by its place in the colonial education system which has trained him as a teacher of 'composition' and literature. Nevertheless, Steve is shown as at least able, through this concept of 'observation', to see the experience around him as material for 'composition', a significant, if limited, advance. The rest of the story constructs an alternative discourse which privileges the 'here and now' over some exterior norm, and the existence of the story itself as literary text confirms this discourse as meaningful and possible practice. It emerges as a series of displacements and limitations on the assessments offered by Mr Blades of Steve's capacities as the story develops.

Mr Blades' privileged position within the story as narrative, as within the consciousness of Steve, remains dominant to the end. It is exposed as inadequate, not within the narrative as closure, but through the narrative as activity. However, as we experience Steve's account of his world and contrast it with Mr Blades' precepts, we begin to detect a significant credibility gap in his assessment of Steve's capacities. Mr Blades has suggested he notice the absence of gates (which he neglected to mention in his composition) but Steve constructs this as a sign of 'freedom':

> I watched the freedom of the fowls among the tall houses, and sometimes the women talked to each other through the windows and smiled. I noticed too, the hills, which were now streaked with the blossoms of the poui, and exultantly I wondered how many people observed this and knew it was a sign of the rains. (15)

Steve sees that the natural world is linked not to abstraction but to experience and to cultural context. Thus his observation of flowers is modified by his ability to relate it to a non-literary code of weather 'lore' (oral in origin) and construct a further meaning from this process. Even at this stage Steve relocates the significance of what he 'learns' in a discourse which refuses to limit its meanings to the categories and codes within which Mr Blades' 'educational' and 'literary' values are circumscribed. In so doing it exposes the limitations of these codes and their power to deny and occlude the full body of experiences and discourses available to the post-colonial child.

The nature of the material Steve continues to find 'inexpressible' (i.e. unacceptable as literary) reveals the limitations of a discourse authorized by this notion of the 'literary', however liberal its purpose:

> The sun was shining brightly now, although there was still a slight drizzle of rain, and I could smell the steam rising from the hot pitch and from the galvanised roofs. 'Rain falling sun shining,' Mr Blades said. And I remembered that *they said at such times the Devil fought his wife*, but when Mr Blades pressed me to tell what I was laughing at I laughed still more and would not say. (emphasis added) (16)

The whole world of speech, of proverb, of talk, the oral world of this society is excluded. From the beginning the discourse empowered by the school denies the existence of such alternative discourses. In Kenneth's first composition we are told how the women of Sandra Street 'could not pass without stopping to talk *as if they had something to talk about*' (emphasis added). The institution is not disinterested but actively processes the experience and licenses it as adequate or not.

Steve as the 'I' of the tale is the formally triumphant figure.
The rich and complex story with its superb placements and
insights 'belongs' to him, not to Kenneth or Mr Blades. In fact,
Mr Blades' 'objective' vision and 'literary' insights are shown to
be unproductive, since he cannot produce what he 'sees' within
a discourse whose perspective is limited to the alternatives of
Sandra Street and 'the other side of town', that is, a discourse in
which anything existing in one experience can only be validated
in terms of some Other. Within the discourses available to him,
Mr Blades cannot write what he so triumphantly sees from the
forest which lies above Sandra Street. He is bound by the
discourse which Steve abrogates in his composition. Thus
the text exposes the inadequacy of Mr Blades' ideology of
'objectivity' and permanent literary values and denies their
'transparency'.

The text significantly emphasizes its theme by repeatedly
positioning Steve and Mr Blades before a window through
which they view the subjects of their compositions. The final
scene is the only one not so placed, suggesting, perhaps, that in
place of Mr Blades' false objectivity a new and subjective norm
has been legitimized. Thus Steve's world, reconstructed out of
the dismantled discourse of authenticity is brought into being
by the transformative power of the imagination. This vision of
Sandra Street is the triumphant product of the text itself – 'Not
far below Sandra Street swept by, bathed in light'. (18) And the
vision is related in Steve's voice, not Kenneth's nor Mr Blades'.

Radical otherness and hybridity: Timothy Findley's
Not Wanted on the Voyage

In *Not Wanted on the Voyage*, Canadian Timothy Findley returns
to the source of a number of persistent western practices crucial
to colonialism and imperialism – those associated with what
Gayatri Spivak terms 'Othering' (Spivak 1985a). These include
the assumption of authority, 'voice', and control of the 'word',
that is, seizure and control of the means of interpretation and
communication. In many post-colonial texts, this is achieved by
means of a 'rewriting' of canonical stories. Findley extends this
method of 'writing back' to the centre of empire by rewriting the
biblical story of Noah and the Great Flood, a source myth in

western civilization for motifs of destruction and salvation – destruction of the many, salvation of the few. As Findley's novel demonstrates, the construction or salvation of any such system, civilization, or tradition as authoritative precludes 'Other' developments; the 'rise' of any culture is not just coincident with the demise of other forms and possibilities, it involves the active suppression and/or annihilation of forms of 'Otherness'. It closes off alternative tropes or modes.

In Findley's radical interrogation of the story of the flood, the great myth of salvation becomes a saga of destruction in the name of minority righteousness and the extension of petty power. Dr Noah Noyes' dedication to the God he has created in his own image results in the annihilation of other life forms in the world – the fairies, the unicorns, the dragons, and the demons – and the marginalization and radical suppression of others – women and animals. To put it another way, once western thinking has been codified in and sanctioned by the book of Genesis, 'Othering' in its most radical form has been achieved. Genesis thus becomes, in Findley's account, not the beginning, but the end, and the story of the Ark a story not of redemption, but of marginalization and destruction. As in *The Mimic Men*, being itself becomes locked at the centre with 'nothingness' at its margins, and the processes of interpretation of reality, literally here of God's word, are the assumptive and self-appropriated bases of Noah's power. Findley's account of Noyes' techniques exposes the ideological processes 'by which knowledge is actuated in the control and surveillance of subject peoples' (Slemon 1987b).

Early in the novel God sends a message to Dr Noyes which he immediately acts upon, without revealing its text to any of the inhabitants of his world, all of whom will be drastically affected by it. This gives him sole interpretative control of events, a control which he extends into supreme authority over those who have already been 'Othered' by his assumption of the authoritative, the axiomatic. Moreover, interpretative power and written record become complicit, so that a particular reading of event and symbol not only gains control of the interpretative 'moment', but is fixed for the future by its inscription in writing as the exclusive meaning of that event or symbol. This process (which is also the way in which Genesis itself operates in the world) is exposed in the early sections of the novel when an apparently inexplicable phenomenon occurs:

> Here it was the end of summer and though it hadn't rained, it had already snowed. Or so it had seemed. Small white flakes of *something* had fallen from the sky and everyone had crowded onto the porch to watch. Dr Noyes at once had proclaimed a miracle and was even in the process of telling Hannah to mark it down as such, when Ham went onto the lawn and stuck his tongue out, catching several of the flakes and tasting them.
>
> 'Not snow,' he had said. 'It's ash.'
>
> Ham, after all, had the whole of science at his fingertips and Mrs Noyes was inclined to believe that it had been ash – but Dr Noyes had insisted it was snow – 'a miracle!' And in the end he'd had his way. Hannah had been instructed to write: TODAY – A BLIZZARD.
>
> (Findley 1984: 21)

From the beginning, the only interpretations to be recorded are Noyes' and hence, as Mrs Noyes had already pointed out, 'the only principles that matter here are *yours*' (13). Even where common sense and knowledge dictate a different interpretation, Dr Noyes will insist on a reading of the event which confirms his position. Principles of ritual and tradition are therefore the self-serving ratifiers of Noyes' views and the basis of his power. Control of interpretative modes facilitates continuing domination and powers of exclusion in ontological as well as material terms:

> The peacock, still maintaining the display of his tail, now lifted his head very high on his neck and gave a piercing scream.
>
> 'You see?' said Doctor Noyes. 'By every sign and signal, my decision is confirmed.' He smiled but had to draw the smile back against his wooden teeth, which had almost fallen out of his mouth.
>
> 'He's only calling to his mate, for God's sake!' said Mrs Noyes.
>
> 'How dare you!' Doctor Noyes was livid. 'How dare you take the name of God in vain! How *dare* you!'

> This sort of rage – more a performance than a reality – was necessary to keep Mrs Noyes in her place. Also, to intimidate the other women, lest they follow her example and get out of hand. (13)

Signs and signals, tradition and ritual, are agents of a sinister power enforcement which, through its self-referentiality, maintains the centrality of Noyes and his control over his family, women, and animals. Such epistemic control ensures that challenges to its validity can only come from *outside* the system; internal challenges immediately find a place within the hierarchy of attempted but always smothered rebellion. The ash has come from the burning of cities in areas outside of Noah's control; indeed, the burnings are a deliberate challenge to Yaweh's power, and therefore to Noah's. But by naturalizing the ash as 'snow', 'a miracle' within his own system, Noah both denatures the outside challenge and actually capitalizes on it by having it bolster his own powers of ascribing meaning. Hierarchies and 'systems' of the kind Noah/Yaweh represents depend for their functioning on rigid categorizations, specifically on binary codifications of the kind embodied in Doctor Noyes' (no/yes) own name; and hence real challenges to his authority can, and do, come from three areas in the course of the novel: from 'marginalized' perspectives on the centrist authority; from the challenges posed by alternative, specifically unconsolidated, 'systems' whose 'model' is that of the network rather than the ladder: and from hybrid or mimic forms which refuse the necessary categorizations of the centrist ruling power.

Not Wanted on the Voyage depicts a multiplicity of relationships between different beings, some realistic, some imaginary. This extension of characters, with the resultant complexity of relationships, implies different ways of being (and knowing) and acts to subvert the establishment of any one notion or way of being as axiomatic. Thus the very *dramatis personae* of the novel counter Noyes' attempts to consolidate a single authoritative structure. In the world of Yaweh and Dr Noyes, all relationships are essentially rigid and hierarchical, reinforced by symbols, ritual, and tradition, so 'the word' passes from God to Noah, to male humans, to female humans, and finally to all lesser beings.

By contrast, the world of animals and of other beings and those humans who cannot or refuse to conform to the rigidities of Noyes' system, is one in which the immanent, the transformative, and the relational underpin meaning and being. In Noyes' world, interpretations (plural) are precluded. In the world of Mottyl, Mrs Noyes, the Unicorn, and Crowe, interpretation occurs by negotiation between differing perspectives and involves not one world, but many, the crossing of whose territories requires debate and discussion, as in the perceptions of the 'angel' by the different species. Brute force does operate in this world, but the key to survival is vigilance through communication. Because of this 'web' of interspecies activity, more senses and therefore more perceptions are available – there is not the determination to exclude that pervades the philosophy of Noyes, but rather the necessity to include. To include, but not to assimilate. Reality thus becomes that which can be negotiated between a multiplicity of groups and possibilities, not a series of differing perspectives on the same reality.

The novel, then, contests the view of Noah and his cohorts that the world offers one reality arrived at through a semiotics which he is privileged to read, in spite of its increasing consolidation of his own power, by suggesting the possibility of an infinite network of negotiation. Noah's will to power almost destroys any such possibility, but it survives in attenuated form through the animals in the Ark and through Mrs Noyes and Lucy (the androgynous fallen angel).

The novel also uses the decentring which results from a multiplicity of perspectives to undermine the self-aggrandizement of Noyes and God. Great moments of investiture or those which might be expected to invoke the high seriousness attendant on manifestations of absolute power are undermined by relativizing perspectives. God's arrival, the climax of the flight of the dove, the sacrifices, and the ritual preparations, are viewed from the angle of Emma, lowest of the low in Noyes' household, and from the perspective of Mottyl, the cat. Both the irreverent (if awed) perceptions of Emma and the assessment available to Mottyl's rather different senses add up to the same thing: the uncanny resemblance between Yaweh and Noyes. 'Man' has indeed created God in his own image:

Yaweh drew a small tin box from somewhere in His robe and opened it. His fingers were not as long as Emma thought they might have been, though part of the reason for this was plainly arthritis . . . Something was lifted from the box – placed against His lips and drawn into His mouth. *God sucks lozenges!* thought Emma, astonished. *Just like Dr Noyes!* . . .

The Lord God Yaweh, who was about to step into the air, was more than seven hundred years older than His friend Dr Noyes, kneeling now in the road before Him. To Mottyl, it was meaningless. Her Lord and Creator was a walking sack of bones and hair. She also suspected, from His smell, that He was human. (66)

In the Noyes scheme of things, 'difference in nature but equivalence in value' (Todorov 1974: 76) is not possible. Hence the hierarchical structures on which his power depends must be policed for 'difference' and everyone/thing rigidly categorized on a scale of value whose successive boundary lines are clear. Noah is below God, his sons below him, the women below them, the animals below them and so on. In this 'Great Chain of Being' there are also angels, between God and man, but some of these, too, are more equal than others. When the novel opens, however, other forms which do not belong to any of the above categories also share the earth: the demons, who are brought into the Noyes kitchen by an as yet unembittered Japeth, and whose heat scorches the furniture; the fairies, who can be seen by Mrs Noyes and the animals, but not by the other humans; the dragons, who stray into the field and whose presence is a source of terror. Then there are those animals who will later be rendered 'extinct', like the Unicorn and his Lady. Above all there are the disturbingly ambiguous 'Lotte children' (ape-children) and the 'fallen' angel Lucy who found the rigid binary classifications of 'Heaven' too boring and unpleasant.

As this voyage of destruction/salvation begins, many forms are lost or deliberately annihilated, drowned, or burned. The fairies are not allowed aboard the Ark and perish in the flood. The Unicorn is brutally 'raped' and murdered through Noyes' use of him as the instrument of rape. The demons are thrown over the side. The dragons haven't made it aboard in the first place. Multiple forms and possibilities of being are lost forever.

Those who survive, including Mrs Noyes, have been brutally 'Othered'. But in *Not Wanted on the Voyage* it is not only the processes of this exclusion and 'Othering' which are exposed and anatomized; the phobias that induce such responses to Otherness, phobias that lie at the very heart of imperialism, are similarly charted.

Anxiety about ambivalence stems from a deep-seated contradiction in the processes by which the Other is constructed, a basis of fundamental contradiction which opens colonial discourse to the possibility of fracture from within (Bhabha 1984b). The dominant discourse constructs Otherness in such a way that it always contains a trace of ambivalence or anxiety about its own authority. In order to maintain authority over the Other in a colonial situation, imperial discourse strives to delineate the Other as radically different from the self, yet at the same time it must maintain sufficient identity with the Other to valorize control over it. The Other can, of course, only be constructed out of the archive of 'the self', yet the self must also articulate the Other as inescapably different. Otherness can thus only be produced by a continual process of what Bhabha calls 'repetition and displacement' and this instigates an ambivalence at the very site of imperial authority and control. Thus there is a kind of built-in resistance in the construction of any dominant discourse – and opposition is an almost inevitable effect of its construction of cultural difference. Of course, what such authority least likes, and what presents it with its greatest threat, is any reminder of such ambivalence. This ambivalence at the very heart of authority is exposed by the presence in the colonial subject of hybridization or colonial mimicry (ibid.).

In *Not Wanted on the Voyage* two elements in particular lie at the heart of Noah's authority anxiety. These are the manifestation of 'Lotte children' in the human community, and Lucy/Lucifer whose gender and human/angel status are ambiguous and hybrid. Though these 'hybrid' forms are either deliberately destroyed or marginalized, their very presence disrupts the apparently axiomatic significatory system which has invested itself with absolute authority over those it has constructed as 'Other'. *Not Wanted on the Voyage*, then, investigates the most fundamental processes of Othering and processes of the centre–margin relation, and does so in a way characteristic of the post-colonial text. It deploys a number of counter-discursive strategies, re-entering the western episteme at one of its most fundamental points of origination to deconstruct those notions and processes which rationalized the imposition of the imperial word on the rest of the world.

Appropriating marginality: Janet Frame's *The Edge of the Alphabet*

Marginality is the condition constructed by the posited relation to a privileged centre, an 'Othering' directed by the imperial authority. But the abrogation of that centre does not involve the construction of an alternative focus of subjectivity, a new 'centre'. Rather the act of appropriation in the post-colonial text issues in the embracing of that marginality as the fabric of social experience. The 'marginal' and the 'variant' characterize post-colonial views of language and society as a consequence of the process of abrogation. The syncretic is validated by the disappearance of the 'centre', and with no 'centre' the marginal becomes the formative constituent of reality. Discourses of marginality such as race, gender, psychological 'normalcy', geographical and social distance, political exclusion, intersect in a view of reality which supersedes the geometric distinction of centre and margin and replaces it with a sense of the complex, interweaving, and syncretic accretion of experience.

Janet Frame's novels draw their energies from a vision of marginality, and particularly of the intersection of different kinds of marginality, which dismantles all notions of a centre to consciousness and self. The 'marginal' and the 'central' are of course psychological constructs, but they have their grounding in the alienation resulting from colonial incorporation. *The Edge of the Alphabet* (Frame 1962) is a narration by 'Thora Pattern' of the journeys of three individuals who meet on a ship travelling from New Zealand to London, and who themselves form the points of intersection of different discourses of marginality: Toby Withers, an epileptic and New Zealander who travels back to London to find his 'centre', Zoe Bryce, a Midlands 'spinster' schoolteacher, and Pat Keenan, a repressed Irish bus-driver. On the surface their alienation appears purely personal; Toby is not 'normal': 'there was just no place for him to fit in' (20); Pat's anxiety was that he 'never "came into his own" . . . one's "own" can be so easily lost!' (60), and there is Zoe Bryce who has never been kissed. The 'kiss' and its absence signify Zoe's marginality as female. Her identity is constituted as negation – she is 'the woman who has never been kissed', and this, in turn, negates her femaleness, because identity is conferred by the kiss from the dominant male world.

But such personal marginality is also an expression of a political and geographical condition. As a New Zealander, Toby is doubly marginalized; when he tells people where he's from, the response is, '"That's somewhere in Australia, isn't it?" Or they said in a dazed way, "New Zealand? I've got a brother who emigrated to Australia"' (180). The colonial dimension of his movement 'back' to the centre is clearly indicated in the title to part 1 of the book, 'A home there'. But both Zoe and Pat identify an earlier state of coloniality and a deeper sense of paradox in relation to the centre. Zoe is a Midlander: 'Shall I go to London? Am I betraying my Midland background by going to London?' she says (170), and Pat is an Irishman who gets very upset at all the 'foreigners crowding the country from left to right':

'But you're not from England yourself,' Zoe said mildly.
'That's different. I'm from Ireland, the real Ireland. We've been under the domination of Britain for long enough. I'm from the real part of Ireland.' (199)

The absurdity of this divided loyalty voiced by the Irishman, the uncertainty of spiritual location imposed by the distinction of centre and margin, is the characteristic of colonial alienation. But as Toby says in an intuitive moment, 'Everybody comes from the other side of the world' (130). The appropriation of the marginal reveals that there is no 'centre', that London is simply an 'other side'.

In one sense the novel is an elaboration of the perception by Naipaul in *The Mimic Men* that London and the home counties are 'the ultimate disorder'. For the centrality they represent, in historical as well as personal and psychological terms, is seen as endlessly deferred, a focus which is ultimately always an illusion. Yet this unabrogated spiritual centrality is an irresistible lure for human beings. 'What mathematical trick', asks Thora Pattern,

'has divided the whole into the sum of so many people, only to set working in our hearts the process by which we continually strive to reduce the sum once more to its invisible whole . . . And what if the person who meets us forever is ourselves? What if we meet ourselves on the edge of the alphabet and can make no sign, no speech?' (300–1).

The 'mathematical trick' is the trick of political and spiritual incorporation, for the centre is always simply composed of further 'edges'. But it constitutes a linguistic trick as well, for available speech comes to us as the language of the illusory centre where we believe 'self' must reside. The periphery of the metropolitan reality denies language because the alphabet always exists elsewhere.

There is a triumph in the dismantling of the centre in this novel which is uniquely post-colonial. The sense of the illusion of the centre occurs first on the ship bound for London. A family which is due to board at Panama becomes a haunting absence at the centre of the life of the ship: '"A table is set aside for them. Their empty cabins are waiting. Can't you see how the life of the ship revolves around them?"' (85). But they are only a 'centre' while they are absent. Once aboard, their mystery is lost; presence confirms their marginality.

But perhaps the most significant decentring of the metropolitan comes when Toby who, never having been to a circus, catches the bus to Piccadilly Circus:

Toby was mystified. The circus must be somewhere, he thought. How can I be there without knowing? Perhaps I'll stand on the corner and watch where this bus goes. It says Piccadilly Circus. I'll know that wherever it stops is the circus.

He watched the bus turn the corner and, still in sight, come toward him, going in the opposite direction. Now that was strange. With a feeling of dismay he read across the front of the bus – *Cricklewood*. (183)

This passage both introduces and dismantles the notion that in not knowing what Piccadilly Circus is, Toby must be 'simple'.

After all, 'the whole world knows about Piccadilly Circus'. The Circus was always employed as the archetypal image of the centre, the 'heart of the Empire' (symbolized by the statue of Eros on the fountain, the centre of the 'centre'). Therefore, Frame's dismantling of the centrality of the Circus is especially resonant. The 'essential' locative and ontological centre of Piccadilly Circus does not exist, it is a fiction perpetuated by language and only those who live on the edge of the alphabet could discover this, for 'what more successful means of avoidance are there than words' (55). The illusion of Piccadilly Circus is symbolic of the fiction of centrality retained in the post-colonial experience, and the centrality of being which it predicates. The focus of 'being' is dismantled by the marginal which sees that the ontological centre is simply the perpetual contiguity of the conditions of 'becoming' and 'having been', like a Piccadilly Circus bus.

However, the process of this discovery involves a return to the centre, in what for Toby is an inevitable *rite de passage*. It is on the one hand a return 'home' to some ancestral certainty. But his main reason for going to London is to write his book *The Lost Tribe* for, after all, this is the centre of the alphabet and at the centre language shall surely elude him no longer. The Lost Tribe lives in the *South* (216) at the edges of the 'real', but the Lost Tribe can only be reproduced as real at the *centre* where words can be controlled. Sitting down to write his book, with the exercise book from Woolworth's and a new HB pencil, Toby discovers, however, that language is no less elusive:

> *The Lost Tribe*, he had written, in slow careful writing. Then he stopped, seized by fear. Perhaps that was his book, just that; three words; nothing else, no chapters or sections or descriptions of people. Could that be so, only three words? (194)

The book, the tangible confirmation of his own real being, is the ultimate assertion of the centre for Toby. But the book is being continually written by his own life. He is one of the lost tribe, 'from the South'. *The Lost Tribe* is the continuous manifestation of absence, the dismantling of any notion of language operating through a structure of 'centre' and 'edges'. The book is a natural artifact of self-realization, for it is through books that the 'real' and the 'valuable' are continually announced in the metropolis.

But as a tangible focus of Toby's world, the book will never be written, for the concept 'book' itself, as closure and final reality, and the irreducible subjectivity which it is intended to confirm, are an illusion.

Pat's orientation to the centre is more ephemeral. He faces north [towards London?] when travelling, 'as facing the north supplied him with the electricity necessary for restful sleep' (59). But the centre of his world are the swans who swim in the concrete-bordered lake in the centre of the common. 'He confessed one evening that he did not know what he would do without the swans' (245), but the permanence of the swans is also illusory. They hatch, they leave each season, they die, they disappear. The swans are never the same swans but always a memory, eliding the absences which surround their fleeting presence:

> What does the swan mean? It is aloof, sour, a snow convention, an annual pageant of suspicious probing with little bags of crusts on the Common. It is Elise, Leda, *any changeful god.* (247; emphasis added)

Zoe Bryce's centre is specifically metonymic of her negation as female. Lying in the ship's sick bay suffering from seasickness Zoe experiences her first kiss when one of the crew furtively kisses her on the lips and disappears. The kiss, the expected conferral of real being on her denies her validity as a person at the very moment of conferral – 'My life has been sucked at last into the whirlpool, made shapeless as water, and here I am trying to carve it as if it were stone. . . . A dirty member of the crew kissed me and like a creature in a fable, stole my identity' (107). But the kiss, in its meaninglessness and casual invasion, becomes an image of that centre which all the characters of the novel are attempting to enclose:

> The kiss is the core of my life. It is my meaning, my tiny precious berry from the one branch of a huge tree in a forest where the trees are numberless. (239)

Whereas Toby and Pat cling to their sense of the centre, however inadequate or illusory it has become, Zoe follows the natural momentum of that illusoriness, producing out of it further foci of deferral and marginality. Sitting with strangers beside a pool she absently picks up a silver cigarette wrapper and twists it into a remarkable silver forest, the ultimate and central creation of her life which she identifies immediately as another version of the casual meaninglessness of the kiss:

> The communication of my life – a kiss in mid-ocean between myself and a half-drunken seaman. The creation of my life – oh my God! – a silver-paper shape fashioned from the remains of an empty cigarette packet! Surely now it is the time for my death? (273)

Zoe's death is not a 'universal human tragedy', but a peculiarly post-colonial dismantling of the fiction of identity. For she has, by rejecting the notion of the centre of the alphabet, transferred even her own identity into a prism through which an exploration of life is made. It is in circling back that we discover Zoe has decentred her own life, that the centre of consciousness of the 'book' *The Edge Of The Alphabet* has been driven to the edges of the alphabet. In returning to the beginning of the book we find the note:

> The following manuscript was found among the papers of Thora Pattern after her death, and submitted to the publishers by Peter Heron Hire-Purchase Salesman. (Prefatory Note)

It was this Peter Heron who as a failed artist had sat with Zoe Bryce by the Serpentine while she created the 'creation of my life', and who became a salesman after her suicide. Thus, through deconstructing the centre, seeing the reality of the alphabet and meaning itself as residing in a 'slippage' of language rather than a distinction of centre and margin, Thora/Zoe/Janet Pattern/Bryce/Frame has deferred reality itself into a continuously expanding horizon of marginal realities. Within this horizon there is no longer any centre, but a fabric of perpetually intersecting discourses of marginality which include the marginality of the author herself.

Appropriating the frame of power: R.K. Narayan's *The Vendor of Sweets*

Within the syncretic reality of a post-colonial society it is impossible to return to an idealized pure pre-colonial cultural condition. The work of Indian novelist R.K. Narayan, which has frequently either been regarded as deeply traditional, or as incorporating the ironic perspective of the English literary tradition, illustrates this problem. For both these readings are based on a false dichotomy. The post-colonial text is always a complex and hybridized formation. It is inadequate to read it either as a reconstruction of pure traditional values or as simply foreign and intrusive. The reconstruction of 'pure' cultural value is always conducted within a radically altered dynamic of power relations.

The Vendor of Sweets (Narayan 1967) tells the story of a small shopkeeper, Jagan, and his relationship with his society and its traditions, traditions which his son Mali (who has studied in America) is determined to change and modernize. Early in the novel we are told how the sweets-vendor, Jagan, collects his money in two separate containers, one representing the sales for the official day ending at 6.00 pm, on which he pays sales tax, and one for money collected 'out of hours' on which he pays none. This money, we are told, he viewed as 'a sort of immaculate conception, self-generated, arising out of itself and entitled to survive without reference to any tax. It was converted into crisp currency at the earliest moment, tied into a bundle and put away to keep company with the portrait of Mr Noble in the loft at home' (10). Earlier in the novel we are introduced to a family relic, the portrait of Mr Noble, the District Collector, who at one time had come to Jagan's father for lessons in astrology, and for whom a chair had been built especially:

> A signed portrait ripening yellow with time was among the prized possessions dumped in the loft; but at some point in the history of the family the photograph was brought down, the children played with it for a while, and then *substituted in its glassed frame the picture of a god* and hung it up, while the photograph in the bare mount was tossed about as the children gazed on Mr Noble's side whiskers and giggled all the afternoon. They fanned themselves with it, too, when the summer became too hot; finally, it disappeared back to the loft amidst old account-books and other obscure family junk.
>
> (8; emphasis added)

Within a metaphoric reading of this trope, the children's action in removing Mr Noble from the frame would seem to serve merely as an ironic device reflecting on the transience of power and the inevitable return of the 'eternal' Indian values, which colonialism merely overlaid. This is how many such 'ironic' moments in Narayan texts are read by nationalist critics who then have some difficulty in reconciling the 'ironic' tonalities within a reading of the text as 'de-colonized' fiction. This is because in Narayan not all the ironies work to the benefit of the Indian verities. Critics have expressed irritation with Narayan's comic if sympathetic treatment of Indian traditional institutions and have found his tone too complex and too ambivalent. Those who seek to totalize the text and read it as an extended metaphor in which Narayan's mythical town of Malgudi functions either as a universal 'great stage of fools', or as a setting for the 'parable of Man from the Indian point of view', will inevitably be forced to 'edit' the text to make it fit such readings. The production of such a stereotype from either perspective must reduce the text to a mere revision or reversal of the colonial perspective and epistemology. Any reading of the trope of the picture frame as total metaphor must reinforce such dependent and colonized practices.

If the trope is read as metonymic and repetitive (Bhabha 1984a) then a different significance is revealed. This early reference to the transition from Mr Noble to household god in the exchange of icons and the 'frame' is repeated in the tale of the 'immaculate money'. When Mali determines, without his father's knowledge, to go to America, and appropriates the air fare from the 'immaculate' undeclared money which Jagan has hidden in the loft 'to keep company with the portrait of Mr Noble', Jagan, though approving of his son's 'enterprise' considers 'transferring' what is left of the untaxed hoard:

> 'It must be very costly,' said Jagan like a prattling baby.
> 'But he has doubtless found the cash for it,' said the cousin.
> 'Naturally. What is the cash worth to me? It's all for him. He can have everything he wants,' said Jagan, making a note mentally to count at the earliest moment his cash hoarded in the loft. He also *considered transferring it all, in due course, to a casket behind the family gods in the puja room.*
>
> (37; emphasis added)

At the level of narrative this transference has the immediate effect of restoring Jagan's economic control, as we discover subsequently when, on Mali's return from America with suitably 'enlarged' horizons he demands 2.5 lakhs of rupees (50,000 dollars) to start his company to manufacture his novel-writing machine. When Jagan refuses Mali is not disturbed. As the cousin reports:

> '. . . he also says he knows where you keep cash not sent to the bank'.
> 'He says so, does he?' said Jagan, laughing within himself at the fact that he had changed the venue of the immaculate cash.
> 'Money is an evil,' he added with great feeling. (61)

But in the novel's larger repetitive insistence on the possibility of appropriating power from the organization and techniques of the colonial and neo-colonial world, the function of the trope is to radicalize the significance of the replacement of Mr Noble by 'the god' in the frame. Rather than a mere substitute of symbols within an unchanging pattern of underlying structures, it signifies an active employment of the symbol to regenerate and reactivate an alternative practice within the historical present. The frame remains but what is empowered within it can now be the product of an active choice. The trope is useful for demonstrating the fact that the processes of abrogation (the rejection of Mr Noble) and appropriation (the retention of the 'frame') inevitably concern the dynamics of power. In this particular example there is a concern not with what is contained within the frame as much as with the way in which reality itself is 'framed' and 'authorized' by the structures of power.

Significantly, of course, the portrait of Mr Noble proves a useless guardian once removed from the 'frame' and consigned to the attic, but the money is successfully protected by the gods who now inhabit the 'frame' of power and active presence. Yet their potency is also produced by the appropriation to them of the 'frame' of power they have inherited from Mr Noble. The same applies to Jagan, who seeks to live by the laws of a modified Gandhian Hinduism but who must always be aware of the changed and hybridized reality within which such changes can be made effective or otherwise. And this is true of both sides of the equation, the traditional prejudices and laws which remain active despite Gandhi's attempted reforms, and the European influences and economic controls which remain in place despite his successful struggle for 'independence'.

Thus when Grace (Mali's Korean–American wife) innocently comments that she had been frightened of prejudice under the caste system before she arrived, Jagan's comments reveal his awareness of the gap between proposed ideal and actuality:

> 'Well, we don't believe in caste these days, you know,' Jagan said generously.
> 'Gandhi fought for its abolition.'
> 'Is it gone now?' she asked innocently.
> 'It's going,' Jagan said, sounding like a politician. 'We don't think of it nowadays,' hoping that the girl would not cross-examine him further. (49)

Such a metonymic reading, whilst it recognizes the significance of Jagan's loyalty to traditional practices, does not do so at the cost of being dismissive of Mali or of his stand against the inadequacies of Jagan's partial and flawed modernization on the Gandhian model.

The present action of the novel is sharply contextualized by the flashback account of Jagan's own courtship, marriage 'in the Indian way' and subsequent struggle to fulfil the demands of his father, his family, and 'the ancient home' (Hindu practice?) they represent. The account of Jagan's journey to the temple with his wife and parents to sacrifice for a son illustrates the inevitable and continuing friction between 'tradition' and changing practice, a friction which is continued in a different way in Jagan's relationship with his own son. Jagan's father is angry at being overcharged by the coconut-sellers who, by custom, supply the sacrifice material:

> 'If I had known the price of things here, I'd have brought all the stuff from home,' he cried irascibly.
> Mother interposed from where she sat, 'That is not permitted. Custom requires . . .'
> 'Yes, yes, it was written in the *Vedas* ten thousand years ago that you must be exploited on this spot of earth by this particular coconut-woman. True, true,' he said cynically, glaring at his son and daughter-in-law . . .

But for the fact that he was a coward, Jagan would have asked his parents, 'Haven't you enough grandchildren? Why do you want more? Why don't you leave me alone?' (131)

In this exchange a continuing dialectical pattern emerges between a traditional insistence on the collective, family, group, and society, and the opposed demands of the European ideology of the independent 'individual' whose social inflection is one of the strongest trace marks left by Europeanization on the post-colonial world. It is a trace whose presence marks the novel with an insistent repetition which spans all three generations of the family, irrespective of their personal concerns and histories. It marks the novel below the level of character and theme, revelatory as it is, not of design or rhetoric, or even of cultural bias or national 'sensibility', through all of whose action critics have sought to 'elucidate' the fiction, but, rather, of the social and cultural formations which produce both the lives of contemporary Indians and the art-forms which are available to record them.

The conditions of production of the book are thus fully and honestly reproduced at all levels of the text, and when these conditions are recognized by an adequate critical practice, the text can be liberated from the domination of partial models of the neo-colonialist or simple nationalist kind and reconstructed as a sign of a distinctive post-colonial practice. We do not have to decide *between* the generations in a moral way any more than we have to endorse or reject their actions. Such a totalizing moral framework would demand a simple collapsing inwards of the novel's paradoxes and pluralities, and would be symptomatic of the reduction of the complexities of the post-colonial Indian text into an approximation (or 'mimicry') of an idealized version of European ethics and philosophical categories masquerading as universals (or, as we have suggested, a falsely 'radical reversal of these which simply exchanges one stereotype for another, as in 'nationalist' readings).

All these symptomatic readings draw attention to the centrality of language and the diverse processes by which the binarism of centre and margin is itself dismantled by the complementary processes of abrogation and appropriation. Texts such as Nkosi's *Mating Birds* and Naipaul's *The Mimic Men* articulate the impossibility of evading the destructive and marginalizing power of the dominant centre and the need for its abrogation. Neither sexual aggression nor social success are sufficient to evade the inherently diminishing force which oppresses the characters. Both texts evidence the destructive qualities and the imitative nature of post-colonial reality. Anthony's 'Sandra Street' and Findley's *Not Wanted on the Voyage* develop other subversive strategies to overpower the forms and themes which constrict them, turning the 'limitations' of their post-coloniality into the source of their formal and thematic originality and strength. Janet Frame's *The Edge of the Alphabet* and R.K. Narayan's *The Vendor of Sweets*, in their different ways, and from the very different perspectives of their societies, illustrate the possibilities of dismantling received epistemological notions once both language and form have been fully appropriated. These become the expression of a society no longer conceived as Other but triumphantly self-defining and self-sustaining, able to reorder the conceptual frame within which power is determined. Symptomatic readings of this kind are not concerned primarily with evaluating one text against another in some privileging hierarchy or canon, nor with 'discovering' their essential metaphoric meaning: but rather with identifying and articulating the symptomatic and distinctive features of their post-coloniality. The post-colonial text is itself a site of struggle for linguistic control, as the power which it makes manifest is yielded up to the appropriating discourse. This struggle, as we have shown, extends to the disputes concerning theme, form, genre definition, implicit systems of manner, custom, and value. A body of indigenous theory which seeks to address the issues implicit here has emerged in post-colonial societies, and it is to a consideration of this that we want to turn next.

4
Theory at the crossroads: indigenous theory and post-colonial reading

All post-colonial countries once had or still have 'native' cultures of some kind. These range from the widespread indigenous literary cultures of India and Pakistan, through the extensive and highly developed oral cultures of Black sub-Saharan Africa, to the Aboriginal cultures of Australia, New Zealand, and Canada. To some extent this is also true of the West Indies, where the Caribs and Arawaks were almost completely annihilated by colonial settlement, but still remain as a ghostly trace on the consciousness of the modern Creolized inhabitants. The creative development of post-colonial societies is often determined by the influence of this pre-colonial, indigenous culture and the degree to which it is still active.

The use of received English has, of course, always been an issue with writers and the choice of language goes hand in hand with indigenous attitudes to the role and function of literature itself in the society. Those theories which emerge in diglossic oral cultures, that is in cultures in which bilingualism is strongly established, for example, in Africa, stem in a direct way from the contrary pull of a native and an imported language which are different in concept and function. In text-based diglossic cultures such as those in India, there is a body of traditional literary critical theory which provides a deep fund of hermeneutic concepts from which a modern indigenous theory can draw inspiration and substance. But the emergence of indigenous theories in monoglossic settler cultures has also been linked to the question of language, of constructing a 'unique' voice, distinct from the language of the centre. Predictably, since the emergence of indigenous literary theories is so germane to the use of language in post-colonial societies, those theories developed in the polydialectical communities of the Caribbean have been amongst the most complex and have displayed the greatest potential for abrogating Eurocentric concepts.

Indian literary theories

Traditional criticism and contemporary use

Indian indigenous criticism has had to form itself in relation to both the dominant aesthetic modes of the colonizing culture, and an indigenous critical tradition at least as old, if not older, than that of Europe.[1] The earliest extant work of Indian criticism in Sanskrit, the *Natya Shastra of Bharata*, dates from *c.* 200 BC and there followed an unbroken tradition of commentary for some two thousand years to the work of Jagannatha (*c.* AD 1780). Literatures in other languages, such as Tamil and Urdu, also have extensive and ancient critical traditions.

Indian scholars and critics have been locked in debate as to how far these traditions can be adapted to the needs of modern criticism for Indian literature. The debate centres on whether or not the 'highly sophisticated theories' propounded by the Sanskrit 'schoolmen' can be, or, indeed, ever were 'applied in the evaluation of works of art' (Krishnamoorthy 1984) and, more specifically, whether the terms of this tradition: *rasa, dhvani, alankara*, etc., are more relevant and suitable than imported terms to the description of contemporary literatures in the Indian vernacular languages and, to a lesser extent, to Indian literatures in english.

This debate has, in part at least, been a debate about decolonization. The attraction of such alternative aesthetic models as the compendium *dhvani–rasa* (suggestion–emotion) theory over imported concerns with ambiguity, symbol, image, etc. (e.g. Krishna Rayan 1984) is in part a concern to reconstitute a sense of the 'Indianness' of the texts considered and to assess their virtue by the standards and assumptions of an indigenous aesthetic. In so far as the traditional indigenous aesthetic is more standardized and codified than any other in the post-colonial world, and in so far as it is the product of a written culture, it lends itself more readily to the discourse of contemporary academic criticism. Although to date there have been few attempts rigorously to apply the traditional aesthetic and its concepts to modern literatures, these concepts may well be a powerful tool for opening up the distinctive features of contemporary Indian texts subsumed under imported critical and generic assumptions.

The main drive in re-employing terms from Sanskrit criticism, such as those listed above, or from ancient Tamil (Ramanujan 1985) has been in assessing the literature produced in Indian vernacular languages where a direct continuity of some essential 'indianness' has been more vigorously asserted. Critics such as K. Krishnamoorthy (1984) claim the existence of a theoretical base common to all Indian literatures, including both post-Sanskrit and non-Sanskrit, a base that is itself the sign of an Indian sensibility. The Kannada-speaking novelist and critic U.R. Anantha Murthy presents a more complex view of the relation between contemporary vernacular texts and the Tamil and Sanskrit canon, a view which takes into account the literatures in english as well as those in Indian languages. He suggests that the relationship of the ancient languages (Tamil and Sanskrit) to the modern vernaculars is analogous to that of Latin and modern English (Anantha Murthy 1986). The Kannada terms *marga / desi*; the *way* and the *earth* are, he claims, potent metaphors for this with Sanskrit as the way (*marga*) and the vernacular (e.g. Kannada) as the earth or ground (*desi*). All texts written in the present mix the two, just as all English texts demonstrate a varying mix of Latinate and vernacular elements (more redolent of the former in the case of, say, Milton, or of the latter in the case of, say, Keats).

By extension, contemporary texts in Kannada may appropriate English words more easily than Sanskrit, since they are part of the rhetoric available to even a village character in the twentieth century, and so the *marga–desi* model may work with an english–Kannada base. Thus, a principle of appropriation from the multiple sources of language is embraced as a positive aim for the modern text in Indian vernaculars. Anantha Murthy (1986) has described his position as being that of the 'critical insider'. The writer remains within his tradition but does so critically, rejecting the idea of a pure unalloyed tradition and embracing the contradictions of his own position as a mark of creative potential, not of a cultural decline or of a continuing colonial domination.

Significantly, a number of writers, even within the Indian vernacular languages, have stressed the extent to which these languages have been altered and hybridized by the presence of alternative discourses, especially that of english, in an age of rapid language change and mass-media influence on everyday speech and habits. Some have found this a feature to be deplored and resisted, others have found it a challenge to fresh appropriation and development. Describing the problems encountered when he decided to return to writing in Tamil after writing in english, the poet R. Parthasarathy wrote:

> My tongue in English chains.
> I return, after a generation, to you.
> I am at the end
> of my dravidic tether,
> hunger for you unassuaged.
> I falter, stumble.
>
> Speak a tired language
> wrenched from its sleep in the *Kural*,
> teeth, palate, lips still new
>
> to its agglutinative touch.
> Now, hooked on celluloid, you reel
> down plush corridors.
> (Parthasarathy 1977: 44)

The process of recovering the past, whether in its earliest or in some arbitrarily designated later form (e.g. 'We should arrive at an intellectual articulation of our literary sensibility as it was before the British advent. Sixteenth or seventeenth century would serve as a promising starting point' – Patankar 1984) has been very tempting to contemporary Indian critics. Despite the obvious objection to such a suggestion – that it merely authorizes, arbitrarily, one moment of culture as 'essential' and so ignores the inevitable syncretic nature of a post-colonial culture – it offers some clear advances in its practice. Although it shares many of the weaknesses of other national models for decolonizing cultures, it does so with the strength of a tradition so extensive and so rich that it has been able to produce powerful abrogating accounts of Indian texts and traditional influences. In practice it has been suggested that such a recovery will work best if the concepts of the traditional aesthetics are subject to adaptation and change. They can be discovered and kept alive, Patankar suggests (ibid.), not by academic study, but by being 'lived' and moulded through use.

It is obviously too early to say whether this will prove to be the case or whether the theories so developed, which, to date, have been mainly concerned with evaluating Indian literatures in vernacular languages, will have a relevance to works in Indian english. But in one important respect they have already done so. The Sanskrit tradition moves from text to a general theory of literature, embracing not only an evaluation and interpretation of the text but also a theory of production and consumption. In one of its most influential forms, the *dhvani–rasa* distinction, such theory lays equal stress on the suggestive possibility within the text (*dhvani*) and the effect of the potential for meaning and feeling in the various realizers: reader/spectator, actor/author, 'character', who collectively embody the text's suggestion in realized emotional states (*bhavas*) according to the traditional classification of emotions (*rasas*). This assertion of literary practice as a dual site of production and consumption makes Indian criticism readily disposed to see much contemporary European and American concern with 'poetics' as less a revolutionary activity than an 'already-given' of Indian indigenous aesthetics. This is a two-edged sword, however, since it creates a climate of acceptance and a sense of *déjà vu* which militate against a radical and innovative appropriation of the traditional to modern conditions.

As a result, the practice of this criticism to date has either described the ways in which Indian concepts pre-date and pre-figure the main terms of twentieth-century European and American aesthetics, and so suggested that Indian critics may be able to 'replace them' in Indian criticism with more appropriate indigenous terms (Paniker 1982) or attempted to reassert an alternative Sanskrit-based aesthetic (Narasimhaiah and Srinath 1984). As important as these developments have been to the process of abrogating the western theoretical hegemony, the problem of trying to recover the illusory essence of 'Indianness' in such theory still needs to be addressed. The assertion that earlier models of post-coloniality (Commonwealth literature, new literatures in English) merely perpetuated the dominance of a renamed but essentially unchanged centre (Patankar 1984), has some credence. But it opens up problems of its own. As we have shown, contemporary syncretic critics in post-colonial societies would reject the assertion that 'Our all-round acceptance of the British hegemony supplies perhaps the only cause for our recent interest in Commonwealth literature and culture' (ibid.). Addressing the problem of writing in India within a post-colonial framework does not imply an acceptance of that hegemony, but rather the opposite – in practice it suggests the only effective way of escaping the control implicit in its very structure.

So far in Indian criticism, the possibility of moving beyond such abrogative stages to the wider possibility of appropriation (an appropriation in which both the possibilities and the limitations of such alternative monolithic cultural models would be interrogated) has only occasionally been voiced. The larger possibilities of the pioneer work of the critics mentioned here as well as many others whom brevity has forced us to leave unacknowledged is still relatively untapped, and its potential as a means to develop that 'critical insider' stance for which U.R. Anantha Murthy has spoken has yet to be fully explored. The Indian traditions are so rich a source that the future of Indian criticism based on the appropriation of traditional aesthetics is difficult to predict. It is impossible, however, not to applaud its project as a political act of rebellion against the incorporating tendencies of European and American neo-universalism.

Problems of contemporary criticism of Indian writing in english

In addition to the development of the possibility of a revived traditional aesthetics, a lively debate has emerged in India about the status, relative value, and possible continuation of Indian writing in english. More than anywhere else in the

post-colonial world, perhaps, the possibility of writing in vernacular languages other than english exists in India as an
immediate and practical choice. For most Indian critics, writing in english represents a small and marginal aspect of the
practice of contemporary Indian writing (George 1986). It is
frequently asserted that the work produced by contemporary
writers in languages as diverse as Maratha, Bengali, Kannada,
Telugu, Malayalam, etc., far outweighs in quantity and quality
the work produced in english. This may well be the case, though
until much more extensive translations into english from these
languages have been produced it is difficult for non-speakers of
these languages to judge.[2]

However, the desire to draw attention to the range and power
of historical and contemporary writing in Indian vernacular
languages need not proceed at the expense of an undervaluing of
the great achievements of Indian writing in english. Any literature which includes, in the last fifty years alone, works as diverse
as the poetry of Nissim Ezekiel, Kamala Das, and A.K. Ramanujan, or novelists as different as Raja Rao, R.K. Narayan, and
Mulk Raj Anand (as well as the more recent work of Arun Joshi,
Kamala Markandaya, and K. Nagarajan, to select only a few),
let alone the large body of nineteenth-century and early twentieth-century writing, which includes such monumental figures
as Rabindranath Tagore and Sri Aurobindo, has already established itself as well worth critical attention.

In fact, the monumental task of creating an effective history of
Indian writing in english was undertaken more than twenty
years ago (Iyengar 1962) and it has been followed up by a series
of studies by both Indian and foreign critics (Mehta 1968;
Narasimhaiah 1969, 1977; McCutcheon 1969; Mukherjee 1971,
1977; Verghese 1971; Naik, Desai, and Amur 1972; Williams
1973, 1976; Harrex 1977; Mokashi-Punekar 1978; Sinha 1979;
Reddy 1979; Naik 1981, 1983; and many others). These studies
have done much to establish the parameters of a discussion of
the nature and role of Indian writing in english, including its
form, its audience, and its effectiveness.

The problem for critics of Indian writing in english has been
that much of their energy has had to go into defending and
justifying the decisions of these authors to write in english at all,
when, it is suggested, they had a more 'authentic' choice of their

vernacular language available. Along with this goes an attack on the subject-matter of these novelists, especially the more recent ones, as being too urban, or too concerned with the experience of an Indian elite whose concerns are removed from the 'essential' India of the rural village.

The best of the criticism has not shirked these issues, but has also tried to indicate that the choice of english, although it

> inevitably affects the style and form of the work, is in no sense a bar to this work being profoundly Indian in concern and potentially as rich a means of reproducing Indian society and thought. This is attested by the proliferation of other post-colonial literatures – an Australian literature, a Canadian literature, a West Indian literature, a South African literature – all written in English, but all as different from each other as American literature is from British. Indo-Anglian literature can be just as separate an entity within its own Indian context.
>
> (Mukherjee 1977)

Since writing in english in India is now more than a century and a half old it is to be hoped that even if the future decrees that it will be replaced entirely by writing in Indian vernacular languages (and this is far from certain, or even likely) that the work already written will justify the continued study and criticism of this corpus as one of the most fascinating bodies of work to have been produced out of the colonial encounter.

African literary theories

Négritude and 'Black literature'

Négritude (see pp. 20–2), was the earliest attempt to create a consistent theory of modern African writing. The Francophone writers Aimé Césaire and Leopold Senghor, in particular, asserted a specific black African nature and psychology which was described by this term. Négritude, as first conceived by these critics in the 1920s and 1930s, would find few totally uncritical adherents today. Nevertheless, it was one of the decisive concepts in the development of modern Black coniess, and is the first assertion of those Black cultures which colonization sought to suppress and deny.

Négritude was never so prominent a feature of the thought of the Anglophone African colonies.[3] The reaction of the first generation of Anglophone writers in the 1960s to the older tradition of French Négritude theory is usefully, if crudely, summed up by the often quoted remark of Wole Soyinka that 'a tiger does not proclaim its tigritude'. Although Soyinka was subsequently to modify this view and to acknowledge the pioneering achievements of Négritude, this jejune remark does place its finger squarely on the essential flaw of Négritudinist thought, which is that its structure is derivative and replicatory, asserting not its difference, as it would claim, but rather its dependence on the categories and features of the colonizing culture.

In the late fifties and early sixties the psychiatrist Frantz Fanon developed one of the most thoroughgoing analyses of the psychological and sociological consequences of colonization (Fanon 1959, 1961, 1967). Fanon's approach stressed the common political, social, and psychological terrain through which all the colonized peoples had to pass. It recognized the potency of such racial characteristics as 'Blackness' at the heart of the oppression and denigration endemic to the colonial enterprise. But it also recognized the essential fictionality of these characteristics, and the readiness with which the assimilated Black colonized could be persuaded to don a white mask of culture and privilege. In essence, Fanon's analysis denied the racist stereotyping at the heart of colonial practice and asserted the need to recognize the economic and political realities which underlay these assertions of racial 'difference', and which were the material base for the common psychological and cultural features of colonized peoples. Unlike the early Négritudinists, Fanon's analysis was always firmly anchored in a political opposition. His theory brought together the concept of alienation and of psychological marginalization from phenomenological and existential theory, and a Marxist awareness of the historical and political forces within which the ideologies which were instrumental in imposing this alienation came into being. From this position Fanon was able to characterize the colonial dichotomy (colonizer–colonized) as the product of a 'manichaeism

delerium' (Fanon 1967), the result of which condition is a
radical division into paired oppositions such as good–evil;
true–false; white–black, in which the primary sign is axiomati-
cally privileged in the discourse of the colonial relationship.
What Fanon perceives is the way this discourse is employed as
mystification and its resulting power to incorporate and so
disarm opposition. But he also recognizes its potential as a
demystifying force and as the launching-pad for a new oppositional stance which would aim at the freeing of the colonized
from this disabling position though the construction of new
liberating narratives. In this respect Fanon's work is a radical
development which takes on board the celebratory and positive
element in the Négritude movement whilst asserting not only
the fictionality but also the historically determined nature of all
racist stereotypes.

In America, Négritudinist ideas and the work of Fanon and
his followers were instrumental in the development of theories
of Black writing and Black identity across the diaspora, but in
Africa they were more usually developed in the geographically
more limited form of pan-African ideology, which sought to
articulate the common cultural features across the differences
between the various national and regional entities which remained as the legacy of colonialism (Awoonor 1975; Irele 1981).

Anglophone social and functional theory

In the same period Anglophone critics and writers were also
asserting the need to recover and build upon uniquely African
views of art – its function, the role of the writer, its traditional
forms – and to stress their differences from the European models
offered by the English Literature departments of universities
such as Ibadan, Lagos, and Makerere (Uganda). This insistence on the social role of the African artist and the denial of the
European preoccupation with individual experience has been
one of the most important and distinctive features in the
assertion of a unique African aesthetic. The *locus classicus* of this
demand is Chinua Achebe's famous essay 'The novelist as
teacher' (1965):

> The writer cannot expect to be excused from the task of
> re-education and regeneration that must be done. In fact he

should march right in front . . . I for one would not wish to be excused. I would be quite satisfied if my novels (especially the ones set in the past) did no more than teach my readers that their past – with all its imperfections – was not one long night of savagery from which the first Europeans acting on God's behalf delivered them. Perhaps what I write is applied art as distinct from pure art. But who cares? Art is important and so is education of the kind I have in mind.

(Achebe 1965: 45)

A related sentiment appeared in the other early essay, 'Africa and her writers' (1963b). Here Achebe stressed that the principal feature which differentiated African artists from their European counterparts was that they privileged the social function of writing over its function as a tool of individual expression. They created their myths and legends, and told their stories for 'a human purpose (including, no doubt, the excitation of wonder and pure delight)', and they made their sculptures to serve the needs of their times. They 'moved and had their being in society, and created their works for the good of that society' (Achebe 1963b: 19). Achebe's sentiments in these early essays are endorsed by similar sentiments in other writers in the sixties (see, e.g. Soyinka 1968) and it remains a consistent feature throughout his work (see also Achebe 1964, 1975, 1978).

In varying degrees this attitude shaped the work of most African critics in the sixties and seventies. Its influence can be seen in nearly all the general accounts of the period, despite their ideological differences (Nazareth 1972; Obiechina 1975; Awoonor 1975; Gakwandi 1977; Ogungbesan 1979; Palmer 1979). They all stressed the need to see African literature in relationship to the society which produced it, and to understand the unique characteristics and function of art in Africa.

The impulse to recover an African social context for the new texts generated a vigorous and persistent debate in African literature between the demand for a recognition of the Africanness of literature and the rejection of universal readings. This was exacerbated by the praise of European and American critics (Larson 1971; Mahood 1977) for those African works which addressed a 'universal audience'. This demand was couched in terms of the avoidance of barriers to 'intelligibility'.

But the cultural and political implications were disturbing, as African critics and writers were quick to point out (Achebe 1975, Armah 1976). In practice 'intelligibility' meant the continuance of Euro-American standards, values, and forms and its praise testified to the refusal of a non-local readership to come to terms with the need to understand the work from within its own cultural context. Achebe summed up the feeling of the time in his seminal essay on 'Colonialist criticism': 'I should like to see the word *universal* banned altogether from discussions of African literature until such a time as people cease to use it as a synonym for the narrow, self-serving parochialism of Europe' (Achebe 1975:13). Just and necessary as this stricture is, the stress on African context sometimes went too far, as, for example, when it was employed in attempts to ban any but locally informed readings of the work as 'inauthentic'. This was to answer universalism with a false essentialism, and to limit the idea of 'meaning' in a dangerously narrow way.[4]

This impulse to resist the cultural incorporation of African writing in the sixties and early seventies has continued in projects aimed at the 'decolonization' of African culture, and in the desire to return to pre-colonial languages and cultural modes (Chinweizu et al. 1983; Ngugi, 1981, 1986).

The demand that African art be seen as distinctive in its social forms was accompanied by the project of recovering a sense of the importance of African oral art as the indigenous equal of the European literary tradition. That African cultures had not, apart from those which had borrowed from Arabic traditions, developed writing beyond the earliest stages by the time of the colonial onslaught should not, it was argued, serve to obscure the fact that African oral art had developed forms at least as highly wrought and varied as those of European cultures. Recognition of this led critics to urge that the study of these forms should be removed from the limiting anthropological discourse within which they were set and be recovered as a legitimate and distinctive enterprise for literary criticism. The study of 'oral performance art' was rescued from such limiting labels as 'traditional' or even 'primitive', and given equal status as a rich, sophisticated artistic tradition. The emergence of terms such as the contradictory 'oral literature' or the later 'orature' were signs of this change in consciousness. A number of accounts stressed the need to 'forge a connection with indigenous poetic traditions of folk tales, conversation and meaningful recounting of personal moments of experience' (Mazrui 1967: 49).

The most influential formulation of this viewpoint was that of the so-called *bolekaja* critics Chinweizu, Jemie, and Madubuike. The name '*bolekaja*' (literally meaning 'come down and fight'), adapted to describe their critical stance, was borrowed from the phrase used by the conductors or 'touts' of Nigerian 'mammy-wagons' (passenger-carrying lorries) in their fiercely competitive vying for customers. Their attacks on many of the leading African writers in english (including Wole Soyinka, John Pepper Clark, and Christopher Okigbo) for 'old fashioned, craggy, unmusical language, obscure and inaccessible diction; a plethora of imported imagery; a divorce from African oral poetic tradition, tempered only by lifeless attempts at revivalism' and their advocacy of the work of Chinua Achebe for its simplicity, directness, and relation to oral traditions, was first published in partial form in the seventies (Chinweizu *et al.* 1975a, 1979) and was published in complete form in 1983.

They argued that Eurocentric criticism of African fiction was based on the perception of the African writer as an apprentice European with no canons other than western ones to emulate (1983: 8). Such criticism, they claimed, refused to concede the autonomy of African literature or to grant it the right to have its own rules and standards based on African cultures and aesthetics. Following Achebe, they rejected 'universal' values as masking provincial European preferences with no validity for African peoples. Instead, they attempted to 'define the proper constituency of African literature', recover the tradition into which it should insert itself, and identify some of the norms which could be transferred from traditional African orature to contemporary literature (4).

The problems seem to begin with the blanket assertion that 'African literature is an autonomous entity separate and apart from all other literatures'. Chinweizu, Jemie, and Madubuike argued that African literature had its own 'traditions, models, and norms', and had historical and cultural imperatives which were radically different from and sometimes quite antithetical to those of Europe, even when written in European languages (4).

Despite their assertions elsewhere that they subscribed to a syncretic view of modern African culture, statements like this seem to imply a refusal to concede that the historical fact of colonialism inevitably leads to a hybridization of culture. Nor does it recognize that the institutionalization of systems of patronage and production profoundly modify and determine the nature of *all* writing in a post-colonial situation (issues of language, of formal properties, and of cultural allegiance apart). There are a number of serious contradictions like this in the various statements of the *bolekaja* group.

These weaknesses allowed Wole Soyinka to make an effective rejoinder to the group's attack on his work in his article 'Neo-Tarzanism: the poetics of pseudo-tradition' (1975). Here, Soyinka highlights the reductionism implicit in Chinweizu and the others' view of 'African reality' and 'African traditional literature'. Referring to their account of the African poetic landscape as a 'landscape of elephants, beggars, calabashes, serpents, pumpkins, baskets, towncriers, iron bells, slit drums, iron masks, snakes, squirrels . . . a landscape portrayed with native eyes to which aeroplanes naturally appear as iron birds' (Chinweizu *et al.* 1983: 29; quoted Soyinka 1975: 38), Soyinka offers a scathing rejection of this as a representation of the modern African experience, failing to see how it proves more acceptable than 'the traditional Hollywood image of the pop-eyed African in the jungle – "Bwana, bwana me see big iron bird"'. He points out that his African world embraces 'precision machinery, oil rigs, hydro-electricity, my typewriter, railway trains (not iron snakes), machine guns, bronze sculpture etc.' (38). These do not exclude a particular ontological relationship with the universe but rather add to its complexity.

Now that the initial heat of the debate has cooled a little it can be seen that the gap between the contestants in this 'fight' was not as great as it seemed to be. In fact, the wrangle between Chinweizu *et al.* and Soyinka in the seventies can now be seen to have been, in essence, a rather old-fashioned dispute about what did or did not constitute 'good' poetry (with the word 'African' inserted between the propositions as an authenticating sign). A number of younger African writers and critics have questioned the formalist nature of this project and its goal of recovering an authentic cultural essence. They are worried by its potential to encourage nostalgic nationalism and cultural exclusivism and are concerned that attention may be diverted from the problems of a contemporary society. As they see it, these societies are still bound to the continuing pressures of imperialism in its neo-colonial form and to the continuing stratification and inherited elitism of post-independence societies. It is the problems arising from this, they argue, which must be urgently addressed (Omotoso 1975; Jeyifo 1979; Sowande 1979; Okeke-Ezigbo 1982; Onoge 1984; Osofisan 1984; and Amuta 1983, 1989).

These more recent essays do not reject the early radical decolonizing thrust of Achebe, Soyinka, Mazrui, Chinweizu, and others, though, in part at least, they are a product of, and a reaction to, the extreme form of this criticism represented by the work of the *bolekaja* critics and the debates they provoked in the mid and late seventies. In this form, the early and necessary claims for a return to African traditional aesthetics and to African forms and themes tended, they argue, to ride over the inescapable political and cultural legacies of the colonial period and its continuing neo-colonial presence in contemporary Africa. The assertion, first made by critics like Mazrui, of the need to value the 'folk' over the 'abstract' seemed to many to have edged over into an overt anti-intellectualism, to lead to a de-politicized reading of African culture and to have embraced a dubious theory of communication which assumed that form and content could be related in a simple reflective model.

For these writers and critics, the issue of the correct formal properties for African verse and the question of an authenticating African traditional content take second place to a concern with the consequences of the social practice of writing. For them, the central issue of a literary work is the strategic value of its content and the effectiveness of its intervention in the struggle to liberate African societies from economic injustice, social backwardness, and political reaction.

A more sophisticated use of Marxist and neo-Marxist critical theory has developed in recent indigenous African criticism, stressing the importance of the material conditions of the production and consumption of the text. More recent Marxist critics of African literature (see essays in Gugelberger 1985)[5] attack obscurantism, elitism, and detachment and this reflects the position and the productions of these younger left-wing writers.

The older Kenyan writer, Ngugi wa Thiong'o has been a powerful influence here too, due to the continued emphasis in his work on the political function of the writer in post-colonial societies (Ngugi 1972, 1986). Ngugi has put forward the argument that 'decolonization' must involve a much more radical movement away from European values and systems, including the language which, as he sees it, carries these values. His development over the last twenty years culminated in his decision to write in Gikuyu or Ki-Swahili rather than english in order to address an audience other than foreigners and the foreign-educated new elite (Ngugi 1981, 1986; see also Riemenschneider 1984 for an account of Ngugi's progress to his present position). This involves a rejection of African writing in english as part of a distinctive 'Afro-European' literature, characteristic of the period of transition between colonization and full independence. Such independence, he argues, requires a 'decolonization of the mind' and this will be the task of the new generation of writers, who have never experienced colonization, and who use African languages. The strength of Ngugi's position is that it is as concerned with the sociological implications of the use of english in terms of the control of production, distribution, and readership which this implies as with any formal idea of the language as 'bearer' of culture. So, even though his case may be flawed by its embrace of an essentialist and representationalist view of language, in terms of its practical politics it is a powerful reminder of the unsolved problems for the African writer in english who desires to speak to and for the people and not just to an educated elite and a foreign readership.

These changes of concern are increasingly reflected in recent criticism. A general account by the Zimbabwean critic, Emmanuel Ngara, offers an historical overview of the development of the African novel from a Marxist perspective (Ngara 1985). Other critics have produced specific accounts of the sociological and ideological practices within which these texts and movements have come into existence (Jeyifo 1979, 1980; Amuta 1983, 1984, 1989) as well as analyses of the continuing pressure of cultural colonization on African writing (Tejani

1979). In this way the emergence of a criticism which sees the text as the site of activity and 'decolonization' as a political action and not as an independent, aesthetic manifestation of some ideal or recovered authentic African literature', has begun to take shape.

Apart from the use made of European Marxist theory by such accounts, the interest in, and employment of, other contemporary European critical models by African critics has not been as widespread as has been the case in India where, as we suggested above, the project of establishing a formal poetics was helped by the example of the traditional Sanskrit critical texts. For example in Africa there have been only isolated examples of structuralist or poststructuralist accounts of writing (Anozie 1970, 1981, 1984) and these have not been very influential in general critical practice (Appiah 1984).

Exceptions to this include JanMohammed's *Manichean Aesthetics* (1983), which develops Fanon's insight into the manichaean dualism of colonial societies and which employs poststructuralist and Marxist theory to offer an account of the construction of Africa in writing over the last century. It generates a reading of colonial period and post-independence African texts in english within a broad political and ideological context. Emmanuel Ngara's *Stylistic Criticsm and the African Novel* (1982) offers an overview of those formalist accounts of African fiction which have been written.

It may be true to say that whilst the stress in Indian criticism has been on formalist accounts, the opposite is true in Africa, where a broader socio-political perspective and a stress on the issue of social commitment in literature has been the dominant critical concern. Thus, though they share common concerns, such as the issues of decolonization, the relationship of the modern writer to traditional practice, and the question of language choice, the critical theories in these two major areas of colonial intervention (India and Africa) have had different emphases.

The settler colonies

The United States, Canada, Australia, and New Zealand

In settler colonies the first task seems to be to establish that the texts can be shown to constitute a literature separate from that of the metropolitan centre. A vast and impressive body of literary histories, thematic studies, and studies of individual literary traditions has accrued over the last one hundred and fifty years or so in the white cultures of settler colonies. In the United States this encompasses a body of texts far too large even to summarize here. Russell Reising's recent guide in this series offers a useful account of the main trends (Reising 1987). Even when a substantial body of texts has been written in the settler colony, the task of compiling a national literary history has usually been an important element in the establishment of an independent cultural identity. Histories of this kind have, therefore, been important landmarks in the critical history of many of the settler colony literatures, for example, H.M. Green's *A History of Australian Literature* (1961); Carl F. Klinck's *Literary History of Canada: Canadian Literature in English* (1965). Later histories have refined and challenged these earlier works, and in this way have also been important in changing the features and boundaries of the national literary self-definition, for example, L. Kramer's *The Oxford History of Australian Literature* (1981) and W.H. New's *A History of Canadian Literature* (1988). These works have been more than simple, neutral compilations; indeed, they have sometimes been the focus of strong controversy. In this sense, they have been the site for formative disputation and discussion.

Collections and anthologies, for example, *The New Oxford Book of Australian Poetry* (Murray 1986) or *The Penguin Book of New Zealand Verse* (Curnow 1960) have also, by the values implicit in their selection, been important sites for recording and even initiating shifts in critical taste and cultural stance. Witness, for instance, the very different bias and temper of Allen Curnow's collection of New Zealand verse and that of the more recent edition edited by Ian Wedde in 1985 (see Wedde 1985a and 1985b).

As well as literary histories and anthologies, the struggle to define the characteristics of the independent literatures has also led to other studies. In Canada these have often stressed thematic concerns considered central to the literature, as in Frye's *The Bush Garden* (1971); Warren Tallman's 'Wolf in the snow' (1960); William New's *Articulating West* (1972), Laurence Ricou's *Vertical Man/Horizontal World* (1973), and John Moss's *Patterns of Isolation in English Canadian Fiction* (1974). More recently, there has been a reaction in Canada against the dominance of thematic criticism, as in Frank Davey's 'Surviving the paraphrase' (1983), B.W. Powe's *A Climate Charged* (1984), or the more positive Russell M. Brown's 'Critic, culture, text: beyond thematics' (1978).

By contrast, thematic studies have been less prominent in Australia and New Zealand, though T. Inglis Moore's *Social Patterns in Australian Literature* (1971), G.A. Wilkes' *The Stockyard and the Croquet Lawn* (1981), and G. Dutton's *Snow on the Saltbush: The Australian Literary Experience* (1984) all have strong thematic elements. In Australia the debate seems to have centred more on conflicting 'traditions' claimed as dominant or characteristic. Thus Wilkes organizes his account through the contrast of the 'genteel' tradition with a populist nationalist mode of writing. In Australia the construction and defence of these conflicting traditions has occupied a good deal of critical space and energy. For example, the nationalist tradition associated with A.G. Stephens and the *Bulletin* magazine in the 1890s and developed around the turn of the century by nationalist writers, such as Palmer (1905), was consciously invoked in the fifties by critics and historians, including Palmer himself, as part of a renewed assertion of Australian identity against the persistent cultural subservience of Australia (Palmer 1954; Phillips 1958; Ward 1958; Moore 1971; Serle 1973). These books sometimes claim to have 'discovered' in the literature of the 1890s and its inheritors the 'essential' Australian national characteristics and values. The refutation of the radical nationalist interpretation in a new trend of academic, text-centred criticism (Kramer, Wilkes, Buckley, Heseltine) beginning in the late fifties, illustrates how the history of recent criticism has remained intimately bound up with the struggle to establish or deny the claim that Australianism is determined by the social and material practices of a post-colonial society (for a lively and contentious, though oversimplified, account, see Docker 1984).

The critical questions raised in these settler colonies cluster around a peculiar set of problems which highlight some of the basic tensions which exist in all post-colonial literatures. The three major issues they raise are the relationship between social and literary practices in the old world and the new; the relationship between the indigenous populations in settled areas and the invading settlers; and the relationship between the imported language and the new place. In critical practice these are often inextricably interwoven.

Constructing 'indigeneity'

White European settlers in the Americas, Australia, and New Zealand faced the problem of establishing their 'indigeneity' and distinguishing it from their continuing sense of their European inheritance. In this respect their situation differs from that of Indians or Africans whose problem was to retrieve or reconstruct their culture at the end of a period of foreign rule.[6] The colonial settlers had to create the indigenous, to discover what they perceived to be, in Emerson's phrase, their 'original relation with the universe' (Emerson 1836: 21).

This 'original relation' ought not to be confused, as Derek Walcott, in the different but contiguous situation of West Indian displacement, points out, with a naive 'return' to (European) origins. The establishment of this new 'Adamic' relation with the world does not represent a simple return to innocence: 'The apples of its second Eden have the tartness of experience' (Walcott 1974b: 5). The relation between the people and the land is new, as is that between the imported language and the land. But the language itself already carries many associations with European experience and so can never be 'innocent' in practice. Concomitantly, there is a perception that this new experience, if couched in the terms of the old, is somehow 'falsified' – rendered inauthentic – at the same time as its value, judged within Old World terms, is considered inferior.

In his 'The foundations of culture in Australia', P.R. Stephensen claims that there are two elements in Australian culture – the imported and the indigenous (Barnes 1969: 211). For Stephensen, the process we would call appropriation was intimately tied up with this duality. He saw Australian indigenous culture as the native plant 'fertilised by phosphates from all countries'. But, he continues, 'it is the plant rather than the phosphates which concern us' (ibid.: 212). Such a plant cannot be 'inauthentic', nor we assume, could it grow properly anywhere else. It is not a branch from the English tree, but a plant rooted 'indigenously' in the new soil. A characteristic result of this perception of an original relation with the New World is the assertion of difference. In these 'New' Worlds there is, as the New Zealand poet Allen Curnow expresses it, 'something different, something nobody counted on' (Curnow 1960: 204). But the only available codes of expression seemed, at first, to be those of the Old World, the 'imported phosphates', and, moreover, since the codes are European there is an impulse to compete, on Europe's terms, for literary recognition which will validate the New World in the eyes of the Old.

Thus, an important site of conflict within post-colonial literary cultures is generated, as the backward-looking impotence of exile and the forward-looking impetus to indigeneity collide. The conflict first emerged in American literature when the desire of early American writers to compete on equal terms with their British counterparts clashed with their desire to repudiate borrowed models and follow an independent path. The works of Charles Brockden Brown in the United States provide excellent examples of such conflict, as do those of James Fenimore Cooper whose novels become a battlefield in the war between the Old World and the New.[7] As Renata Wasserman puts it, the early writers had both to legitimize the American and differentiate it from the European, stressing 'the difference in nature and equivalence in value' between the New World and the Old. The task was made easier by the fact that they were writing in English, but at the same time it was rendered problematic by the fact that the language of the metropolis came with its own 'connotational and ideational baggage' (Wasserman 1984: 131).

This problem with the use of the language – 'easier yet more difficult' – distinguishes the literature of the settler colonies. Whatever the particular nature of colonial oppression in Africa or India, and whatever the legacy of cultural syncretism, the *differences* confronted as a result of colonialism were palpable, and their literary expression required no great feat of meta-physical disentanglement. In the settler colonies, however, difference from the inherited tradition and the need to assert that difference was felt equally strongly. However, the manner and matter of the assertion remained the central problem for these post-colonial literatures.

The result was, until recently, a post-colonial theory which dealt with such different issues from those of European theory that it was simply not granted the status of theory. For example, the fundamental issue was the existence and nature of the literature itself, rather than its specific content or strategies. Furthermore, the unease with the 'gulf' between imported language and local world became in time a radical questioning of the relationship between language and the world, an inves-tigation into the means of knowing rather than into what is, or can be, known. One of the more interesting features of settler colonies, in which intellectual life is so relentlessly characterized as an extension of European culture, is that from the earliest times some of the most important theoretical writing emerged in creative texts. These texts explore, in their figures, themes, and forms, the conceptual dimensions of the act of writing itself, and the tensions and issues traversing the institution of literature in marginalized societies. Novels like *Such is Life* can be seen to function in this way (as we have argued above in ch. 2, pp. 73–5) as can, in one sense, all post-colonial texts (as we argue in ch. 3, p. 83). This is especially the case, though, in settler colonies where difference is only inscribed (apparently) in subtle changes of language and where the absence of an alternative pre-colonial metaphysic makes the assertion of 'Otherness' more difficult.

A concomitant perception, one shared with the other post-colonial areas in which it was more immediately obvious, is that of the political operation of language, the exercise of European hegemony through 'the word'. Thus, as Kenneth Dauber notes (Dauber 1977: 55) the primary concern of American literature has always been its own nature. As a colonial literature, defined within the literature of the mother country, as a 'branch' or 'tributary', it was unsure of itself from the beginning, and the result was self-consciousness. As in other post-colonial areas, then, the subject of the writer's work became its own process.

Any problem was incorporated 'within their text as a "problematic" or principle inhering in the writing that embodied it' (ibid.). This, says Dauber, is the literary root of American pragmatism, and the reason why American literature has been the object of so few serious philosophic investigations. 'Grounded in writing itself, American writing, in effect, has no ground'. Until philosophy itself turned to an attack upon the founding of discourse on anything outside discourse 'we had no language capable of dealing with it' (ibid.).

Like early American tourists, American writers and critics at first had to choose the 'European plan' of literary history, interpreting their concern with their own literature as a sign of 'immaturity', and this model has been successively applied since to other post-colonial literatures. Post-colonial literatures would apparently demonstrate their maturity when they stopped talking about themselves and got on with more 'universal' (i.e. European) concerns. The radically subversive questions raised for British literature and European philosophy by, for instance, Melville's *Moby Dick* or Hawthorne's *The Scarlet Letter*, and later by Joseph Furphy's *Such Is Life* or G.V. Desani's *All About H. Hatterr*, went largely unrecognized.

But in the questions which post-colonial texts posed, in their radical attempts to address the issues of language, reality, and their inherited and now troubling epistemological assumptions, there was a necessarily subversive element. If European preconceptions about the relation between language and reality were called into question by these 'original relations', then the assumed universality of their theoretical bases was similarly vulnerable. What was expressive of the dilemma of the post-colonial writer, philosopher, or theoretician was at the same time subversive of inherited axioms. Gary Lee Stonum notes the 'shock of recognition' experienced by American critics of American literature as contemporary European post-structuralist theories spread to the US. Their reaction was far more 'tumultuous' than American critics of British or continental literatures, because the 'roomy folds of post structuralist thinking' seemed to hold a great and unexpected promise. 'What in its native European context avows itself to be the subversive underside of dominant cultural traditions', Stonum claims, 'appears strangely central to the American canon' (Stonum

1981: 3). Such features of American literature which post-structuralist theory is now describing and appropriating have, according to Stonum, 'always been acknowledged to exist, [but] they have often been maligned as inept, uncouth, or perverse' (ibid.).

What is being acknowledged here is the persistence of European critical and theoretical domination of the study of post-colonial literatures long after the literatures themselves had begun exploring the fields now incorporated into, and legit-imized by, the European theoretical hegemony. When Dauber claims that until the recent post-structuralist theoretical revol-ution 'we had no language capable of dealing with [our litera-ture] in a rigorous way' (Dauber 1977: 55), he is merely perpetuating the dominance of that hegemony. Creative writers in the United States and in other post-colonial areas had been successfully creating that very language since the beginning of colonial and post-colonial cultures. Ironically, it is only with the fashion in Europe for subversive theory, and the slow acknowl-edgement of cultural relativity in value ascription, that post-colonial literatures have begun (again on the tail of a European movement) to give credence to their own theories. The Canadian critic Diana Brydon makes a similar point. With refer-ence to the work of 'the last two decades in contemporary critical theory' she notes, with a certain wryness, that 'We of course have been writing about these dangers for years, but in a discourse marginalised by its status as "Commonwealth litera-ture" and by its reliance, until recently, on the language of monologist or monocentrist criticism' (Brydon 1984b: 387).

In the early stages of settlement and national assertion there were, in the United States, Australia, New Zealand, and Canada, concerted calls for a 'native literature' and 'native' critical tools with which to assess it. Creative writers in all areas, like Melville, Hawthorne, Emerson (USA), Marcus Clarke (Australia), and Major Richardson (Canada) began exploring in their essays and fiction the nature of the 'original relations' in which they found themselves. The advent of New Criticism in these areas as well as in the West Indies, India, and Africa, at a time when post-colonial literatures other than American were first beginning to be taken seriously both at home and abroad, can be seen as a major development in the critical self-awareness of these literatures.

Language, place, and theory

Language and 'space' in conjunction indicate one creative site of conflict in the writing of settler colonies. The problem of imported language and the 'alien' native landscape is taken up by Judith Wright (1965), in her Preface to *Preoccupations in Australian Poetry*, as 'Australia's double aspect'. Here she is continuing a long debate in Australia, from assertions, on the one hand, that the country had the wrong historical, cultural, and physical environment for 'great literature' (Sinnett in 1856 and Cowling in 1935; see Barnes 1969: 9–10), to claims, on the other, that 'through this country a great many people walk as aliens' (Palmer 1905: 168). Allen Curnow in his influential Introduction to the *Penguin Book of New Zealand Verse* (1960) raises some of the same problems and in similar terms. The history of New Zealand poetry is 'the record of an adventure or series of adventures, in search of reality', a search initiated by that colonial 'gulf' between 'the land and the book, the mind and the hand' (25). 'Reality must be local and special at the point where we pick up the traces' (or, as the Australian critic Vance Palmer put it a little more ingenuously at the turn of the century: 'Our art must be original as our own flora and fauna are original' – 1905: 169).

What Curnow interprets as a recoil of the European imagination from (colonial) realities receives more sophisticated attention from the Canadians, Dennis Lee and Robert Kroetsch. They, like a number of other post-colonial writers (Melville in *The Confidence Man*, for instance, or Furphy in *Such Is Life*) began to see the problem as more than a simple mismatch between language and landscape, which might solve itself in time through progressive familiarity with the land and adaptation of the language into it. To them it was a situation in which the perceived 'inauthenticity' of the spoken New World/Word became the site of investigation and expression – not as the preliminary to a possible 'adaptation', but as a continuing dynamic of the use of 'alien' words in 'colonial space' (Brydon 1981). As Robert Kroetsch writes:

At one time I considered it to be the task of the Canadian writer to give names to his experience, to be the namer. I now suspect, that, on the contrary, it is his task to un-name . . . the Canadian writer's particular predicament is that he works with a language within a literature, that appears to be his own. . . . But . . . there is in the Canadian word a concealed other experience, sometimes British, sometimes American.

(Kroetsch 1974: 43)

The problem appeared to reside in a radical 'inauthenticity' in the word, and the key to the relation between land and language lay first of all, as Randolph Stow noted in Australia, in silence, and then, in Kroetsch's terms, in 'unhiding the hidden', in 'unnaming'.

Expressed in terms we have introduced above, this silence is caused by the failure to 'control the means of communication':

Beneath the words our absentee masters have given us, there is an undermining silence. It saps our nerve. And beneath that silence, there is a raw welter of cadence that tumbles and strains toward words and that makes the silence a blessing because it shushes easy speech. That cadence is home . . .

The impasse of writing that is problematic to itself is transcended only when the impasse becomes its own subject, when writing accepts and enters and names its own condition as it is naming the world.

(Lee 1974: 165, 166)

What Lee proposes here is that not only should the control of communication be appropriated, but that silence itself should be adopted as the fruitful basis for an indigenizing literature.

Lee describes his own experience of seeing writers all around him using words while he simply 'gagged'. Writing had become a problem in itself, 'it had grown into a search for authenticity, but all it could manage to be was a symptom of inauthenticity'. His own decision was to write only if he could also establish, 'like a key in music', the particular inauthenticity of the words he used (1974: 156, 158). For Lee, this problem of 'inauthenticity' and its ultimate insolubility (for the post-colonial writers a condition of *in*authenticity is inescapable) generates that obsession with being a victim which novelist Margaret Atwood documents in her account of Canadian literature, *Survival* (1972).

The Canadian 'victim position' is occasioned not just by the obvious political circumstances of domination by the USA or, earlier, by Britain and France, but by the radical problem of the 'word'. Canadians in Lee's terms do not have their own language, but are forced to use the language of others, in a position closer to that of the Africans brought to the Caribbean once their ancestral languages were no longer recuperable, or, as feminist theorists have frequently pointed out, to that of the position of women.

> The colonial writer does not have words of his own. Is it not possible that he projects his own condition of voicelessness into whatever he creates? that he articulates his own powerlessness, in the face of alien words, by seeking out fresh tales of victims? Over and above Atwood's account of it, perhaps the colonial imagination is driven to recreate, again and again, the experience of writing in colonial space . . .
>
> The language was drenched with our non-belonging . . . words had become the enemy.
>
> (Lee 1974: 162, 163)

The 'first necessity for the colonial writer', Lee notes, echoing Judith Wright's essay, is for the 'imagination' to 'come home'. But this is not possible for the colonial, because the 'words of home are silent':

> Try to speak the words of your home and you will discover – if you are a colonial – that you do not know them . . . To speak unreflectingly in a colony then, is to use words that speak only alien space. To reflect is to fall silent, discovering that your authentic space does not have words. And to reflect further is to recognise that you and your people do not in fact have a privileged authentic space just waiting for words; you are, among other things, the people who have made an alien inauthenticity their own. You are left chafing at the inarticulacy of a native space which may not exist. . . .
>
> But perhaps – and here was the breakthrough – perhaps our job was not to fake a space of our own and write it up, but rather to find words for our space-lessness . . . Instead of pushing against the grain of an external, uncharged lan-

guage, perhaps we should finally come to writing *with* that grain.

(Lee 1974: 163)

Lee's 'solution' at least partly answers the problem of the transplanted/transported post-colonial territories whilst avoiding the untenable nationalist position.

Indigenous textuality

One of the more complex features of settler colonies has been the relationship between the Indigenous and settler populations. The first consequence of this for the writing, apart from the use of Aborigines as subjects in literary texts (Healy 1978; Goldie 1984; Monkman 1981), was the attempt by the settlers, in the process of 'constructing indigeneity', to incorporate or utilize a pre-existing aesthetic dimension identified with the Indigenous occupants of the country. For example, the Jindyworobak movement in Australia in the 1930s and 1940s (Elliott 1979) was a loose attempt to develop an identifiable Australian aesthetic from the rich fabric of Aboriginal culture. *Jindyworobak* is an Aboriginal word meaning 'to annex, to join', and it was used to describe the process of an enriching cultural appropriation.

Although this movement is usually taken to be the major attempt in Australia to assimilate an Aboriginal aesthetic it was long foreshadowed in the twenties by the artist Margaret Preston, and by K.S. Prichard's rediscovery of the Aborigines as a valid subject of fiction in *Coonardoo* (1929), and accompanied by Xavier Herbert's classic *Capricornia* (1938). Rex Ingamells' 'Conditional culture' (1938) declared that the poet could best divest himself of the cloak of English assumptions and appropriate a new innocence by adopting the Aboriginal outlook, which 'sublimated through our thought' could allow us to achieve 'something of a pristine outlook on life' (Barnes 1969: 264). Despite the fact that the Jindyworobak movement faced the issue of the existence of an Indigenous culture and its identification with the difference of the country, the relative historical transience of the movement shows that such radical Indigenizing strategies have yet to find fertile soil in these societies.

In terms of their own developing writing, however, the position of groups such as the Maoris, Inuit, and Australian Aborigines is a special one because they are doubly marginalized – pushed to the psychic and political edge of societies which themselves have experienced the dilemma of colonial alienation. For this reason they demonstrate a capacity, far greater than that of white settler societies, to subvert received assumptions about literature.

The source of this subversive capacity in Australian Aboriginal writers, for instance, stems from the unique conception of textuality in traditional Aboriginal culture. The land itself is constituted as a text of the Dreaming and that text is intimately bound up with the life and experience of each individual. The Aboriginal painter does not represent space nor signify the visual in a 'European' way, but symbolizes both the mythic time of the Dreaming and its embodiment in the land. Aboriginal art and performance are a reworking of the basic text of mythic experience which is 'written on' the land itself (see Benterrak *et al.* 1984).

In New Zealand the continuance and growth of a powerful modern tradition of Maori language usage sets up a challenge of a different kind (one more analogous for the Maori to the condition of a writer in a diglossic culture such as Africa or India with the possibility of language 'choice'). The *pakeha* (white person) is, of course, only able to incorporate Maori elements as 'markers of difference' in the english text. But, as writers like Patricia Grace and Witi Ihimaera have shown, those Maori writers who choose to do so can both appropriate english to their own usage and as a result influence the discourse of New Zealand literature in a more effective way than that achieved by the white writers associated with the Jindyworobak movement in Australia. Aboriginal writing in english in Australia [for example in the work of prose writers Bobbi Sykes, Mudrooroo Narogin (Colin Johnson), Archie Weller and Sally Morgan, playwrights Robert Merritt and Jack Davis, or poets Oodgeroo Noonuccal (Kath Walker) and Kevin Gilbert] also seems likely to establish a strong dialogue with writing by white Australians as it appropriates the language of the settlers to its own specific political and cultural needs (Shoemaker 1989).

The link with the land and its effects on Indigenous notions of textuality may well serve as an interesting generator of change in all indigenous communities as writers from these societies seize the post-colonial means of communication in a different way from its appropriation in settler cultures. Indigenous writing has suffered many of the general historical problems of post-colonial writing, such as being incorporated into the national literatures of the settler colonies as an 'extension' rather than as a separate discourse. But, locked into the process of appropriation through which Indigenous groups write is an alternative metaphysic, as well as a political rage, which has proved a powerful creative stimulant.

Finally, the arrival in settler colony cultures of large groups of migrants who continue to employ their language of origin has led to the development of texts which are written and read within national and post-colonial practices and yet which are organized from within alternative language and culture groupings, themselves marginalized within the societies which have produced them. Such writing, especially in Canada and Australia, seems likely to grow and is already the subject of criticism and debate (Blodgett 1982; Gunew 1985).

Caribbean theories

It is, however the Caribbean which has been the crucible of the most extensive and challenging post-colonial literary theory. Here the crucial issues are least obscured. Behind the Chinweizu–Soyinka debate or the demands for social relevance in West Africa, behind the question of 'which language' in East Africa, or the greater suitability of the aesthetics of *rasa-dhvani* in India, behind the problematic of writing itself in the settler colonies, lie the central and unavoidable questions of the relationship between the imported European and the local, between ancestry and destiny, and between language and place. These questions remain at the heart of the creative conflicts and possibilities inherent in all post-colonial writing and theory.

In the Caribbean, the European imperial enterprise ensured that the worst features of colonialism throughout the globe would all be combined in the region: the virtual annihilation of the native population of Caribs and Arawaks; the plundering and internecine piracy amongst the European powers; the deracination and atrocities of the slave trade and plantation slavery, and the subsequent systems of indenture which 'stranded' Chinese and Indians in the Caribbean when the return clauses of indenture contracts were dishonoured. The present-day population of the West Indies consists of a variety of racial groups all more or less in ancestral exile, and all still subject to the hegemonic pressures of their former European owners, and, more recently, to that exercised in the region by the USA. Issues which initially remained cryptic in the settler colonies, and which could be avoided by calls for a pre-colonial regeneration in colonies of intervention (that is, colonies which were forcibly occupied by European invasion) were of immediate and inescapable importance in the Caribbean.

From the early days of slavery, cultural clash and miscegenation formed the brutal texture of Caribbean life. The history of the slave trade and its social patterns made it impossible for the slaves to be unaware of the significant part language played in their continuing enslavement. Where possible, slaves were isolated from their common language group and transported and sold in 'mixed lots', as a deliberate means of limiting the possibilities of rebellion. This policy of language suppression was continued on the plantations of the New World wherever it could be implemented. The result was that within two or three generations (sometimes within one) the only language available to the Africans for communication either amongst themselves or with the master was the European language of that master. African slaves could not avoid an awareness of the cruel pressure of an imposed language and the loss of their own 'voice', a loss incurred, moreover, in an alien landscape. So, subject to a tragic alienation from both language and landscape, the transplanted Africans found that psychic survival depended on their facility for a kind of *double entendre*. They were forced to develop the skill of being able to say one thing in front of 'massa' and have it interpreted differently by their fellow slaves. This skill involved a radical subversion of the meanings of the master's tongue.

Edward Brathwaite and Creolization

It is clear, from Caribbean history, that race and ancestry were issues of supreme and inescapable importance, crucial not just to philosophy but to the dynamics of day-to-day survival. This had to be so in a society which bore the permanent traces of conflict, repression, immigration, and forced migration. In the West Indies, where British educational policy deliberately excluded any reference to slavery or to the African ancestry of the slaves (absences imaginatively documented in George Lamming's *In the Castle of My Skin* (1970: 38–88) it has in some cases been seen to be necessary to revive that lost ancestral link before the Caribbean present can be understood, before the islands become 'home'.

The view expressed by poet and critic Edward Kamau Brathwaite on the importance of the African connection has sometimes obscured his increasing concern with Creolization. For him, the recognition of an ancestral relationship with a folk or aboriginal culture, whether African or Amerindian, involves the artist in 'a journey into the past and hinterland which is at the same time a movement of possession into present and future'. Through this movement, he says, 'we become ourselves, truly our own creators, discovering word for object, image for the word' (Brathwaite 1974: 42). But his stress on African (and Amerindian) ancestors over the European as a way of recuperating an identity swamped by the imposed cultural 'norm' does not deny the role of the European presence in Creolization.

Brathwaite's 'model of Creolization' is extended to include a more comprehensive sense of cultural interaction not only among all elements of the 'tropical plantation' but also between these elements and certain metropolitan aspects of the continent (1977: 41). In his view of Caribbean social history, Brathwaite invokes a cross-cultural time–space dynamic which also provides the basis for an indigenous literary theory in essays like 'Jazz and the West Indian novel' (1967–8) and 'The love axe' (1976), or poems such as 'Sun poem' (1982). As in the settler colonies, a fundamental aspect of the cross-cultural dynamic is the relationship to land, to place. For Brathwaite, Creolization is a cultural action based upon the 'stimulus–response' of individuals to their environment and, within culturally discrete white–black groups, to each other. 'The scope and quality of this response and interaction was dictated by the circumstances of the societies' formulation and composition' (1971: 296). Thus Brathwaite's concept of a distinctive 'Sun aesthetic' includes place as a dynamic factor in the contemporary Caribbean reality.

Denis Williams and catalysis

In the essays and art of Denis Williams, cross-culturality, language, and landscape – 'Langscape' (McGregor 1985) – are also inextricably interwoven. Williams proposes the 'catalysis' model of Guyanese society against a 'filiastic' tendency which he sees as retarding creativity in the settler post-colonial cultures of Australia, Canada and New Zealand. In these societies the stress on lineage ensures that the relationship with the imperial power is a subservient–subclass one, fixed always in relation to the 'parent'. But the attachment to the parent, the 'security of being thoroughbred', is not for New World cultures. Rather, a catalytic interaction occurs in which 'each racial group qualifies, and diminishes, the self-image of the other'. For Williams, Guyanese society presents the image of post-colonial catalysis, with its sense of psychic erosion and self-questioning within a totality of groups greater than their sum. Such a 'psychic unease' which stems from a lack of union with the ancestral gods of the soil is not, he claims, characteristic of Old World cultures. It is therefore 'the supreme paradox of the colonial condition that all experience is articulated in the forms and institutions of the Old World' (Williams 1969: 19).

Williams proposes a theory of art based on this catalysis, one which stresses the creative meaning of the present in terms of the individual. The post-colonial self-image is different from that of people in the Old World, he claims, and to assess one's condition in the light of Old World values and institutions is to diminish this self-image, to engage in a kind of self-annihilation. 'Reality for us hinges in the fact of the human in infinite process of catalysis.' The individual in the post-colonial society has no guarantee to anything but the present and it is the minute nature and definition of this present viewed by the individual consciousness which seems to Williams to be crucial in 'realising this situation in our works of art' (34–5).

Wilson Harris and the syncretic vision

For Williams, Wilson Harris is the practitioner of Caribbean catalysis *par excellence*, and it is not surprising to find an analysis of some of his early works as the climax of Williams' essay. Harris, as he notes, 'confounds the understanding . . . bred on the intellectual conventions of the European novel'. For these, 'Wilson Harris has no use whatsoever – he stands in no kind of relationship at all to the European novel' (Williams 1969: 37). Before attempting to give some assessment of Harris's remarkable achievement, it is important to establish one other Caribbean antecedent to his work.

In September 1956, at the first Congress of Negro Writers and Artists, Jacques Stephen Alexis had faced the interesting problem of presenting, to an organization understandably devoted to brotherhood across cultures (and not within or between them), the idea that Haitian culture was not in essence Black African, however important the African element in it might be, but was an Afro-Amerindian–European syncretism. To opt for a monolithic solidarity throughout the African diaspora, was, as Alexis saw it, to be unable to speak for Haiti or Haitian peoples' art. His essay, 'Of the marvellous realism of the Haitians' is a masterpiece of daring and tact, given the forum in which it was presented. Distrustful of the concept of 'universality' which he recognized as a hegemonic European critical tool wielded to designate 'inferior and superior cultures', he nevertheless supported the notion of cross-culturality, of cultural syncretism and, perhaps most interesting of all, he linked it to forms in fiction. Again Alexis went against the grain in rejecting realism as a suitable mode for Black–Haitian expression. In the synthesis of European, African, and Amerindian which forms the genesis of Haitian art, 'social realism has joined forces with revolutionary romanticism' to shed more light on the 'contradictory character of human consciousness'. For him, Haitian art has been enriched by, but will transcend, that of the west. Order, beauty, logic, controlled sensitivity have all been received, but will be surpassed. Haitian art presents the 'real' along with its accompaniment of 'the strange and fantastic, of dreams and half-light, of the mysterious and the marvellous' (Alexis 1956: 267). Alexis was careful, however, to draw out the political implications of 'marvellous realism' and to distinguish it from 'the cold-blooded surrealistic researches' and 'analytical games' of Europe. Invoking Césaire, he emphasized that 'Haitian art leads always to man, to the fight for hope and not to free art and the ivory tower' (268).[8]

Twenty years after Alexis, J. Michael Dash, examining the apparent failure of the Négritude movement, attributes that failure to the need to reject the colonial past, an understandable and even necessary impulse, but one which appeared to condemn the Caribbean to a radically uncreative pastlessness (Dash 1973). Elaborating on the positions of some of the earlier commentators, Dash proposed a basis for Caribbean art in which the antagonistic energies of that past transform themselves, in the present, into a creative syncretism. It is the literature of the French Caribbean, the poetry of Walcott, and above all the works of Wilson Harris which underwrite this view.

In the course of almost thirty years, Harris has written two books of poetry, eighteen novels, two volumes of short stories, numerous articles of literary criticism and theory, cultural and aesthetic commentary, and two volumes of literary theory, *Tradition, the Writer and Society* (1967) and *The Womb of Space* (1983). Because his output has been so prolific, the following necessarily oversimplifies Harris's principal views. First, Harris has a profound belief in the possibilities of (individual and communal) psychic regeneration through catastrophe. By the transforming powers of the imagination, what appears to have been irretrievably lost may be recuperated – indeed in the very energy involved in violent and destructive acts reside the seeds of creativity. It is as if, for instance, race hatred and race oppression by their own energies savagely deconstruct themselves, seeking to 'consume their own biases' (Harris 1985: 127), and to dismantle their binary oppositional bases. Moving away from the values enshrined in the beliefs of ancestral cultures, Harris opts for the transformative power of the imagination to effect 'genuine change' rather than for genetic inheritance or traditional institutional and cultural avenues. In the time-scale of 'the womb of space' the original human ancestors are ancestors of all. The annihilation of the Caribs and the atrocities of slavery energize one field of historical activity which eventually results in the contemporary Caribbean mixing of all peoples, returning them to an original 'shared' ancestry.

Second, Harris, like Williams, believes that the racially mixed populations of the Caribbean, and Guyana in particular, offer unique possibilities for cross-cultural creativity and philosophy *unavailable* to monocultural societies, or to those which aspire to monoculturalism.

Third, Harris sees language as the key to these transformations. Language must be altered, its power to lock in fixed beliefs and attitudes must be exposed, and words and concepts 'freed' to associate in new ways. There are, he points out, two kinds of relationship to the past – one which derives from the past, and one which is a dialogue with the past. The nature of tradition is in one sense a 'ceaseless question about the nature of exploitation' – self-exploitation, as well as the exploitation by others, of one culture by another. The question which arises from this is 'what kind of dynamic breakdown of tradition, bringing about an unpredictable release of energies, arises within homogeneous and self-sufficient bodies making them susceptible to exploit each other or to be exploited by each other?' Furthermore, is there within exploitation itself 'a curious half-blind groping into a conception of heterogeneous community beyond static cultural imperatives?' (Harris 1973: 45).

Harris relates these questions specifically to the novel form. For the art of fiction as 'architectonic scale', as an alteration of the inherited novel form, involves a dialogue with values 'through' appearances:

> Appearances are given, are apparently objective. The mystery of the subjective imagination lies, I believe, in an intuitive, indeed revolutionary, grasp of a play of values as the flux of authentic change through and beyond what is given to us and what we accept, without further thought, as objective appearances. It is not a question of rootlessness but of the miracle of roots, the miracle of a dialogue with eclipsed selves which appearances may deny us or into which they may lead us.
>
> (1973: 47)

Consequently, for Harris, the 'comedy of manners' novel of, say, the nineteenth-century British tradition, or contemporary works of any culture having claims to a realist mode, merely perpetuate the problems they purport to address. Harris's principal views are elaborated most fully (and applied in specific literary analysis) in *The Womb of Space* (1983). In this text, which is subtitled *The Cross-Cultural Imagination,* he gives extended 'intuitive readings' of works such as Faulkner's *Intruder in the Dust,* Poe's *Narrative of A. Gordon Pym,* Jean Toomer's *Cane,* Juan Rulfo's *Pedro Paramo,* Jean Rhys's *Wide Sargasso Sea,* Paule Marshall's *The Chosen Place, the Timeless People,* Patrick White's *Voss,* and Raja Rao's *The Serpent and the Rope.* Harris also includes some discussion of the poetry of Césaire, Walcott, Edward Brathwaite, and Zulfikar Ghose. The cross-cultural elements in the works are stressed, indeed these are precisely what energizes their open interpretative potential:

> The paradox of cultural heterogeneity, or cross-cultural capacity, lies in the evolutionary thrust it restores to orders of the imagination, the ceaseless dialogue it inserts between hardened conventions and eclipsed or half-eclipsed otherness, within an intuitive self that moves endlessly into flexible patterns, arcs or bridges of community.
>
> (1983: xviii)

In his analyses of *Voss* and *The Chosen Place, the Timeless People* Harris demonstrates the ways in which certain 'persistent intuitive elements' in the texts conspire to undermine the imperialism which governs the surface texture of character and event. He is not concerned with whether these 'elements' are an intentional part of the writer's design – he clearly thinks that they are not in Poe, that they are in Rhys and White, and that their 'intent' remains problematical in Marshall's novel. But for Harris, whether they are 'intended' or not, they exist in all cross-cultural creative works as significant internalizations of the post-colonial impulse which constantly 'seeks to consume its own biases'. The surface 'historical reality' is of a destructive and continuing imperialism, but its exploration inevitably exposes an underlying imaginative imperative towards cross-culturality, Creolization, hybridization, and catalysis. Imperialism, the prevailing political reality of these works, is thus perpetually undermined by a persisting regenerative seed, masked perhaps as intuition or dream. The implications for literary modes and forms are profound, indicating a surface realism creatively fractured by the intrusive irrational, by dream and madness.

Harris's extensive fictional explorations, which have culminated in his recent theoretical writing, chronologically overlap Derrida's investigation of the limitations of the western philosophical tradition, and the resulting development of his theory of language '*différance*'. Harris's earliest novel, *Palace of the Peacock* (1960) predates Derrida's translation of Husserl by two years and the French publication of *Of Grammatology* (Derrida 1967a) and *Writing and Difference* (Derrida 1967b) by seven years. The relation between the two is therefore not one of influence but of a separate, similar, though finally diverging approach to the problem of language and meaning. Although Harris finds the apparent meaning of 'the word' constantly 'deferred' in a sense, and his critical practice involves the explosion of the text from the site of a 'fissure' in its apparently seamless texture, such 'deferrals' and 'fissures' are not for him, as for Derrida, the inescapable characteristics of language and textuality itself, but the ambi/valent 'limbo gateway' (Harris 1970a: 9) to the de-imperialization of apparently monolithic European forms, ontologies, and epistemologies.

The works of Wilson Harris comprise the most radical experiment in post-colonial cultures of any revolutionary rewriting, through fiction, of concepts of 'language' and of 'history'. All Harris's novels as well as his critical and theoretical writings form one cohesive body of work, but they are 'cohesive' in a peculiarly paradoxical manner. The potential authority of any single text is eroded by its successor, while, as Gregory Shaw has noted, its general insights are preserved and extended, often dialectically, in relation to previous works (Shaw 1985). 'Persons' and 'events' exist only as a state of process, in a world of becoming which escapes fixity of bias or episteme, and which is emphatically not preliminary to the re-establishment of any fixed system. Destructive binaries are impossible to sustain, character escapes fixity both within and between texts, even the life and death of characters are not absolutes, and no text is ever finally written. Each new text, whether novel or commentary, both builds upon its predecessor and by a series of 'paradoxical juxtapositions' deconstructs the earlier work by recasting and re-distributing its elements.

All his works, from *Palace of the Peacock* (1960) to *The Infinite Rehearsal* (1987) deliberately dismantle and unmask concepts and forms complicit in the construction of historical and textual monoliths, demonstrating the possibilities of alter/native ficto-historical texts which can create a world in process while continually freeing themselves from their own biases. Harris's work thus provides a model for a new post-colonial conception of history, language, and textuality.

The strategies of subversion and appropriation outlined above are crucial in the development of post-colonial theory, but they also indicate another important consideration. One result of European intervention and settlement throughout the world was a mixing of different peoples whose philosophies, languages, and ways of seeing and valuing were crucially tied to a belief in monoculturalism, to ancestry and purity of race or lineage. Much innovative philosophical and theoretical debate in post-colonial areas centres on the relationships between pure ancestry and cultural and racial hybridization, and it is again not surprising to find that it is in the Caribbean in particular that these issues have generated the most intensive discussion. Whether in linguistics, philosophy, or literary theory, post-colonial theories operate recursively and subversively to dismantle received assumptions in European theories. The complexities occluded by unitary assumptions of monism and universality are unravelled by the constant pull of marginality and plurality, so that through displacement, theory is 're-placed'.

5

Re-placing theory: post-colonial writing and literary theory

Post-colonial literatures and postmodernism

Post-colonial writing and literary theory intersect in several ways with recent European movements, such as postmodernism and poststructuralism, and with both contemporary Marxist ideological criticism and feminist criticism. These theories offer perspectives which illuminate some of the crucial issues addressed by the post-colonial text, although post-colonial discourse itself is constituted in texts prior to and independent of them. As many post-colonial critics have asserted, we need to avoid the assumption that they supersede or replace the local and particular (Soyinka 1975). But it is also necessary to avoid the pretence that theory in post-colonial literatures is somehow conceived entirely independently of all coincidents, or that European theories have functioned merely as 'contexts' for the recent developments in post-colonial theory. In fact, they clearly function as the conditions of the development of post-colonial theory in its contemporary form and as the determinants of much of its present nature and content.

Despite the recognition of this relationship, the appropriation of recent European theories involves a number of dangers, the most threatening of which is the tendency to reincorporate post-colonial culture into a new internationalist and universalist paradigm. This incorporative practice is shared by both the apparently apolitical and ahistorical theories of poststructuralism and the socio-cultural and determinist theories based in contemporary Marxist thought. Conversely, it is arguable that dominant European movements, such as postmodernism, which have sought in recent times to reabsorb post-colonial writing into an international postmodern discourse, may themselves, in fact, be more indebted to the cultural effects of the material practice of colonization and its aftermath than is usually acknowledged. In fact, the history of literary and critical movements in the twentieth century is, as one might expect, deeply determined by an interaction with imperialism. Indeed such interaction is characteristic of our century.

Modernism and the colonial experience

Modernism and the sudden experimentation with the artistic forms of the dominant bourgeois ideology, such as late nineteenth-century realism, are themselves, in part, products of the discovery of cultures whose aesthetic practices and cultural models were radically disruptive of the prevailing European assumptions. Europeans were forced to realize that their culture was only one amongst a plurality of ways of conceiving of reality and organizing its representations in art and social practice.

Central to this perception was the encounter with African culture in the period of the so-called 'Scramble for Africa' in the 1880s and 1890s. Even while the dominant cultures were engaged in violently suppressing the 'savage' cultures they encountered in West and East Africa they were importing into Europe, as loot, the revelation of an alternative view of the world in the form of African masks, carvings, and jewellery – artefacts which were, for the most part, stored away in the basements of the new museums of ethnology and anthropology. It was this material which, placed on display in the early decades of the next century, was to inspire the modernists and encourage them in their attempts to create the images of an alternative and radically 'unrealistic' art. The great interest in African art recovered from the punitive expeditions against Benin which were stored and catalogued by the British Museum was directly responsible for the inclusion of images of African art in novels such as D.H. Lawrence's *The Rainbow* (1916). Similarly, the collections which were to form the basis for the Musée de l'Homme in Paris were the source of the inspiration of such works incorporating African elements as Picasso's 1907 painting *Les Demoiselles D'Avignon* (Ruthven 1968).

Although the movement which underlay this interest in collecting the artefacts of 'primitive' cultures was much older, with its roots in the pre-romantic concerns with the culture of the *Ur-volk* of the various European nations, the renewed force of this interest evinced by the primitivist movements of the late nineteenth century received a great fillip from the discovery of cultures whose artefacts were not only totally 'new', but whose art proceeded on radically different principles, which called into question the basic assumptions of European aesthetics. Universalist claims of taste and function for art were hard pressed by such alternative cultural artefacts. Yet primitivist interest in peasant cultures and in the art of the pre-literate communities of their own European cultures had been present, as we have said, since the pre-romantic period. In addition, such interests had increased rapidly in the late nineteenth century as the Austro-Hungarian empire (last secular remnant of the concept of a unified Christendom) disintegrated under nationalist and economic pressures. The Slavic nationalism which followed led to a search for the primitive origins of Slavic cultures. The geographical position of these societies, readable from either a European or an Asiatic perspective, made them an important component in the questioning of the idea of culture which had prevailed up until this time. They were amongst the earliest signifiers of the Other both as a positive and negative force in European culture's concept of itself and of its 'uniqueness' and value. This was reflected in all the arts through the late nineteenth and early twentieth centuries (in the poetry of the Russian symbolists such as Blok, the music of Smetana and Dvorak, the art of Bakst and Goncharow, etc.). African artefacts, then, together with art-works from such apparently 'similar' cultures as New Guinea, the South Sea Islands, the North American Indians and Inuit, New Zealand Maoris, and Australian Aboriginals were viewed as examples of cultures 'preserved in time', of the primitive and aboriginal impulses common to all men. This art reflected a 'stage' in the development towards civilized art. However, from the earliest times this ethnographic view was accompanied by a more radical, fearful, and complex vision in which 'primitive' art was seen as expressive of the 'other side' of the European, civilized psyche, the 'dark' side of man. This is the fear which is expressed in such works as Conrad's *Heart of Darkness* and which is summed up in Yeats's comment after seeing Jarry's *Ubu Roi*: 'After us, the Savage God.'

This comment of Yeats is of particular significance, since he was a leading figure in the primitivist movement's search for the roots and origins of cultures. In his comment on Jarry he is implicitly distinguishing the legitimate search for the 'origins' of civilization from the frightening alternative of discovering in the 'primitive' the true and permanent face of the Other, that 'rough beast' whose turn, come round at last, threatens to overwhelm high European civilization.

In the reaction of artists and writers as diverse as Jarry, Rousseau, Rimbaud, Artaud, Lawrence, and Picasso a more radical critique is formulated; one in which the claims of European art to universal validity are questioned, and in which the constructed and impermanent nature of 'civilization' is exposed. Significantly, the African 'loot' of the eighties and nineties comes to light at the moment of profound crisis for this image of enduring and permanent civilization, during and immediately after the First World War.

Here, at the moment of formation of the central texts of modernism, and especially of those modernist texts which point towards the possibilities of the post-modernist deconstruction of the stability and authority of form *per se*, the encounter with the Other in the form of non-European cultures is crucial. From now on the 'discovery' of cultures essentially different from Europe in their basis and development is a central factor in the production and reproduction of European art itself. In this sense the emergence of post-colonial art and its engagement with European models is, from the beginning, part of a radical process affecting both European and non-European cultures.

The 'discovery' of African culture in the eighties and nineties is of especial significance since, unlike the earlier alternative cultures, such as China and India, encountered in the great

period of European expansion from the sixteenth century onwards, Africa was not perceived as a decayed remnant of
an alternative, earlier, and now superseded model for 'high
civilization'. The 'respect' paid to cultures such as India and
China by such diverse developments as the establishment of
Sanskrit and Chinese studies, the fashions for chinoiserie and
Indian styles in furnishings and decorations, the orientalist
imitations in literature and the adoption of such exotic drugs as
opium and hashish was also a way of asserting the ability of the
superior European civilization which was 'on the side of history'
to absorb and surpass their achievements.

African cultures, on the other hand, whose 'literature' was
non-existent; whose 'art' challenged the conventional ideas of
durance and decoration to the point where European critics
could not recognize them as art objects; and whose social
organizations seemed so utterly alien that the philosopher
Hegel could define the continent as being 'outside history',
offered a much more radical challenge. This challenge could
only be absorbed into the European frame as a mirror image, or
more appropriately, the negative of the positive concept of the
civilized, the black Other to the white norm, the demonic
opposite to the angels of reason and culture. Or, in what is really
only a false converse to the same Eurocentric viewpoint, African
culture could be viewed as the liberating Dionysiac force which
could shatter the Apollonian certainty of nineteenth-century
bourgeois society. For the early twentieth century, Africa was
an image which offered either absolute horror (of the Kurtzian
variety found in Conrad's *Heart of Darkness*) or an absolution
from the decayed and destructive fragments of a 'civilization'
whose bloodthirsty hypocrisies and violent contradictions had
been exposed on the battlefields of the Somme and Verdun. The
dying Rimbaud being carried through French Somaliland by
his native bearers is the ultimate image of the simultaneous
closeness and distance in the European concepts of Africa
during the nineteenth and early twentieth centuries. Rimbaud's
last journey, a sort of inverted and ironic version of Living-
stone's, sums up the limitations of the new European response
to Africa, and to the non-European world in general as the
ultimate exotic setting for European culture's search for a
theatrical extinction.

Africa is the source for the most significant and catalytic images of the first two decades of the twentieth century. In one very significant way the 'discovery' of Africa was the dominant paradigm for the self-discovery of the twentieth-century European world in all its self-contradiction, self-doubt, and self-destruction, for the European journey out of the light of Reason into the Heart of Darkness. As such, the more extreme forms of the self-critical and anarchic models of twentieth-century culture which modernism ushered in can be seen to depend on the existence of a post-colonial Other which provides its condition of formation.

New Criticism and post-colonial theory

The influential modern movement known as the New Criticism was itself largely a product of a post-colonial USA intent on establishing the legitimacy of its literary canon against the persistent domination of the English tradition. As Dauber asserts, the Americans, lacking tradition, and distrusting literature as an institution, could never believe in the reality of received 'categorizations'. New Criticism methodized this disbelief, 'to force us to begin again with each work' (Dauber 1977: 59). It emphasized the *individual work* from the post-colonial world, and so in a peculiar way bestowed on it a 'validity denied the literature in general' (ibid.).[1] Although New Criticism was almost immediately assimilated as Anglo-American, its roots were post-colonial, and in certain ways it served to allow the passage of post-colonial writers, whose traditions were by European definitions 'childish', 'immature', or 'tributary' (to adopt the most favoured metaphors of the period), into the English canon, which by the 1960s was in dire need of fresh fodder.[2] William Walsh's books on Commonwealth writers are an example of the way in which New Criticism facilitated the 'adoption' of individual post-colonial authors by the 'parent' tradition (Walsh 1970, 1973).

But New Criticism had a profoundly negative impact, too, rendering its effects on post-colonial culture deeply ambiguous. The assimilation of post-colonial writers into a 'metropolitan' tradition retarded consideration of their works within an appropriate cultural context, and so seriously militated against the development of a 'native' or indigenous theory. This tendency was consolidated by the New Criticism's misleading claims to objectivity. It was also, of course, the critical practice imposed by a British education system throughout the colonial world at a time when many post-colonial literatures were undergoing rapid development and needed consideration in the context of their own cultures. In this respect New Criticism prevented them from being seen as innovative, distinctive, and subversive of imported European values.

Cliff Lashley explains, in the Jamaican instance, that 'the birth of West Indian literature and the education of the majority of contemporary West Indian men of letters coincided with the ascendency of. . . New Criticism'. By about 1950, says Lashley, when West Indian criticism was born, the New Critical claim to objectivity and assertion of autonomy of the literary work had become the ruling and apparently unchallengeable orthodoxy (Lashley 1984: 11). The influence of the practice of New Criticism throughout the English-speaking world has been inestimable, and in spite of its post-colonial genesis and potentially liberating impetus, it remains one of the principal factors retarding the development of indigenous literary theories.

Nevertheless, New Criticism drew attention to features of individual texts which, when considered nationally and collectively, could be styled as unique, distinctive, or characteristic. Thus, from an empirical base, post-colonial criticism began to move towards the investigation of a set of theoretical 'problematics', focusing on what was again perceived to be different from the Anglo-European model. With the growth of comparative post-colonial studies between two or more areas, what had often been regarded as nationally or regionally unique was revealed to be more generally post-colonial, and a broader base for investigating theoretical questions was thus provided.

Postmodernism and the post-colonial experience

Such revisions of political critical 'history' question the objective categories of historical discourse itself and expose their formations as culture specific rather than universal. Hayden White (1973) has noted how a long line of European thinkers from Valéry and Heidegger to Sartre, Lévi-Strauss, and

Foucault have cast doubts on the claims of an objective historical consciousness and stressed the fictive nature of 'historical
reconstructions'. A similar challenge to the epistemological
status and cultural function of historical thought has been
mounted, from a different direction, by Anglo-American
philosophy. As a result

> it is possible to view historical consciousness as a specifically
> western prejudice, by which the presumed superiority of
> modern, industrial society can be retroactively substantiated.
>   (White 1973: 1–2)

Such challenges go far beyond the kind of rereadings of moments of historical crisis suggested above and argue that the
enterprise of 'reconstruction' is profoundly vitiated at source
and reflects, above and beyond its conscious categories, the
Eurocentricity of its formations. This accelerated qualification
of monocultural thinking has been closely associated with
so-called postmodern writing and poststructuralist literary
theories, that is, with the 'crisis of authority' in European
forms:

> Decentred, allegorical, schizophrenic . . . however we choose
> to diagnose its symptoms, postmodernism is usually treated,
> by its protagonists and antagonists alike, as a crisis of cultural
> authority, specifically of the authority vested in Western
> European culture and its institutions. That the hegemony of
> European civilisation is drawing to a close is hardly a new
> perception; since the mid-fifties, at least, we have recognised
> the necessity of encountering different cultures by means
> other than the shock of domination and conquest.
>   (Owens 1983: 57)

However, despite the theoretical investment in the question
of 'Otherness', certain tendencies within Euro-American structuralism and poststructuralism have operated in the same way
as the Western historicizing consciousness, to appropriate and
control the Other. This is hidden by the fact that it simultaneously performs a major cultural redemption, that is, the
reformation or revolutionizing of western epistemological codes
and cognitive biases.

'Post-colonial', 'postmodern', and 'poststructuralist' are

inconvenient labels which cover a wide range of overlapping literary and cultural practices. Arguments raised by the recent debate as to whether American culture is post-colonial makes this process of overlap clearer (Stonum 1981. See ch. 4, pp. 138–9 above). Whilst the recent American critical models have been profoundly influenced by Europe, with Derridaian and Foucaultian theories being whole-heartedly adopted by American critics, the Americans are now beginning to recognize that their own post-coloniality had already provided the ground for similarly subversive views of language and culture. Rather than the postmodernists and poststructuralists being seen as decentring forces, undermining the categories of a universal authority, they are beginning to be viewed as confirmations of the essentially subversive nature of much American literature throughout its development: subversive, that is, of the authority of the European centre and its forms and expectations. Thus the long-term importance of the postmodernist and poststructuralist impacts in America may well be in allowing the Americans to recapture and appropriate their own writing from a false history of explication. Until recently most Americans stressed the absence of a concern with the English centre and contrasted themselves in this respect with other post-colonial societies at large. Such a difference, they suggested, was the product of the reversed power structure obtaining in the last half-century or so. It is significant, then, that more recently American critics have seen the possibility of rereading American literature as metonymic of a continual process of subversion and appropriation which predates the concerns of modernism and postmodernism and which may well be centred in their post-coloniality. An acceptance of post-coloniality as part of the American formation is then no longer 'a badge of shame' or of immaturity, but a sign of distinction and difference, a difference which has been potent in American culture as a creative force.

The New Zealand critic Simon During, in an article entitled 'Postmodernism or postcolonialism?' (in which he uses the term 'postcolonial' to refer to something rather different from our use, centred on the older nationalist models of identity crisis and post-independence legitimacy), has argued that this interest in recent poststructuralist discourse is symptomatic of postcolonial societies in general. But for him it is the result of a negative condition, the product of what he defines as 'the indirection, illegitimacy and emptiness of post colonising [in his sense of the term] discourses'. During argues that in post-colonial countries, 'one finds a crisis of emptiness' (During 1985). Intellectuals in post-colonial societies thus reveal an urgent need to define themselves both against the identity given them by their colonial past and against international postmodernism. Speaking in particular of Australians he says, 'there is no strong postcolonised discourse by which they can mirror themselves as themselves'. Thus

> there is big business in . . . 'import rhetoric'. Those theorists, such as Foucault, Baudrillard and Derrida who have attacked the imperialism of Western thought from within, have currency there. Indeed Australians have been active in translating and circulating Foucault and Baudrillard internationally.

> (ibid.)

However, although this diagnosis is an astute one, it is worth returning to the point made by Stonum about the 'shock of recognition' experienced by critics of American literature when they encountered contemporary European theories. As this suggests, these theories, seen as disruptive, subversive, and innovative, were instantly recognized by critics in both settler colonies and colonies of intervention, such as India, as expressive of much of their situation, and quite consistent with the direction of most of their existing literature and criticism. It is perhaps an indication of the persisting hegemony of Europe that theories such as poststructuralism are adopted more readily than similar views derived from the conditions of post-colonial experience.

In a critique of the inappropriate adoption of recent European critical models in Nigeria, Wole Soyinka made a similar point about radical Marxist ideological criticism of culture and society. Comparing Marxist critics with the earlier generation of Christian converts, Soyinka regrets what he characterizes as their 'self-negation, the first requirement for a transcendentalist (political or religious) fulfilment'. The problem as he sees it is to avoid the two extremes of a national or racial essentialism (such as Négritude) and an international posture which denies 'self-apprehension'. As Soyinka says: 'To refuse to participate in the creation of a new cult of the self's daily apprehended reality is one thing; to have that reality contemptuously denied or undermined by other cultic adherents is far more dangerous and arouses extreme reactions.' The adherent of Marxist 'import rhetoric', like the Christian convert, is equally a victim of the doctrine of self-negation. Above all, 'the new ideologue has never stopped to consider whether or not the universal verities of his new doctrine are already contained in, or can be elicited from the world-view and social structures of his own people' (Soyinka 1976: xi, xii). It is in this spirit and with these strictures in mind that contemporary post-colonial intellectuals have usually responded to the attractions of the new critical movements from Europe.

Post-coloniality and contemporary European theory

The concern of postmodernist writers and post-structuralist critics to dismantle assumptions about language and textuality and to stress the importance of ideological construction in social–textual relations finds echoes in post-colonial texts. The concerns of these discourses are therefore increasingly interactive and mutually influential. Jean François Lyotard's critique of the enterprise of western science, for example, is traversed by similar preoccupations to those of post-colonial criticism (Lyotard 1979). It lays stress on narrative as an alternative mode of knowledge to the scientific, and draws out the implications of this for our view of the relationship and privileging of contemporary scientific ideas of 'competence' over 'customary knowledge' (19–23). Lyotard is aware, as a result of these perceptions, that in oral societies where narrative dominates, ways of knowing are legitimized as a product of actual social relations and not valorized and reified as a separate 'objective' category above and beyond other categories (as the western category of science is separated from those of ethics or politics, for example):

> Narratives . . . determine criteria of competence and/or illustrate how they are to be applied. They thus define what has the right to be said and done in the culture in question, and

since they are themselves a part of that culture, they are legitimised by the simple fact that they do what they do. (23)

Science, as Lyotard notes, is in opposition to such self-legitimizing narrative statements (even though it employs them covertly in the form of *petits récits*) and, as such, is a primary means of legitimizing the 'Occident' and its 'right to decide what is true' (8). Science, as he argues, classifies the narrative dominated oral world as belonging to a different mentality, 'savage, primitive, undeveloped'. From this view develops 'the entire history of cultural imperialism from the dawn of Western civilisation. It is important to recognise its special tenor, which sets it apart from all other forms of imperialism: it is governed by the demand for legitimisation' (27).

Although Lyotard's account questions the western enterprise of 'knowledge', it also refuses to entertain the possibility of an unproblematic recuperation of the traditional:

> there is no question here of proposing a 'pure' alternative to the system: we all now know ... that an attempt at an alternative of that kind would end up resembling the system it was meant to replace. (66)

Thus, for Lyotard, the establishment of concepts such as the postmodern (or, by analogy, the post-colonial) would not be designed to set up 'new metanarratives', that is, would not be constituted in the attempt to re-establish a single, monolithic, and legitimizing discourse, but rather in the attempt to articulate a weave of practices grounded in the particular and the local. As one reviewer of Lyotard has put it:

> Lyotard, in a manner similar to Derrida, conceives truth to be 'local', for 'knowledge is no longer the subject but the servant of the subject'. . . . A socially mediated truth, simply put, has at least as much legitimacy as one that is abstract. The difference, however, is that the former is 'anti-colonial' (Derrida) . . .
>
> (Murphy 1987)

Post-coloniality and discourse theory

The concept of discourse, as developed in the work of Michel Foucault and in those who have extended and questioned his formulation (Said, Althusser, Pêcheux, Terdiman etc.), has been useful in locating the series of 'rules' which determine post-coloniality. A discourse in the Foucaultian sense is best understood as a system of possibility for knowledge. What rules, for instance, allow the construction of a map, model, or classi-factory system? What rules allow us to identify certain indi-viduals as authors, to identify certain texts as 'literature'? (e.g. Foucault 1966, 1969, 1977a).

Edward Said's proposal of orientalism as the discourse which constituted the Orient in the consciousness of the west offers an influential analysis of how the world was constructed in the European mind. The Orient is not merely there, says Said:

> Just as the Occident itself is not just there either. We must take seriously Vico's great observation that men make their own history, that what they can know is what they have made, and extend it to geography: as both geographical and cultural entities – to say nothing of historical entities – such locales, regions, geographical sectors as 'Orient' and 'Occident' are man-made.
>
> (Said 1978: 5)

Just as the two geographical entities, the Occident and the Orient, in Said's terms, 'support and to an extent reflect each other', so all post-colonial societies realize their identity in difference rather than in essence. They are constituted by their difference from the metropolitan and it is in this relationship that identity both as a distancing from the centre and as a means of self-assertion comes into being.

To speak of a post-colonial discourse in Foucault's or Said's sense, then, is to invoke certain ways of thinking about lan-guage, about truth, about power, and about the interrela-tionships between all three. Truth is what counts as true within the system of rules for a particular discourse; power is that which annexes, determines, and verifies truth. Truth is never outside power, or deprived of power, the production of truth is a function of power and, as Foucault says, 'we cannot exercise power except through the production of truth' (Foucault 1977b: 12). The discourse of the post-colonial is therefore grounded on a struggle for power – that power focused in the control of the metropolitan language (Foucault 1982). Power is invested in the language because it provides the terms in which truth itself is constituted.[3] The struggle for power over truth in some senses 'mimics' the metropolitan impulse of dominance, and post-colonial critics such as Homi Bhabha have sought to address this problem (Bhabha 1984a). Only by stressing the way in which the text transforms the societies and institutions within which it functions (its 'transformative work') can such a mimicry be avoided and replaced by a theory and practice which embraces difference and absence as material signs of power rather than negation, of freedom not subjugation, of creativity not limitation.

The relationship between European discourse theory and the post-colonial has been viewed in various ways. Critics like the Canadian Diana Brydon argue that critiques of imperialist and patriarchal discourse constructed in terms of general European theory (Said 1978; Spivak 1985b, 1987; Moi 1987 etc.) can provide useful allies for post-colonial counter-hegemonic theory. Expressed more positively, it is possible to argue that post-colonial discourse may appropriate what it requires from European theory. Discursive formations are not hermetically sealed, they overlap and intersperse in ways that may be fruitfully and reflexively utilized. It is, after all, at the point of intersection with other discourses that any discourse becomes determined.

Counter-discourse: Richard Terdiman

Richard Terdiman's recent account of counter-discourse (Terdiman 1986) begins from a notion of language functioning in practice and usage, thus fully acknowledging the material site of the text's production. In this, Terdiman echoes the concerns of post-colonial linguistics with the practical orientation of language. His starting-point, however, is Louis Helmslev, who, as Terdiman reports, 'problematised Saussure's distinction between *langue* and *parole* by introducing a positive, concrete term – "usage" – between them'. 'Usage', Terdiman comments, is

> more than a compromise or an attempt to strike an average. It upsets the idea that language systems can usefully be split into a system on the one hand, and nonsystematic, somehow

degraded or irrational manifestations on the other. . . . It projects not a private, unique *act* but a pattern *active* in a community, a pre-established set of determinate possibilities and limits. (30)

Terdiman also 'detects within (Saussurian) binary opposition a *hierarchy*, socially determined and determining' (33) and so concludes with Foucault that culture is a 'field of struggle'. For Terdiman, the multi-accentuality of the sign suggests that 'no discourse is ever a monologue . . . it always presupposes a horizon of competing, contrary utterances against which it asserts its own energies' (36). So discourses come into being in a structure of counter-discursive practices. This implies that 'the inscription of conflict is no longer conceived as a contamination of the linguistic but as its properly defining function' (37). So Foucault's perception that the 'history which bears and determines us has the form of a war rather than that of a language: relations of power, not relations of meaning' (40), can now, Terdiman argues, be evolved further to allow us

to radicalise even Foucault's striking formulation. For against his own antinomic posing of the linguistic and military alternatives themselves, and in our own counter-discursive formulation of a fundamental model for cultural analysis, we would need to assert that *the form of language itself is contradiction*. (40)

Clearly a discourse such as post-colonialism, which runs 'counter' to the established canon and privileges usage and syncreticity, can very readily appropriate from Terdiman the idea that the sign obtains its meaning in conflict and contradiction and apply it to post-colonial texts and societies (Slemon 1988).

Post-coloniality and theories of ideology

The work of Marxist critics such as Louis Althusser, Michel Pêcheux, and Fredric Jameson is of particular relevance to the problematic of the relationship between language and literary practice addressed by post-colonial critics (see Bhabha 1984a: 257 and *passim*) and to the problem of constituting identity within the self–Other division imposed by imperialism.

Foucault's late attempt to 'create a history of the different modes by which in our culture, human beings are made subjects' (Foucault 1982) grew out of his perception of the relation between such ideological constructions and the determining structure(s) of power. It clearly reflects Althusser's seminal definition in the famous essay on 'Ideology and ideological state apparatuses (notes towards an investigation)' (1970). This proposed the idea that subjects are interpellated (called into being) within ideologies and that this is inescapable; that is, that we become conscious under the power of construction resident in imaginary subjection: 'Ideology interpellates individuals as subjects' (ibid.). Michel Pêcheux extends and develops this insight into the creation of subjects through ideological practices and extends the investigation more fully to the areas of semantics and linguistics.

He argues that there are three modes in which subjects are constructed. The first mode is that of 'Good' subjects who result from 'Identification'; they 'freely consent' (in Althusser's terms) to the discursive formation which determines them. The second mode produces 'Bad' subjects who result from 'counter-identification'; they refuse the image offered and turn it back on the offerer. In this mode 'the reversal leaves linguistic traces; "what *you* call the oil crisis", "your social sciences", "your Virgin Mary" . . .' (Pêcheux [1975] trans. 1982: 157). Or, as we might add; 'your literary values', 'your aesthetics', 'your civilization'. This is an important and radical mode and yet, for Pêcheux, it is finally limited. Implicit in it is the danger of 'counter-determination', that is it may inadvertently support what it seeks to oppose by confirming a 'symmetry' between the two (as could be claimed, for instance, of Négritude). As Pêcheux sees it, such counter-determinations remain locked within the mode of thought they seek to deny. It is arguable that the moment of abrogation in post-colonial discursive practices and the nationalist or racist criticisms which this encourages is such a 'counter-identification' and so is 'counter-determined' in the same way. The third mode Pêcheux characterizes as 'disidentification'; this is the product of political and discursive practices which work 'on and against' the dominant ideologies. Pêcheux's third modality, then, recognizes that dominant ideologies, whilst they are inescapable (to suggest otherwise is to embrace the political myth of the 'end of ideologies'), are transformable. 'Disidentification constitutes a *working* (transformation-displacement) of the subject form and not just its abolition' (169).

Pêcheux's concept has two useful features for post-colonial studies. First, it permits an understanding of the 'subjective appropriation of knowledges' (as well as the politics to which they give rise). So we are able to recognize that the effects of these (for example, educational practices, and 'civilizing' missions) rest on pre-existent meanings produced by discursive formations which are 'always-already-there'. Second, Pêcheux's formulation is useful in the way it displaces a concern for the constituting subject to lay its stress on meaning and discourse as formed in and through material struggle. For Pêcheux, meaning does not reside in language *in itself*, but linguistic meaning has a material character produced by the position of the language as a signifier in social, political, and cultural struggle. 'Words, expressions, propositions etc. . . . change their meaning according to the positions held by those who use them, which signifies that they find their meaning by reference to these positions' (111). This has, of course, been a recurrent and noticeable feature in post-colonial discourse from the beginning of the imperial–colonial relation.

Fredric Jameson's work (Jameson 1971, 1981) on narrative as a socially symbolic act has also been influential on developing theories of textuality and social process in post-colonial societies. For example, Jameson's characterization of literature as informed by the political unconscious and so as an activity which 'must be read as a symbolic meditation on the destiny of community', a reading whose function is 'the unmasking of cultural artefacts as socially symbolic acts' (Jameson 1981: 70, 20) has been the basis for some important accounts of post-colonial aesthetics (e.g. JanMohammed 1983). JanMohammed employs Jameson's account of literature's relationship to ideology and to social and cultural practice in order to emphasize the need in post-colonial texts to '[rewrite] the literary text in such a way that the latter may itself be seen as the rewriting or restructuration of a prior historical or ideological *subtext*' (Jameson 1981: 81–2).[4]

Jameson's account is useful to post-colonial discussion of the role of narrative fictions in simultaneously articulating and deconstructing the 'Manichean aesthetic' of post-colonial societies. This aesthetic expresses the binary divisions of centre–margin, self–Other, good–evil, Black–white which, he argues, is the characteristic feature of such societies and their art. Jameson provides post-colonial critics seeking to develop Fanon's analysis of Manichean duality with the necessary model of a reflexive relationship between social process and text, a model which emphasizes that the text's relationship with 'the historical subtext' is an *active* one. It is the text which transforms the historical subtext which it draws up into itself and this transformation constitutes what Jameson characterizes as the 'symbolic act' of the narrative. So the text, paradoxically, 'brings into being that very situation to which it is also, at one and the same time, a reaction' (Jameson 1981: 81–2). This Jamesonian model can then be used to show the generic rather than the idiosyncratic relationships which exist between authors and their societies.[5]

Contemporary accounts such as these argue that the 'truth' of post-colonial societies, like that of other oppressed, or repressed, or silenced communities is ideologically determined. It stems from a construction of the self as subject in relation to the Other. In oppressed communities, however, this relationship is not viewed in Sartrean terms as a reciprocity: 'in and through the revelation of my being-as-object for the Other. . . . I must be able to apprehend the presence of his being-as-subject' (Sartre 1957). Such a reciprocity allows mutual relations between self and Other in which both may at various times willingly function as objects for the Other. But in post-colonial societies, the participants are frozen into a hierarchical relationship in which the oppressed is locked into position by the assumed moral superiority of the dominant group, a superiority which is reinforced when necessary by the use of physical force. Such accounts, too, are grounded in an awareness of the struggle between discourses as the fundamental constitutive mode of such relations.

Given the extent to which European postmodernist and poststructuralist theories have invested in cultural relativity as a term in some of their most radical insights, it is ironic that the label of 'postmodern' is increasingly being applied hegemonically to cultures and texts outside Europe, assimilating post-colonial works whose political orientations and experimental formations have been deliberately designed to counteract such European assimilation (and, it might be argued, have themselves provided the cultural base and formative colonial experience on which European theorists have drawn in their apparent radicalization of linguistic philosophy). The dialectic of self and Other, indigene and exile, language and place, slave and free, which is the matrix of post-colonial literatures, is also an expression of the way in which language and power operate *in the world*. Assimilation of these texts into 'postmodernism', or of their insights into the importance of text and word as a means of control into European poststructuralism invokes a neo-universalism which reinforces the very European hegemony which these works have been undermining or circumventing. Thus the so-called 'crisis of (European) authority' continues to reinforce European cultural and political domination, as the potential relativization of European systems of thought acts through such labelling once again to make the rest of the world a peripheral term in Europe's self-questioning.

Marxism, anthropology, and post-colonial society

Marxist theory, in particular, has had many uses and much appeal for post-colonial societies, and for post-colonial theory with its stress on the political construction of cultural events. But Marxist theory has been limited, until recently, in its dealings with these societies by its own unconscious Eurocentricity. However there are signs that recently, Marxist anthropological theory is developing a greater awareness of the need for sensitive adaptation in arguing that such categories as 'class' are applicable to all societies. The work of Louis Althusser is again crucial here, providing, as it does, in its development of Marx's theory of 'mode of production', a more flexible account of the relationships ('articulations' is Althusser's term) between the several interlinked structures making up any specific 'mode of production' in a specific society. Althusser's model, together with the work of M. Godelier, who pointed to the Eurocentric limitations of Marx and Engels' knowledge and account of pre-capitalist societies, initiated this development (Godelier 1977, 1978). Godelier was also the first Marxist anthropologist to note that unilinear views of history are untenable, and in fact were never held by Marx himself.

The need for these modern revisions stems primarily from the dominance in earlier Marxist anthropology of a radically simplified version of Engels' theory of pre-capitalist societies in *The Origin of the Family, Private Property and the State*, developed under Stalin and imposed by him and the Comintern as official policy for most European Communist Parties. Since Godelier and Althusser, a number of anthropologists in Europe and, significantly, in Latin America have sought to develop more sophisticated accounts and have taken as their project 'the separation of the general theory from the specific case so that the theory could be used to analyse non-capitalist systems' (Bloch 1983: 152). Naturally though, despite this post-Althusserian orientation, contemporary Marxist anthropology still rejects the 'empirical' approach of an out-and-out pluralism. That is, it continues in the Marxist tradition to understand social and historical phenomena not in their 'own terms' but in terms of 'an *underlying* system of structural relations, which because it contains within it internal mechanisms tensions and contradictions, is the source of historical transformation' (ibid.: 155). However, using this more flexible model, anthropologists such as Rey (1971) and Terray (1975) have argued that 'With this kind of analysis the Marxist notion of class, the key to Marxist social theory, does apply to pre-capitalist societies, and indeed, reveals with great exactness their character' (Bloch 1983: 164).

Feminism and post-colonialism

Women in many societies have been relegated to the position of 'Other', marginalized and, in a metaphorical sense, 'colonized', forced to pursue guerrilla warfare against imperial domination from positions deeply imbedded in, yet fundamentally alienated from, that *imperium* (Spivak 1987). They share with colonized races and peoples an intimate experience of the politics of oppression and repression, and like them they have been forced to articulate their experiences in the language of their oppressors. Women, like post-colonial peoples, have had to construct a language of their own when their only available 'tools' are those of the 'colonizer'.

As in post-colonial theory, language, 'voice', concepts of speech and silence (Duras 1973), and concepts of mimicry (Irigaray 1985a, 1985b) have been important in feminist theory, together with the connections between literature and language, political activity, and the potential for social change. Recognizing that aesthetic value is not universal, that it does not reside within the text, but is historically and culturally specific, feminist critics reject the patriarchal bases of literary theory and criticism and seek to subvert them and show them to be relative, not absolute or axiomatic. Starting from potentially essentialist positions in the 1960s and 1970s feminist critics have moved away from biologistic stances (often based on white, Anglo-Saxon norms) towards more complex subversive positions and towards increasing recognition that the principle of 'difference', lying as it does at the very heart of their construction as 'Other', is basic to any contemporary feminist theory. Exclusivist or essentialist definitions which acted to marginalize other races or classes have increasingly been eroded, particularly through the work of influential critics like Alice Walker (for instance in her rewriting of Virginia Woolf's famous reflections on the fate of Shakespeare had he been born a woman, 'Judith Shakespeare' (Walker 1983) or in the earlier work of Tillie Olsen (1978). Such writers criticize feminist theory for being middle class and Anglo-American in its assumptions. As a result, intersections of race, class, and gender have become increasingly important within the discourse of feminism (Spivak 1981; Willis 1985; Zimmerman 1985).

Thus the history and concerns of feminist theory have strong parallels with post-colonial theory. Feminist and post-colonial discourses both seek to reinstate the marginalized in the face of the dominant, and early feminist theory, like early nationalist post-colonial criticism, sought to invert the structures of domination, substituting, for instance, a female tradition or traditions in place of a male-dominated canon. But like post-colonial criticism, feminist criticism has now turned away from such simple inversions towards a questioning of forms and modes, to unmasking the assumptions upon which such canonical constructions are founded, moving first to make their cryptic bases visible and then to destabilize them.

In addition, both feminist and post-colonial critics have reread the classical texts (Jones 1985), demonstrating clearly that a canon is produced by the intersection of a number of readings and reading assumptions legitimized in the privileging hierarchy of a 'patriarchal' or 'metropolitan' concept of 'literature'. This offers the possibility of reconstructing the canon, and not simply replacing it in an 'exchange of texts', since both discourses recognize that to change the canon is to do more than change the legitimized texts. It is to change the conditions of reading for all texts. It is important to note that in both cases these more sophisticated, reflexive possibilities only emerge after an initial (and understandable) resistance to theory itself, to that formalism which 'sets theory above experience in its claims to dominance'. As Sydney Janet Kaplan expresses it,

> there may always be a split between the theoretical impulses of criticism practised 'in the university' and those passions of love and anger that resist its categorisations.
>
> (1985: 56)

The subversion of patriarchal literary forms themselves has also been an important part of the feminist project. As in the post-colonial texts this subversion may not be a conscious aim of the authors. It may be generated, inescapably, by the ideological conflict that inevitably takes place in the text. On a wider scale, there has also been a radical questioning of the basic assumptions of dominant systems of language and thought. Here feminist criticism has drawn upon deconstruction theory (Furman 1985: 74–6) to disentangle polarized concepts in the dominant language, such as terms like Black and White, which some critics have argued install a false separation within the women's collective.

As one might expect, such practice has not been uncontentious. Although Julia Kristeva finds that 'modern breaks with tradition and the development of new forms of discourse are harmonious with the women's cause', Gayatri Spivak cautions that the unsettling of meaning *per se* will not necessarily promote a feminist future nor escape the historical determination of sexism (Spivak 1981: 154–84). There is, for instance, as in the example above, the problem that in rejecting the binary structures of patriarchal discourses we may also lose sight of the political, social, and ideological force of (for instance) racism in our society. Hence feminist theory stresses the need for the deconstructive and the political to go hand in hand. It opposes sexism, where women write as a biologically oppressed group, and endorses feminism as part of a political project, to raise and transform consciousness. This latter point also demonstrates another significant parallel between feminist discourse and the post-colonial in that their projects are oriented towards the future, positing societies in which social and political hegemonic shifts have occurred. Concomitantly it is generally true that both discourses link a disruptive involvement in books with a project towards revolutionary disruption in society at large.

Feminism has not in general provided post-colonial criticism with a model or models because its development has been rather as a coincident and parallel discourse. But intersections between the two are crucial, for instance in the work of writers such as Henry Handel Richardson, Jean Rhys, Alice Walker, Doris Lessing, Buchi Emecheta, and Margaret Atwood. Increasingly, too, critics are beginning to draw the two discourses together (see, for instance, Holst-Petersen and Rutherford 1985; Spivak 1987).

The politics of theory: decolonizing colonialist discourse

The development of recent theories of colonialist discourse (Bhabha, Spivak, JanMohammed etc.) has clearly been one of the most influential results of the appropriation of contemporary post-structuralist accounts to the field of post-colonial writing. These critics have sought to offer ways of dismantling colonialism's signifying system and exposing its operation in the silencing and oppressing of the colonial subject.

Spivak, particularly in her accounts of the double subjection of colonized women and her discussion of the silencing of the muted native subject, in the form of the 'subaltern' woman, ha_ testified to the fact that 'There is no space from where / subaltern (sexed) subject can speak' (Spivak 1985c: 122) implication, the silencing of the subaltern woman extends whole of the colonial world, and to the silencing and muting of all natives, male or female.

Bhabha has similarly asserted that the colonized is constructed within a disabling master discourse of colonialism which specifies a degenerate native population to justify its conquest and subsequent rule. Unlike Spivak, though, Bhabha has asserted that the 'subaltern' people can speak, and that a native voice can be recovered. His introduction of the ideas of mimicry and parody as both a strategy of colonial subjection through 'reform, regulation and discipline, which "appropriates" the Other', and the native's inappropriate imitations of this discourse, which has the effect of menacing colonial authority (Bhabha 1984b: 126–7) suggests that the subaltern has, in fact, spoken, and that properly symptomatic readings of the colonialist text can and do 'recover a native voice'.

Such contemporary theories of colonialist discourse, like the poststructuralist accounts of language from which they derive, have been subject recently to criticisms which assess the implications of their politics. These criticisms have drawn attention to the negative effects which may stem from such discourse, stressing as it does, for example, 'the absence of a text that can "answer one back" after the planned epistemic violence of the imperialist project' (Spivak 1985a: 131). For example, Benita Parry asks what the politics might be of a criticism in which discourse is privileged as the primary form of social praxis (Parry 1987: 37). 'What are the politics', she asks,

> which dissolve the binary opposition colonial self/colonized other, encoded in colonialist language as a dichotomy necessary to domination, but also differently inscribed in the discourse of liberation as a dialectic of conflict and a call to arms? (29).

In other words, such critics question whether or not the models which stress the inescapability of the discourse which constitutes colonizer–post-colonized are not in fact only a sophisticated mask over the face of a continued, neo-colonial domination, another aspect of what Parry has characterized as the 'protean forms of imperialism', of which colonialism was only one historical stage.

Parry invokes Fanon as a classic and effective alternative

model, whose position she characterizes as constructing a 'politically conscious, unified Self, standing in unmitigated antagonism to the oppressor' (30). She rejects the work of colonialist discourse theorists as apolitical; although, paradoxically, concedes that the work of critics such as Spivak and Bhabha, connecting as it does signifying systems with social forces, cannot have the 'charge of political quietism . . . levelled against [it]' (32). The crux of her quarrel with these critics, despite this disclaimer, remains their political ineffectiveness and even reactionary implications. For Parry, Fanon (properly read) and presumably other decolonizing critics engaged in writing what she characterizes as 'nationalist liberationist narratives' (e.g. Ngugi 1986) address the issue of the next stage beyond the limits imposed by the 'silencing' effect of colonialism: the stage in which a sufficient space can be created so that 'the colonised can be written back into history' (39).

The warning in Parry's essay of the dangers of theories of colonialist discourse 'becoming a coloniser in [their] turn' is a very useful one. But it does seem to assume that the choice between a 'seductively inclusive political humanism' and the 'affirmation of multiple forms of "native difference"' necessarily involves some variety of total decolonization. Parry totally rejects syncretism, by which she seems to mean any acknowledgement of a mutual interaction of colonizer and colonized, although she has applauded Fanon's project to use the past 'to put an end to the history of colonisation – the history of pillage – and to bring into existence the history of the nation – the history of decolonisation' (Fanon 1961: 51), and has enthusiastically embraced Jonathon Dollimore's idea of 'the reversal of the authentic/inauthentic opposition . . . and the subversion of authenticity itself (as presumably, separate) stages in a *process of resistance*' (Dollimore 1986: 190). Despite this clear signalling of the necessity of distinguishing distinctive and different stages of what we have termed 'abrogation' and 'appropriation' in acquiring control of the processes of 'self-apprehension' (to use Soyinka's term), such creative syncretism can be characterized, for Parry, only as 'cultural esperanto' and dismissed as merely a subtle device for the reintroduction and reincorporation of native 'difference' into a new hegemonic totality (cultural neocolonialism is implied, though she does not use the term).

In constructing this critique, it is significant that the only intellectual form other than European influenced discourse criticism that Parry refers to in the contemporary period is the equally Europeanized and now very outdated '"common-wealth studies" and its progeny "commonwealth literature"' (1987: 32). This she rightly attacks as the characteristic product of a disguised humanist reincorporation, but it seems clear that her critique of syncretism, made largely in terms of its use by post-colonial deconstructive critics like Spivak and Bhabha and using examples drawn exclusively from colonies of military intervention such as Africa and India, does not take account of the more complex model of syncretic post-colonial culture proposed by West Indian and settler colony critics.

Despite the force of critiques like Parry's it is hard to go along, finally, with their belief in the practical possibility of decolonizing projects which can avoid the pitfalls of a 'reverse discourse replicating and therefore re-installing the linguistic polarities devised by a dominant centre'. This difficulty is not only experienced by those 'concerned with deconstructing the text of colonialism'. It is arguably installed in the very practices and politics of everyday existence in post-colonial societies. Syncret-ism is the condition within which post-colonial societies oper-ate, and accepting this does not, in any simple sense, involve hiding the role culture plays in the continuing neo-colonial hegemonic formation of the day-to-day experience of those societies.

It is quite understandable that many post-colonial critics have felt an urgent need to reject European theory (and even 'theory' as such) as irredeemably Eurocentric in both its assumptions and political effect. But to reject the possibilities of appropriation in this way is to refuse to accept that the same condition of hybridity as exists in the production of the post-colonial text also exists in the production of theory. Critical texts as well as creative texts are products of post-colonial hybridity. In fact, it is arguable that to move towards a genuine affirmation of multiple forms of native 'difference', we must recognize that this hybridity will inevitably continue. This is a prerequisite of a radical appropriation which can achieve a genuinely transformative and interventionist criticism of con-temporary post-colonial reality.

Post-colonial reconstructions: literature, meaning, value

Post-colonial theories of literature emerge from a view of language grounded in an assertion of the importance of practice over the code, the importance of the 'variant' over the 'standard'. There is also a sense in which post-colonial writing itself, as well as the systematic indigenous theories, offers a broader, non-Eurocentric perspective on some traditional questions of theory. What kinds of writing 'fit' or could be considered to fit into the category 'literature'; how do texts 'mean'; by what criteria could or should these texts be evaluated; how do they dismantle the process of ascribing 'merit' through critical practice; and how applicable are the universalist assertions of European theory to the growing body of post-European literatures. This perspective does not necessarily exclude conclusions which may be reached within Eurocentric theory, but its very existence questions the circumscribed range of that theory's project.

'Literature'

The interaction of english writing with the older traditions of orature or literature in post-colonial societies, and the emergence of a writing which has as a major aim the assertion of social and cultural difference, have radically questioned easy assumptions about the characteristics of the genres we usually employ as structuring and categorizing definitives (novel, lyric, epic, play etc.). Our sense, not only of that which ought to enter the canon, but also of what could be given the name 'literature', has been altered by writers incorporating and adapting traditional forms of imaginative expression to the exigencies of an inherited english language. For example, African literatures, as a result of their interface with traditional oral narratives, have offered a number of alter/native ways of conceiving narrative structure. These have influenced both the structure and features of 'novels' produced in english in that continent (Fritschi, 1983),[6] and insisted on the inclusion of many forms of performance art in any effective cross-cultural discussion of the structure and form of narrative. The perspective of cross-cultural literatures has given explicit confirmation to the perception that genres cannot be described by essential characteristics, but by an interweaving of features, a 'family resemblance' which denies the possibility of either essentialism or limitation.

Any writer may extend the 'boundaries' of a genre, but the writer who incorporates forms from other traditions articulates more clearly the constant adjustments we make to our perceptions of what is admitted to the category of 'literature'. Most English literary forms evolved in an historical environment quite alien to the cultures of most post-colonial countries. In one sense, the European forms created a basis on which the indigenous literature in english could develop. But this is more a marriage of convenience than a deep cultural commitment to the received genres. Once writing in english is established as a regular social practice, it begins to adapt itself to the traditional ways of formulating the imaginative arts. The received forms do not remain the authentic centre of this complex of practices, but, in time, become one series of forms among many. Inevitably the sensibilities of individual writers will be influenced by the literary and aesthetic assumptions of their own cultures. More often the use of the local tradition will be quite conscious and deliberate; for example, the use of traditions derived from oral performance art and religious epic in the Indian novel, orature and proverb in West Africa and, in settler colonies, various forms of ritual from indigenous speech, such as the 'yarn' in Australia.

Clearly, wherever they exist, traditional pre-colonial indigenous forms are especially important both in the syncretic practice which develops and as an expression of a renewed sense of identity and self-value in the independence period. Ghanaian poet and novelist Kofi Awoonor, for example, claims that the artist must return to traditional sources for inspiration itself. His work makes full use of traditional forms like the dirge, which 'opens with a statement of the mourner's condition, develops through a series of images of the causes of grief, or of the nature of mourning itself, usually ending with a message or plea' (Colmer 1977: 6). Another traditional form employed by contemporary writers is the song of abuse, which opens with a direct address to the person being abused, develops through a catalogue of his or her vices, particularly those that affect the author, and closes with a declaration of the poet's independence. Clearly, the allowable variations of content in the song of abuse offer wide possibilities for any contemporary African poet writing in english. The purpose of using such traditional forms, for Awoonor, for example, is to knit the existing motifs and forms in to an artistic whole so that the artist 'is ultimately restored, to a community sensibility, to a resolution, a restoration of calm and quietude' (Awoonor 1973: 88).

The use of traditional forms has not been limited to short poetic pieces. The first Maori novel, Witi Ihimaera's *Tangi* (1973), a novel 'about' his father's death and the subsequent Maori funeral *tangi*, is in fact a sustained lament incorporating all the traditional oral features of repetition, eulogy, and oratory. The lament transposed into novel form achieves remarkable power as a profound celebration of Maori culture, community, and family life. But it puts particular pressure on received notions of what actually constitutes a novel as well as on the received processes of evaluation. To a western reader, used to the tradition of linear progression, character development, and novel form, this lament could seem tedious, repeating as it does the writer's sense of loss and desolation in a book of circular structure. But such a reaction alerts us immediately to the Eurocentric nature of such an evaluation and the need to incorporate cultural context into any assessment of literary worth.

Ideas of narrative structure are also altered. Salman Rushdie has made it quite clear that the techniques of the novel *Midnight's Children* reproduce the traditional techniques of the Indian oral narrative tradition. In an interview he says:

> Listening to this man (a famous story teller in Baroda) reminded me of the shape of the oral narrative. It's not linear. An oral narrative does not go from the beginning to the middle to the end of the story. It goes in great swoops, it goes in spirals or in loops, it every so often reiterates something that happened earlier to remind you, and then takes you off again, sometimes summarises itself, it frequently digresses off into something that the story teller appears just to have thought of, then it comes back to the main thrust of the narrative . . .
>
> So that's what *Midnight's Children* was, I think, and I think

everything about Laurence Sterne, Garcia Marquez, and all that, comes a long way behind that, and that was the thing that I felt when writing it that I was trying to do.

(Rushdie 1985: 7–8)

This technique of circling back from the present to the past, of building tale within tale, and persistently delaying climaxes are all features of traditional narration and orature. Witness this account of the narrative technique of the traditional clown–narrator (the 'Vidushka') in the ancient Indian performance art of *Kuttiyattam*:

The Vidushka can take all kinds of liberties; in fact he is expected to and encouraged to do so. He can indulge in any kind of extravagance, provided he can come back to the main thread of the narrative without getting lost in his own elaborations. He could turn his narrative into a string of short stories or take one of these stories and lengthen it for hours or days. Thus the oral narrative can easily achieve the length of a novel – if length is a criterion at all.

(Paniker 1986: 21–2)

This oral technique, itself grafted onto the fragments of ancient Sanskrit written texts which form the basis for *Kuttiyattam* performance, illustrates the possibilities of undoing the assumptions of logocentric texts in post-colonial practice. Rushdie can employ similar graftings in the development of the relationship between the narrator and 'listener' (Padma) in *Midnight's Children*. Rushdie assures us that such techniques from orature are consciously part of his writing. Also, of course, there are many literary sources in traditional Indian written narrative we could look to as unconscious influences which are far older than Sterne; for example the fourth century Brhatkatha of Gunadhya (Krishnamoorthy 1986). In fact, to anyone familiar with traditional Indian writing and orature it is clear that Rushdie's text is profoundly intertextual with the whole of the Indian narrative tradition.

Post-colonial texts like *Midnight's Children* (or Amos Tutuola's *The Palm-Wine Drinkard* three decades earlier) have been subjected to a schizophrenic form of critical dismissal. On the one hand contemporary nationalist critics dismissed these texts because in their view they only reproduced in a translated or 'plagiarized' form the traditional techniques of narration and so failed the test of 'authenticity'; on the other hand, European critics, out of ignorance, failed entirely to record the debt of these texts to African and Indian traditional forms. What neither position did was to engage with the text as an extreme example of that hybridity which is the primary characteristic of all post-colonial texts, whatever their source.

Meaning

Another question posed by post-colonial literatures is 'Could the *concept* of meaning itself be Eurocentric?' Our understanding of the concrete nature of languages with no written script, for instance, suggests at least the necessity for a greater questioning of the way in which the meanings of words function. But post-colonial writing has provided a distinct approach to the question of meaning because in these texts the 'message event' itself is so important. Whereas the history of European literary theory has been an arena in which the three poles of any meaning exchange – the language, the utterer or writer, and the hearer or reader – have been locked in a gladiatorial contest over the ownership of meaning, the nature of post-colonial writing has helped to reveal that the situation is not so simple. All three 'functions' of this exchange participate in the 'social' situation of the written text. The insistence of post-colonial critics that writing is a social practice with an indelible social function suggests the possibility that meaning, too, is a social accomplishment characterized by the participation of the writer and reader functions within the 'event' of the particular discourse.

The discursive 'event', which includes all the features of its production and consumption as 'communication', therefore becomes of paramount importance in post-colonial literatures because the 'participants' are potentially so very 'absent'. Indeed, unlike spoken discourse, the central problematic of studies of writing is *absence*. It is not so easy to see the written meaning as the 'situated accomplishment' of participants because the message 'event' occupies the apparent social fissure between the acts of writing and reading, the discursive space in which writer and reader as social actors never meet. No matter what the species of writing, it is the written text which stands apart in its own material integrity, apparently unrelated to persons, to language or to social systems in any purely mechanical or isomorphic way. How meaning is constructed in the writing by its absentee users becomes a much clearer question in cross-cultural writing systems, in which writer and reader might have ranges of experience and presuppositions which may not be expected to overlap greatly, if at all.

Thus the perspective brought to this discussion by post-colonial literatures is their accentuation of this phenomenon of *distance*: they present us with writers and readers far more 'absent' from each other than they would be if located in the same culture; they present a situation which in some cases (because the genre of continuous prose is so removed from some cultures) provides a totally ambivalent site for communication.[7] But most importantly, as we demonstrated (ch. 2, pp. 51–9) they provide, through the metonymic function of language variance, a writing which actually installs distance and absence in the interstices of the text.

Clearly, in this respect post-colonial theory concurs with aspects of the poststructuralist position. Post-colonial texts confirm that writing, by freeing language from the contingent situation, paradoxically gives language its greatest permanence, whilst, at the same time, giving meaning its greatest volatility because it opens up horizons within which many more sets of relations than those pertaining to the contingent situation can be established. Writing does not merely inscribe the spoken message or represent the message event, it becomes a new event.[8]

Post-colonial writing reveals this most clearly when its appropriation of english, far from simply inscribing either vernacular or 'standard' forms, creates a new discourse at their interface. This is a constitutive feature of english in which the notion of a standard 'code' is dismantled by the continuum of practice in which the language is formed. However, what occurs at the moment of such a dismantling is not endless deferral but the possibility of a meaning which functions in and through variance and usage rather than in opposition to it.

Of course, the immense 'distance' between author and reader in the post-colonial (cross-cultural) text certainly does act to undermine the privilege of both subject and object and to open meaning to a relational dialectic which 'emancipates' it (Derrida 1967b: 12). But this emancipation is limited by the 'absence' which is inscribed in the cross-cultural text, by that gulf of silence installed by those strategies of language variance which signify its difference (see ch. 2, especially pp. 61–77). The post-colonial text therefore does not 'create meaning' through the mere act of inscribing it, but rather indicates a potential and shifting horizon of possible meanings. Its capacity to 'mean', though, is circumscribed finally by that post-colonial silence (described above in chs 2, 3, and 4) which cannot be over-whelmed by any interpretation.

It is this concept of silence, not any specific cultural concept of meaning, which is the active characteristic linking all post-colonial texts. It is this same silence which also challenges metropolitan notions of polysemy, and which resists the absorption of post-colonial literatures into the new universalist paradigms which emerge in the wake of post-structuralist accounts of language and text. For this reason the post-colonial text raises very important questions for the current debate about meaning. It presents one of the clearest examples of the distance traversed when authors write and readers read in order to engage in communication. But it also serves to make it clear that the distance is traversed and that effective communication of important social and cultural issues does occur. It reminds us that all writing comes into being at the difficult meeting point between the acts of production and consumption; and that, although the 'social relationship' of writer and reader (the two absent subjects) is only ever really a function of their rela-tionship to the 'situation' of writing, nevertheless meaning is accomplished within the three-fold interaction between situation, author (function), and reader (function).

Value

Post-colonial literatures, spanning considerably diverse cul-tural traditions, have revealed with unequivocal clarity that value, like meaning, is not an intrinsic quality but a relation between the object and certain criteria brought to bear upon it. For instance, it is apparent that those people who have a strong link with an oral tradition judge literature quite differently from those who continue a written tradition. The presence of features of African orature in novels which, viewed with European assumptions about novel structure, may look like simple, even imitative reproductions of existing styles, must change our valuation of the text's 'originality' or its 'success'. For example, European critics have generally regarded the Malawian novelist David Rubadiri's *No Bride Price* (1967) as a simple, sociological account and a classic realist text. Yet criticism informed by an understanding of African oral performance and orature has shown how it reflects the pattern of traditional drum narratives which have been built into the structural features of the text (Shadle 1981). Faced with the vastly different criteria which people from diverse cultures obviously bring to bear upon all matters of judgement, we are presented with clear and extraordinary confirmation of the tenuousness of the notion of 'intrinsic value'.[9]

For Homi Bhabha, the process of evaluation in universalist and nationalist theories, which are overwhelmingly representationalist, becomes a process of establishing a mimetic adequacy. Because such theories propose a predominantly mimetic view of the relation between the text and a *given* pre-constituted reality, evaluation becomes the business of establishing the representative 'truth' of the text:

> The 'image' must be measured against the 'essential' or 'original' in order to establish its degree of *representativeness*, the correctness of the image. The text is not seen as *productive* of meaning but essentially reflective or expressive.
>
> (Bhabha 1984a: 100)

Consequently it is broadly within these empiricist terms that the discourses of universalist and nationalist criticism circulate and pose the questions of colonial difference and discrimination, and this is the essentially limiting factor which initiates their practice.

An 'intrinsic' value, linked as it is with an 'essential' meaning, is crucial to the operation of the universalist conception of the literary. The intrinsic and essential must, by definition, be universal, and of course the universal is the province of the discourse which imposes its criteria. In the evaluation of post-colonial literatures it is the centre which imposes its criteria as universal, and dictates an order in terms of which the cultural margins must always see themselves as disorder and chaos.

Post-colonialism as a reading strategy

The subversion of a canon is not simply a matter of replacing one set of texts with another. This would be radically to simplify what is implicit in the idea of canonicity itself. A canon is not a body of texts *per se*, but rather a set of reading practices (the enactment of innumerable individual and community assumptions, for example about genre, about literature, and even about writing). These reading practices, in their turn, are resident in institutional structures, such as education curricula and publishing networks. So the subversion of a canon involves the bringing-to-consciousness and articulation of these practices and institutions, and will result not only in the replacement of some texts by others, or the redeployment of some hierarchy of value within them, but equally crucially by the reconstruction of the so-called canonical texts through alternative reading practices.

Shakespeare's *The Tempest* has been subject to many such readings, for example George Lamming's in *The Pleasures of Exile* (1960), or Aimé Césaire's reworking of the play in an African context (Césaire 1969) or Jonathan Miller's famous 'colonial' 1970 production, and these continue to the present day.[10] Perhaps the most influential rereading of the play has been George Lamming's (1960) which dismantles the hierarchy of Prospero, Ariel, and Caliban. Caliban is no longer seen as the creature outside civilization 'on whose nature / Nurture can never stick' (IV.i.188–9), but as a human being (specifically a West Indian), whose human status is denied by the European claims to an exclusive human condition. Along with this goes a rereading of the political allegory of *The Tempest* in which the text's concern with the issue of 'good government' is extended to encompass Lamming's sense of the injustice of Prospero's dispossession of Caliban's inheritance – 'this island's mine, by Sycorax my mother'. Finally, this reading shows the duplicity and hypocrisy by which this dispossession is effected and stress is laid on the eagerness and willingness with which Caliban initially offers to share the fruits of the island with the ship-wrecked Prospero and his child. Prospero's assertion that in exchange he has given Caliban the gift of language is undercut in Lamming's reading by this fact of material dispossession, and thus Lamming stresses the justice of Caliban's response: 'and my profit on't / Is, I know how to curse' (I.ii.425–6).

Leslie Fiedler's *The Stranger in Shakespeare* concerns itself with the 'stranger', 'the borderline figure which defines the limits of the human'. It includes, as well as studies of the woman, the Jew, and the witch in Shakespeare, a study of the 'savage man of Ind' as 'stranger', centred on a reading of *The Tempest*. For Fiedler the play concerns the myth of America and of the Indian, who is the last stranger in Shakespeare – 'the last stranger, in fact, whom this globe can know, until we meet on his own territory, or in ours, the first extraterrestrial, whom until now we have only fantasised and dreamed' (Fiedler 1973: 208). This develops Fiedler's early perception of America (Fiedler 1968) as the first encounter of Europe with figures unaccommodatable within the medieval idea of a closed tripartite world (Europe, Afrique, and Asia). It does so in the context of Fiedler's reading of influential critics such as Fanon, from which he concludes that 'no respectable production of the play these days can afford to ignore the sense in which it is a parable of transatlantic imperialism, the colonisation of the West' (209). Although Fiedler's reading represents the more extreme claims for *The Tempest* as a visionary, indeed prophetic, play, a large number of other readings are prepared to go beyond the local, immediate life of the text to emphasize its New World imagery. For a useful account of the history of these readings see Frey (1979).

The Tempest has been perhaps the most important text used to establish a paradigm for post-colonial readings of canonical works. So established are these readings that in contemporary productions 'some emphasis on colonialism is now expected' (Griffiths 1983). In fact, more important than the simple re-reading of the text itself by critics or in productions has been the widespread employment of the characters and structure of *The Tempest* as a general metaphor for imperial–margin relations (Mannoni 1950; Dorsinville 1974) or, more widely, to characterize some specific aspect of post-colonial reality. For example, Chantal Zabus (1985) extends Lamming's reading of *The Tempest* to show how writers throughout the post-colonial world, particularly writers of the Anglophone and Francophone white and Black diasporas, have written answers to *The Tempest* from the perspectives of Caliban, Miranda, and Ariel. Lamming himself has re-written *The Tempest* from a post-colonial perspective in his novel *Natives of My Person*, and in *Water with Berries*. Joan Kirkby surveys American literature by identifying the hero figure as a Prospero-type who places himself over nature and seeks to subdue it by a massive exercise of his will (Kirkby 1985). She argues that Prospero remains the prototype for the order-imposing figures who permeate the works of such writers as Poe, Hawthorne, Melville, and James. Stephen J. Greenblatt has argued that the play is an example of the impact of a lettered culture on an unlettered one, and that Caliban's rejection of Prospero's gift of language is fully justified (Greenblatt 1976). There is, of course, a whole tradition of earlier American criticism which stresses the New World imagery of *The Tempest* and which can be read as part of that preoccupation in American culture, from Emerson onwards, with 'original relations' and 'brave new' concerns. In these readings Prospero's move outside society to the 'pastoral' retreat, from the social to the natural, is stressed (e.g. Marx 1964). This tradition is itself, as we have argued above (ch. 1 and ch. 4, pp. 34–5 and 135–6) paradigmatic of the post-colonial concern with the replacing of culture, and the renewal of the Walcottian 'Adamic' vision when social, cultural, and linguistic practices are exposed to radical and subversive change by their transportation to a New World. Prospero's experience in his New World certainly has that 'tartness' of experience which Walcott stresses as characteristically post-colonial.

A range of different ways of engaging with texts from the English and European canons have emerged in recent years. Eldred Durosimo Jones' *Othello's Countrymen* (1965) for example, presents a series of studies of the African in a range of Renaissance drama texts. More recently, David Dabydeen has examined the representations of the Black in English art and literature (Dabydeen 1985a; 1985b). *Hogarth's Blacks* (1985b), for example, details the iconography of the African in eighteenth-century English culture and again stresses the deprivileged and dehumanizing presentation of the African, typically placed in a socially inferior position and oppressed by his placement in the formal construction of the painting. Studies like this show how concepts of the inferiority of the African have been constructed in European art and literature over the last 300 years. Significantly, as the Marxist historian Basil Davidson has pointed out in a recent television series *Africa*, such a presentation did not occur in pre-Renaissance art. He draws attention to several instances of the presentation of Black saints in medieval carvings and statuary in cathedrals throughout Europe. (For a more scholarly account of this, see Devisse 1979). It is perhaps not erroneous to draw the conclusion that later pejorative constructions of Africanness went hand in hand with European expansion from the sixteenth century onwards.

Diana Brydon's 'Re-writing *The Tempest*' surveys a number of Canadian versions of the play and argues that in that context it is internalized, as opposed to the usual externalized post-colonial response in which there is an identification of the colonial with Caliban. For Canadian rewritings, at least in Canadian english, the emphasis has been on Miranda. Brydon suggests that this is consistent with english-speaking Canada's view of its colonial relationship with the motherland as 'dutiful daughter'. Significantly, Québecois rewriting, as she notes, follows African, Afro-American, and West Indian readings in externalizing the colonizing power as Prospero and identifying with Caliban (Brydon 1984a). Readings of this kind have, of course, not been restricted to *The Tempest*. Allan Gardiner (1987) and Helen Tiffin (1987) discuss the ways in which Caribbean and South African writers have redeployed the terms of Daniel Defoe's *Robinson Crusoe* to interrogate those originary tropes of invasion and colonization. Stephen Slemon (1986) has explored the radical re-writing by Wilson Harris of Dante's *Divine Comedy*, while John Hearne (1974) and other commentators have drawn attention to the appropriateness of Jean Rhys' strategies of writing back to Charlotte Bronte's *Jane Eyre* in *Wide Sargasso Sea*.

Once this kind of reading strategy is engaged, the possibilities for reconstructing the more or less hidden potentialities of other English literary texts, such as those of Austen, Thackeray, and

Swift, are revealed. Yasmine Gooneratne (1986), for example, has reread Jane Austen's *Mansfield Park* to uncover the silences of the text and its repression of the economic basis on which polite society erects its civilized practices. The 'dead silence' which greets Fanny's enquiries to her uncle, Sir Thomas Bertram, as to the slave trade is a resonant reminder of the hidden anguish and torture on which estates like Mansfield Park are raised. This silencing of the discussion of the source of the family's wealth is metonymic of the profounder silencing of the 'marginal' world of the slave both in this novel and, by implication, in the discourse of the novel in the period. At a time when slavery and emancipation were burning issues and the burden of a large body of evangelical Anglican and nonconformist pamphlets and tracts, the novel, as a form, is unable to handle this issue as a direct subject of the text. As Gooneratne notes,

> we are not allowed to trouble ourselves with such speculations. 'Let other pens dwell on guilt and misery,' writes Jane Austen, beginning the last chapter of *Mansfield Park*. 'I quit such odious subjects as soon as I can.' Her direct reference is to the sexual guilt and misery of Maria Bertram (now Rushworth) and Henry Crawford, but there are other sources of 'guilt and misery' (such as the barbaric trade in human flesh upon which the solid structure of Mansfield Park has been built) which have already been skirted delicately by her, or glossed over. (1986: 11–12)

From a post-colonial reading perspective such unspoken subjects may well become the crucial announcements of the text.

Reading strategies which have produced such analyses of specific texts and authors also have wider implications for post-colonialism as a general discursive practice. Some contemporary critics have suggested that post-colonialism is more than a body of texts produced within post-colonial societies, and that it is best conceived of as a reading practice. They argue that the post-coloniality of a text resides in its discursive features, and that modes of representation such as allegory or irony are transformed as a practice by the development of a post-colonial discourse within which they construct counter-discursive rather than homologous views of the world (Slemon 1987b).[11]

The first and most important result of the development of post-colonial theory has been to describe the features and projects of the substantial body of texts which exist in these societies and the ways in which these have appropriated the practice of writing from the centre. It would not be too much to claim that post-colonial writing now dominates, at least numerically, and perhaps in other ways too, the publication of literature in the english language. Second, in critical theory, the growth of important indigenous theories, and the adaptation of aspects of European theory to the analysis of post-colonial english writing have been important developments leading to the questioning of basic critical assumptions in all societies. Finally, post-colonial readings of traditional English literary texts and, more importantly, perhaps, the effects on the practices of reading by which such texts are canonized, are inevitable products of a changed world in which it is no longer possible to preserve repositories of a fixed and immutable system of values.

Post-colonial criticism appears to be following two major paths at present: on the one hand, via the reading of specific post-colonial texts and the effects of their production in and on specific social and historical contexts, and on the other, via the 'revisioning' of received tropes and modes such as allegory, irony, and metaphor and the rereading of 'canonical' texts in the light of post-colonial discursive practices. The former has been more closely associated with the traditional domain of the field, but the latter has begun, more recently, to produce powerfully subversive general accounts of textuality and concepts of 'literariness' which open up important new areas of concern.

Conclusion:
more english than English

The contemporary art, philosophy, and literature produced by post-colonial societies are in no sense continuations or simple adaptations of European models. This book has argued that a much more profound interaction and appropriation has taken place. Indeed, the process of literary decolonization has involved a radical dismantling of the European codes and a post-colonial subversion and appropriation of the dominant European discourses.

This dismantling has been frequently accompanied by the demand for an entirely new or wholly recovered pre-colonial 'reality'. Such a demand, given the nature of the relationship between colonizer and colonized, its social brutality and cultural denigration, is perfectly comprehensible. But, as we have argued, it cannot be achieved. Post-colonial culture is inevitably a hybridized phenomenon involving a dialectical relationship between the 'grafted' European cultural systems and an indigenous ontology, with its impulse to create or recreate an independent local identity. Such construction or reconstruction only occurs as a dynamic interaction between European hegemonic systems and 'peripheral' subversions of them. It is not possible to return to or to rediscover an absolute pre-colonial cultural purity, nor is it possible to create national or regional formations entirely independent of their historical implication in the European colonial enterprise.

Hence it has been the project of post-colonial writing to interrogate European discourse and discursive strategies from its position within and between two worlds; to investigate the means by which Europe imposed and maintained its codes in its colonial domination of so much of the rest of the world. Thus the rereading and the rewriting of the European historical and fictional record is a vital and inescapable task at the heart of the post-colonial enterprise. These subversive manoeuvres, rather than the construction of *essentially* national or regional alternatives, are the characteristic features of the post-colonial text. Post-colonial literatures/cultures are constituted in counter-discursive rather than homologous practices.

What is more, post-colonial literature and its study is essentially political in that its development and the theories which accompany this development radically question the apparent axioms upon which the whole discipline of English has been raised. Not only the canon of 'classical texts', the disruption of which by new, 'exotic' texts can be easily countered by a strategy of incorporation from the centre, but the very idea of English Literature as a study which occludes its own specific national, cultural, and political grounding and offers itself as a new system for the development of 'universal' human values, is exploded by the existence of the post-colonial literatures.

In spite of the fact that the situation still leaves much to be desired and that there are still many struggles for control to be won, there are three inescapable conclusions that post-colonial literatures force on the future of english studies and its institutions. First, in the same way that the existence of varieties of english has meant that the concept of a standard English has been exploded, the very existence of post-colonial literatures completely undermines any project for literary studies in english which is postulated on a single culture masquerading as the originating centre. Second, as a further implication of this decentring, the English canon is radically reduced within a new paradigm of international english studies. The works from the traditional canon which remain may reflect a radical revision and rereading. For example, what texts from the 'tradition' are selected for consideration and study may alter greatly. Kipling and Haggard may well take the place of George Eliot and Hardy, since their relationship to historical and political realities may come to seem more important. Post-colonial reading strategies acknowledge that readings and the formations which bring them into being are corrigible. They are not immutable 'truths' but changeable social and political constructions. Finally, the concept of literary studies in general will be revitalized by the perception that *all* texts are traversed by the kinds of complexities which the study of post-colonial literatures reveals.

Readers' guide

Theoretical and comparative studies

These texts either offer the most useful general accounts of the field, deal with seminal concepts or models of a theoretical nature in post-colonial criticism, or provide some of the most important statements about the provenance and direction of post-colonial literatures.

Achebe 1975   Chinua Achebe. *Morning Yet on Creation Day*. New York: Doubleday.
> An invaluable collection of essays by one of Africa's leading novelists and critics. One of the first writers to question Eurocentric perspectives in criticism and to call for a specifically African critical position.

Ashcroft 1978   W.D. Ashcroft, 'The function of criticism in a pluralist world', *New Literature Review*, no. 3.
> Discusses the function of criticism from a post-colonial perspective with particular attention to the operation of language and the communicability of cultural experience.

Barker *et al.* 1985   Francis Barker (ed.). *Europe and its Others*. Colchester: University of Essex.
> A two-volume collection of contemporary theoretical essays investigating the relationship between Europe and the rest of the world. Specifically looks at the way in which Europe through writing and mapping constituted the rest of the world as 'Other'.

Benterrak *et al.* 1984   Krim Benterrak, Stephen Muecke, and Paddy

Roe. *Reading the Country: Introduction to Nomadology*. Fremantle, W.A.: Fremantle Arts Centre Press.

A unique and fascinating discussion of the way in which the land can be seen to be a text on which the experience and identity of the Australian Aboriginal people is written. Raises issues of general import for the reappraisal of ideas of 'textuality' and land in pre-European indigenous cultures throughout the post-colonial world.

Bhabha 1984a   Homi K. Bhabha. 'Representation and the colonial text: some forms of mimeticism'. In *The Theory of Reading*. Ed. Frank Gloversmith. Brighton: Harvester, pp. 93–122.

A very important theoretical essay which argues for the transformation of the imitative element in 'colonial' writing. It stresses the metonymic function over the metaphoric and argues for the development of readings which stress the text as symptomatic of the post-colonial condition.

Brahms 1982   Flemming Brahms. 'Entering our own ignorance – subject–object relations in Commonwealth literature'. *WLWE*, 21 no. 2 Summer, 218–39.

From a sociological perspective this essay addresses the problems of inherited critical traditions with particular focus on concepts such as the wilderness experience, value system confusion, and 'demonization' (the radical and pejorative descriptions of other cultures which results from imperial aggression).

Brathwaite 1967–8   Edward Kamau Brathwaite. 'Jazz and the West Indian novel', *Bim*, 44, 275–84; 45, 39–51; 46, 115–26.

Suggests that an activity like jazz provides a better basis for the analysis of West Indian writing than Anglo-centred critical assumptions. Although this deals only with the West Indian novel, its search for the way out of a European aesthetic suggests the presence and possibility of similar attempts in other post-colonial writing.

Brathwaite 1984   Edward Kamau Brathwaite. *History of the Voice*. London: New Beacon.

This study, which Brathwaite describes as 'the development of nation language in Anglophone Caribbean poetry' directly addresses the issue of indigenizing 'voice' in english writing. The points he makes are generally applicable across the post-colonial literatures.

Brydon 1984   Diana Brydon. 'The thematic ancestor: Joseph Conrad, Patrick White and Margaret Atwood', *WLWE* 24, no. 2 Autumn.

Develops Macherey's approach in 'The thematic ancestor' and adapts its implications to post-colonial texts. Acknowledges the usefulness of poststructuralist and Marxist readings to these texts, but also vigorously asserts the prior existence of such constructions and concerns in post-colonial criticism itself.

Chinweizu, Jemie, and Madubuike 1983   Chinweizu, Onwuchekwa Jemie, and Ihechukwu Madubuike. *Towards the Decolonisation of African Literature*. Washington: Howard University Press.

An influential though contentious work which attempts a definitive view of African culture in the context of an active programme of cultural decolonization.

Coombes 1974   Orde Coombes (ed.) *Is Massa Day Dead? Black Moods in the Caribbean*. New York: Doubleday. (See especially Walcott, 'The muse of history' and Brathwaite, 'Timheri'.)

An indispensable collection of essays which examine crucial questions of cultural and literary decolonization.

Dash 1973   J. Michael Dash. 'Marvellous realism – the way out of Négritude', *Caribbean Studies*, 13, 57–70.

Develops Alexis's critique (see Alexis 1956 in gen. bib.) of the social and ideological implications of social realism and Négritude in the post-colonial world and proposes the need for an imaginative transformation of literary form as a project of post-colonial writing. Although this deals with Black writing in the Caribbean and Africa, its argument against the dichotomy asserted to exist between 'metaphysical' and 'social realist' traditions has implications for many other literatures and it has been widely influential outside the immediate area of its concerns.

Dathorne 1981   O.R. Dathorne. *Dark Ancestor: The Literature of the Black Man in the Caribbean*. Baton Rouge: Louisiana State University Press.

Example of an African writer discussing West Indian literature and suggesting the common ancestral cultural links of the Black diaspora; see also in this respect Omotoso 1984 and Ngugi 1972.

Docker 1984   John Docker. *In a Critical Condition*. Ringwood, Vic.: Penguin.

An idiosyncratic and contentious work which examines the development of criticism in Australia as a contest between various orthodoxies which have all oversimplified literary and critical issues. A provocative account of the progress of theoretical debates, particularly since the 1950s.

Dorsinville 1974   Max Dorsinville. *Caliban Without Prospero*. Erin, Ont.: Press Porcepic.

Develops a unique inter-cultural comparison between Québecois (French–Canadian) literature and that of the Black diaspora and from the evidence of these literatures argues for the distinction between 'dominated and dominating' forces as the principal determinant of literature.

Durix 1987   Jean-Pierre Durix. *The Writer Written: The Artist and Creation in the New Literatures in English*. Westport: Greenwood.

Discusses images of the artist in post-colonial literatures and considers specific works from New Zealand, the Caribbean, and Australia.

Fanon 1959   Frantz Fanon. *Black Skin White Masks*. London: Paladin 1970.

Develops the argument of his earlier work *The Wretched of the Earth* that colonization imposes a pattern which determines the individual and collective psychological features of post-colonial societies and argues the continuity of this pattern in such societies after independence, and the ongoing need to oppose this.

Frye 1971   Northrop Frye. *The Bush Garden*. Toronto: Anansi.

Well-known collection of essays on Canadian literature which has some broader relevance to post-colonial literatures.

Gates 1984   Henry Louis Gates Jr. (ed.). *Black Literature and Literary Theory*. London and New York: Methuen.

A collection of theoretical essays from various perspectives which examine Black writing and propose the emergence of a specific Black literary theory.

Griffiths 1978   Gareth Griffiths. *A Double Exile: African and West Indian Writing Between Two Cultures*. London: Marion Boyars.

An inter-cultural comparison which argues for the existence of a shared condition of cultural and linguistic 'exile' as a feature in both African and West Indian literatures. Also provides accounts of the major writers and introduces their work.

Gurr 1981   Andrew Gurr. *Writers in Exile: the Identity of Home in Modern Literature*. Brighton: Harvester.

Offers a definition of 'exile' as a constitutive feature in a wide variety of modern writers in english including those from the West Indies, Africa, Australia and New Zealand.

Harris 1983   Wilson Harris. *The Womb of Space; The Cross-Cultural Imagination*. Westport: Greenwood.

An indispensable and pioneering study of a syncretic view of culture which presents cross-culturality as the energizing imaginative factor in post-colonial writing, through a series of analyses of contemporary texts.

Holst-Petersen and Rutherford 1985   K. H. Petersen and A. Rutherford (eds). *A Double Colonization: Colonial & Post-Colonial Women's Writing*. Aarhus: Dangaroo.

A collection of essays illustrating the contiguity of colonization and sexist repression in the production of texts by women in post-colonial societies.

JanMohammed 1983   Abdul JanMohammed. *Manichaean Aesthetics: The Politics of Literature in Colonial Africa.* Amherst: University of Massachusetts Press.
   Discusses the presentations of Africa in white colonial and Black African writing and uses these to critique the privileged binary opposition at the heart of the European notion of Africa and the implications of this for contemporary African writing.

Jeyifo 1980   Biodun Jeyifo. *The Truthful Lie: Towards a Radical Sociology of African Literature.* London: New Beacon.
   A theoretical account of African literature and drama which argues the need to move beyond concerns with identity divorced from a radical political perspective. It also offers the only extensive account of the work of younger Nigerian writers such as Osofisan, Omotoso, Sowande.

King 1974   Bruce King (ed.). *Literatures of the World in English.* London: Routledge.

King 1980   Bruce King. *The New Literatures in English.* London: Macmillan.
   Two introductory accounts. The first offers discussions of national and regional literatures, the second provides an historical account readers may find useful for considering relationships between various post-colonial literatures.

Lamming 1960   George Lamming. *The Pleasures of Exile.* London: Allison and Busby.
   A personal account of Lamming's response to being a West Indian in the metropolitan centre of London which raises several issues, such as exile, margin–centre relations and canonicity, which are generally relevant to writers and critics in post-colonial literature. This includes the very influential essay on *The Tempest* which deals with the discursive effects of such canonical texts throughout the post-colonial world.

Lee 1974   Dennis Lee. 'Cadence, country, silence: writing in colonial space', *Boundary* 2, 3, 1, Fall, pp. 151–68.
   An important account of the relationship between language and place in colonized cultures.

Matthews 1962   John P. Matthews. *Tradition in Exile.* Toronto: University of Toronto Press.

Comparison of Australian and Canadian poetry that is still a pioneering study and the starting-point for comparative work in the field.

Maxwell 1965   D.E.S. Maxwell. 'Landscape and theme' in John Press (ed.). *Commonwealth Literature*. London: Heinemann, pp. 82–9.
Seminal essay in post-colonial literary criticism positing the inextricable relationship of language and place in these cultures.

McCrumb 1986   Robert McCrumb. *The Story of English*. London: Faber and Faber.
A popular and informative account of the spread of English throughout the world and its emergence as a world 'lingua franca'. It was based on a BBC television series which provoked controversy for its 'subversive' views when aired in 1986, though its assertions seem relatively conservative from a post-colonial perspective.

McDougall and Whitlock 1987   R. McDougall and G. Whitlock (eds). *Australian/Canadian Literatures in English: Comparative Perspectives*. North Ryde: Methuen.
A collection of comparative essays on Canadian and Australian literatures which deals with questions of general interest to all settler colony literatures.

Memmi 1965   Albert Memmi. *The Coloniser and the Colonised*. New York: Orion Press.
An early and influential sociological study of the destructive relationship between colonizers and colonized which, like Fanon, proposes a continuing and inevitable dialectic between these two elements of the post-colonial world.

New 1975   W.H. New. *Among Worlds*. Erin, Ontario: Press Porcepic.
An important survey which, although it has chapters on separate national literatures, is informed throughout by an awareness of the shared features, themes, and forms which traverse the field. In particular, there is a significant argument for the existence of certain techniques as characteristic post-colonial features, e.g. irony.

New 1978   W.H. New. 'New language new world' in *Awakened Conscience* ed. C.D. Narasimhaiah. Delhi: Sterling, pp. 360–77.
A widely comparative paper focusing on language and arguing that 'literature in the Commonwealth is an oral art'.

Ngugi 1986   Ngugi wa Thiong'o. *Decolonising the Mind: the Politics of Language in African Literature*. London: Currey.
The most cogent and powerful account advocating the need to 'decolonize' cultures, including the return to writing in pre-colonial languages. An essential text in the debate which has emerged on these issues in many post-colonial societies.

Ong 1982   Walter J. Ong. *Orality and Literacy: The Technologising of the Word*. London: Methuen.
A useful and comprehensive account of the relationship between written and oral forms of communication which offers a survey of the main ideas in the development of modern revisions of orality as a social and literary practice.

Schipper 1984   Mineke Schipper. 'Eurocentrism and criticism: reflections on the study of literature in the past and present', *WLWE*, 24, 1, Summer, 16–26.
A discussion of the Eurocentric nature of concepts of universality in literary criticism. (See also Larson 1973 in Bibliography.)

Slemon 1987b   Stephen Slemon. 'Monuments of empire: allegory/counter-discourse/post-colonial writing', *Kunapipi*, 9, 3, 1–16.
Argues that allegory as employed in post-colonial texts is not a conservative mode used to display existing structural and value assumptions but is a site for the struggle between colonialist discourse and post-colonial counter-discourse. Allegory employed thus is seen as a characteristic post-colonial form. Post-colonial writing is therefore seen as an important and distinctive form of interventionist textual and cultural criticism.

Soyinka 1976   Wole Soyinka. *Myth, Literature and the African World*. Cambridge: Cambridge University Press.
An influential and much-quoted account of the philosophic and aesthetic bases upon which African art and culture is constituted. It offers a critique of such diverse ideas as Négritude and contemporary ideological criticism, and develops Soyinka's individual and influential defence of the need for a 'local' but not essentialist stance in African criticism.

Spivak 1987   G.C. Spivak. *In Other Worlds: Essays in Cultural Politics*. New York and London: Methuen.
The essays collected in this volume examine some of the intersections between gender, class, and racial difference from the perspective of the post-colonial subject. Spivak's readings in 'subaltern' studies are especially relevant to the theory of post-coloniality.

Tiffin 1983   Helen Tiffin, 'Commonwealth literature: comparison and judgement' in Riemenschneider 1983, pp. 19–35.
Gives a brief account of the history of the development of Commonwealth literature and argues the need to move beyond evaluative accounts of post-colonial texts to a symptomatic account which stresses the post-colonial characteristics of the text.

Wasserman 1984   Renata Wasserman. 'Re-inventing the new world: Cooper and Alencar', *Comparative Literature*, 36, no. 2 (Spring), 130–45.

This essay compares North and South American writing in ways which have widespread relevance to the writing of settler cultures. In particular the problem of asserting difference whilst establishing equivalence in value between the literatures of the Old World and the New World literatures they were creating. Studies like this point the way towards the future development of inter-language studies in post-colonial societies.

Williams 1969   Denis Williams. *Image and Idea in the Arts of Guyana*. Georgetown, Guyana: National History and Arts Council. Ministry of Information.

An analysis of the development of 'catalysis', Williams' term for an indigenous Caribbean way of conceiving the creative hybridity within post-colonial cultures.

Zabus 1985   Chantal Zabus. 'A Calibanic tempest in Anglophone and Francophone new world writing', *Canadian Literature*, 104, Spring, 35–50.

Shows how writers through the Anglophone and Francophone white and Black diasporas have written answers to *The Tempest* from the perspective of Caliban, Miranda, and Ariel. An example of how the Empire has 'written back' through post-colonial readings of the classic canon.

A reading programme

Here is a suggested order for starting to read the material listed above. The following texts: King 1974 and 1980, New 1975 and 1978, Maxwell 1965, Tiffin 1983, Schipper 1984, Wasserman 1984, Fanon 1970, and Memmi 1965 offer a useful starting-point to large-scale formulations of the field and offer 'overviews'. These might usefully be read first. The essay on 'Colonialist criticism' in Achebe 1975 and the essays in Lamming 1960 are also useful starting texts following on from these.

Those of Chinweizu *et al.* 1980 and Ngugi 1986 argue the need to undertake a 'decolonizing' of post-colonial literatures. This is an important argument to read before the formulations of those who believe this to be a desirable but impossible project.

The texts by Matthews 1962, Gurr 1981, Griffiths 1978, Durix 1987, Dorsinville 1974, McDougall and Whitlock 1987, and Holst-Petersen and Rutherford 1985, offer useful comparative perspectives which open up ways in which critics have sought to combine and compare the various post-colonial literatures in constructing larger critical and cultural connections between them.

Ong 1982, McCrumb 1986, and Ashcroft 1978 offer accounts of language issues in the post-colonial world which help to define and refine the issues raised in the critical texts. They offer overviews of language and culture which are useful to read before the texts cited below are tackled.

Brathwaite 1967–8, Brydon 1984, Dash 1973, Slemon 1988, analyse some of the features, tropes, and modes by which post-colonial language and literatures order their new perceptions of their place, of time and history, and of the literary formulations of these.

Williams 1969, Frye 1971, Brathwaite 1984, JanMohammed 1983, Jeyifo 1980, Lee 1974, Coombes 1974, Soyinka 1975, and Docker 1984, though they each centre on a particular national or regional literature, analyse this from an important theoretical point of view which has implications for other post-colonial literatures.

Finally, the following texts reach out to a wide reading of post-coloniality across a range of literatures or address central critical issues which apply to all the literatures of the post-colonial world. They would best be read when some of the other material had been absorbed. We have included here, too, those essays and collections which draw most strongly on contemporary European critical theory and suggest the way in which this theory is being appropriated to the analysis of post-colonial societies and writing, though some of the accounts mentioned earlier draw on this theory in less comprehensive ways: Gates 1984, Harris 1983, Spivak 1987, Brahms 1982, Bhabha 1984a, Barker 1985, Benterrak *et al.* 1984, Zabus 1985.

Studies of national and regional literatures

This is a brief selection from the many specific accounts of national and regional literatures available. They are selected to introduce readers to some of the main writers and issues so that they can follow up the issues raised by the theoretical work in specific traditions. More extensive and specialist reference is available in the general bibliography but even this can only be a selection of the vast amount of material we might have included.

Africa

Cook 1977   David Cook. *African Literature: A Critical View.* London: Longmans.
   A wide-ranging survey of contemporary African writing in english, covering most areas and giving accounts of the leading authors and texts. Good starting-point.

Palmer 1979   Eustace Palmer. *The Growth of the African Novel*. London: Heinemann.

An introductory account of the development of the African novel, and the social and political background. It gives basic accounts of the major writers and movements.

Goodwin 1982   K.L. Goodwin. *Understanding African Poetry: a Study of Ten Poets*. London: Heinemann.

A useful account of modern poetry with detailed readings from the works of the major figures.

Gurr and Zirimu 1973   Andrew Gurr and Pio Zirimu. *Black Aesthetics*. Nairobi: East African Literature Bureau.

Despite its title, this is really a regional account of East African writing and the need to recognize and articulate a separate and distinctive aesthetic in the region separate from West African models which seemed dominant at the time. For East African writing see also the entries for Ngugi and Gurr & Calder in the Bibliography.

Gray 1979   Stephen Gray. *Southern African Literature: An Introduction*. London: Rex Collings.

An account of Black and white writing in Southern Africa. Gives an historical overview of the development and interaction of the various traditions of English and Afrikaans writing, and of the relationship between Black and white accounts.

Barnett 1983   Ursula A. Barnett. *A Vision of Order: A Study of Black South African Literature in English*. London and Amherst: Sinclair Brown / University of Mass. Press.

A more comprehensive account of Black writing in South Africa which covers the main figures and periods in greater detail than Gray.

Awoonor 1975   Kofi Awoonor. *The Breast of the Earth: a Survey of the History, Culture and Literature of Africa South of the Sahara*. Garden City: Doubleday.

An eminently readable personal account by one of Ghana's leading poets and novelists. It offers a broad historical survey of the development of African cultures.

Irele 1981   Abiola Irele. *The African Experience in Literature and Ideology*. London: Heinemann.

Introduces the main intellectual and ideological movements which have developed in Africa and relates them to literary production.

Gikandi 1987   Simon Gikandi. *Reading the African Novel*. London: James Currey.

An up-to-date survey of the main writers and ideas; provides a reliable introduction to the field.

Amuta 1989   Chidi Amuta. *The Theory of African Literature: Implications for Practical Criticism*. London: Zed Books.

An account of the issues raised by African writing from a modern Marxist perspective and the implications of this for contemporary critical practice.

Australia

Barnes 1969   John Barnes (ed.). *The Writer in Australia: 1856 to 1964*. Melbourne: Oxford University Press.

A valuable collection of critical works written since 1856 which indicate some of the major and continuing theoretical concerns of Australian criticism. Most useful for the period up to the 1950s.

Ferrier 1985   Carole Ferrier (ed.). *Gender, Politics and Fiction: Twentieth-Century Australian Women's Novels*. St Lucia: University of Queensland Press.

Goodwin 1986   Ken Goodwin. *A History of Australian Literature*. London: Macmillan.

A clear and readable account of the major developments in Australian literature.

Hergenhan 1988   L. Hergenhan (ed.). *The Penguin New Literary History of Australia*. Ringwood: Penguin.

A collection of essays on particular periods and movements. Useful because it collects a wide range of expertise in the various literary historical areas.

Kiernan 1974   Brian Kiernan. *Criticism*. Melbourne: Oxford University Press.

A short but useful history of literary criticism in Australia.

Moore 1971   Tom Inglis Moore. *Social Patterns in Australian Literature*. Sydney: Angus and Robertson.

One of the most systematic demonstrations of the 1950s 'nationalist' school of criticism in operation. A study which discusses various persistent traditions and 'essential' characteristics in Australian literature.

Shoemaker 1989   Adam Shoemaker. *Black Words White Page: Aboriginal Literature 1929–1988*. St Lucia: University of Queensland Press.

The first comprehensive account of all considerations of Indigenous literatures in post-colonial societies.

Wilkes 1981   G.A. Wilkes. *The Stockyard and the Croquet Lawn*. Melbourne: Edward Arnold.

A thematic account of Australian literature which proposes the existence of the 'genteel' and the populist nationalist traditions as the major opposing forces in its development.

Turner 1986   Graeme Turner. *National Fictions: Literature, Film and the Construction of Australian Narrative*. Sydney: Allen and Unwin.

An important innovative and cross-disciplinary account of narrative forms in Australian literature.

Canada

Atwood 1972   Margaret Atwood. *Survival: A Thematic Guide to Canadian Literature*. Toronto: Anansi.

Characterizes Canadian literature through various 'victim positions' which are adopted as strategies of survival for those oppressed within the colonial situation.

New 1989   W.H. New. *A History of Canadian Literature*. London and Toronto: Macmillan.

A broadly chronological, comprehensive account of Canadian literature. New's awareness of a post-colonial comparative framework informs his national/regional discussions.

Ricou 1973   Laurence Ricou. *Vertical Man / Horizontal World: Man and Landscape in Canadian Prairie Fiction*. Vancouver: UBC Press.

A thematic account of modern Canadian writing.

Moss 1974   John Moss. *Patterns of Isolation in English Canadian Fiction*. Toronto: McClelland & Stewart.

Argues for the dominance of the theme of isolation in Canadian fiction.

Blodgett 1982   E.D. Blodgett. *Configuration: Essays on the Canadian Literatures*. Ontario: ECW Press.

Essays in this volume take up 'other' Canadian literatures breaking down the older binary divisions, and substituting a 'polysemous/polyvalent' reading of the tradition.

Davey 1983   Frank Davey. *Surviving the Paraphrase: Eleven Essays on Canadian Literature*. Winnipeg: Turnstone.

A collection of essays on Canadian writing which, amongst other things, questions the dominance of the thematizing tendency in Canadian criticism.

Caribbean

Ramchand 1970   Kenneth Ramchand. *The West Indian Novel and Its Background*. London: Faber & Faber.

One of the earliest and still among the most comprehensive accounts of the sociology and literary provenance of West Indian fiction. It offers accounts of individual writers but relates these to an examination of the questions of audience and of literary production.

Ramchand 1976   Kenneth Ramchand. *An Introduction to the Study of West Indian Literature*. London: Faber & Faber.
A valuable introduction to the literature of the Caribbean.

Gilkes 1981   Michael Gilkes. *The West Indian Novel*. Boston: Twayne.
An up-to-date survey of the main prose fiction writers.

King 1979   Bruce King (ed.). *West Indian Literature*. London: Macmillan.
Useful essays on the history and background of West Indian literature and on eight major writers.

Brown 1978   L.W. Brown. *West Indian Poetry*. New York: Twayne.
An account of the main West Indian poets and their work.

Baugh 1978   Edward Baugh (ed.). *Critics on Caribbean Literature*. London: Allen and Unwin.
A collection of essays which covers important language and literary issues in the Caribbean.

Dance 1986   Darryl Cumber Dance (ed.). *Fifty Caribbean Writers: a Biobibliographical Critical Sourcebook*. New York: Greenwood.
An invaluable recent reference work offering accounts of all the major Caribbean writers.

India

Iyengar 1962   K.R. Srinivasa Iyengar. *Indian Writing in English*. Bombay: Asia Publishing House.
The pioneering account of Indian writing in English which offers a comprehensive survey of the field from the earliest times to the 1960s. It remains an indispensable reference book, despite the emergence of updated accounts in recent years.

Harrex 1977   S.C. Harrex. *The Fire and the Offering: the Modern Indian Novel in English*. Calcutta: Writers Workshop.
Comprehensive two-volume survey of modern Indian novelists, tracing themes and movements and offering critical accounts of the major figures.

Mukherjee 1971   Meenakshi Mukherjee. *The Twice-Born Fiction*. New Delhi and London: Heinemann.
A readable critical account of the main novelists in english in recent times in India. Deals with the language issue and with the characteristic features of the major novelists.

Narasimhaiah and Srinath 1984   C.D. Narasimhaiah and C.N. Srinath (eds). *A Common Poetic for Indian Literatures*. Mysore: Dhvanyāloka Publications.
Examines the idea that Indian writing in the various languages may offer the opportunity to rethink concepts of literature, meaning,

value, etc. in the light of Indian traditional and contemporary critical theory and practice.

Naik 1981   M.K. Naik. *A History of Indian Writing in English*. New Delhi: Sahitya Akademi.

A useful update of the work of early literary histories such as Iyengar, which also offers critical assessments of many of the leading poets, novelists etc.

McWatt 1985   Mark McWatt (ed.) *West Indian Literature and Its Social Context*. Barbados: Department of English, University of the West Indies.

Like the Baugh this is a collection which grounds literary analyses.

New Zealand

McCormick 1959   E.H. McCormick. *New Zealand Literature: a Survey*. Oxford: Oxford University Press.

A good guide to the earlier period up to the 1950s, though now out of date. An updated *Oxford History of New Zealand Literature* is in preparation.

Curnow 1973   Wystan Curnow. *Essays on New Zealand Literature*. Auckland: Heinemann.

A collection of essays which seeks to offer a coherent view of the literature and its development. It gathers material dealing with individual writers, New Zealand literary history, and Maori writing. A number of the essays move towards a theory of New Zealand literature.

Stead 1981   C.K. Stead. *In a Glass Case: Essays on New Zealand Literature*. Auckland: Oxford University Press/Auckland University Press.

This is a collection of Stead's essays on individual writers written between 1957 and 1981. A section on fiction writers and one on poets is followed by 'A poet's view' which contains the interesting early essay 'For the hulk of the world's between'.

United States

Reising 1987   Russell Reising. *The Unusable Past: Theory and the Study of American Literature*. New York and London: Methuen (New Accents), 1986.

A critical account of the development of a distinctive American literary criticism, its stages and periodization, and the significance of these for contemporary American critical accounts.

Fiedler 1960   Leslie Fiedler. *Love and Death in the American Novel*. New York: Stein & Day.

Although now a little dated, this still remains a classic for its heady readability and for its construction and exploration of the crucial differences between the American and British literary traditions.

Fussell 1965   Edwin Fussell. *Frontier: American Literature and the American West*. Princeton: Princeton University Press.

Argues that the experience of a new landscape and the condition of marginality fostered by the idea of a 'frontier' society was the overriding condition within which American writing developed its characteristic features.

Marx 1964   Leo Marx. *The Machine in the Garden: Technology and the Pastoral Idea in America*. New York: Oxford University Press.

Stresses the importance of the 'pastoral' as an aesthetic pattern in American writing and suggests that American culture is based on the idea of a redemptive journey away from society towards nature. It argues that *The Tempest* thus anticipates prophetically the moral geography of American Literature.

Boelhower 1987   William Boelhower. *Through a Glass Darkly: Ethnic Semiosis in American Literature*. New York: Oxford University Press.

An account which stresses the importance of the inscription of ethnicity in American literature.

Dearborn 1986   Mary Dearborn, *Pochahontas' Daughters: Gender and Ethnicity in American Literature*. New York: Oxford University Press.

Details and comments on the importance of such discourses of marginality as gender and race in the constitution and development of American Literature.

Pacific

Subramani 1985   Subramani. *South Pacific Literature: From Myth To Fabulation*. Suva: University of the South Pacific Press.

An analysis of South Pacific writing with particular reference to the importance of the oral tradition for the development of contemporary texts.

Subramani 1979   Subramani. *The Indo-Fijian Experience*. St Lucia: University of Queensland Press.

A collection of stories and critical articles articulating the experience of Fijian Indians.

Tiffin 1978   Chris Tiffin (ed.). *South Pacific Images*. St Lucia: SPACLALS.

A collection of critical essays on South Pacific topics, about half of which deal with Australia and half with the other literatures of the Pacific region.

Singapore/Malaysia

Thumboo 1976   Edwin Thumboo. *The Second Tongue*. Singapore: Heinemann Asia.

> The introduction to this anthology remains a useful overview of the issues posed by writing in this multicultural region.

Thumboo *et al.* 1985   *The Poetry of Singapore: an Anthology of ASEAN Literatures*. Singapore: ASEAN Committee on Culture and Information.

> Again an anthology, but with useful connecting essays and comments. So far no general history of the literature of the region has been produced.

Singh 1986   Kirpal Singh. *Critical Engagements: Focus on Singapore Poetry*. Singapore: Heinemann Asia.

> A collection of essays on Singapore poetry.

Fernando 1986   Lloyd Fernando. *Cultures in Conflict*. Singapore: Grahame Brash.

> A useful collection of essays by a leading Malaysian writer and critic, contains a number of accounts of the literature of the region and the social and linguistic forces involved in its development.

Hyland 1986   *Discharging the Canon: Cross Cultural Readings in Literature*. Singapore: Singapore University Press.

> A useful recent collection of articles on writing in the region.

Journals

Much of the most important material in this field may be found in the following journals. Although there are many journals which specialize in one or another of the national or regional literatures, they are too numerous to list here and so we restrict our list to those which address the field as a whole.

Kunapipi

A general journal of post-colonial writing, edited by Anna Rutherford, published in Aarhus, Denmark by Dangaroo Press. It has an annual issue which gives bibliographical regional surveys of the year's significant work. It also publishes important special issues in book form.

World Literature Written in English (WLWE)

A general journal of post-colonial writing first published in the United States, now edited by G.D. Killam, and published in Guelph, Canada. Also contains bibliographical updates from time to time.

The Journal of Commonwealth Literature (JCL)
One of the oldest journals in the field, currently edited by Alistair Niven. Despite its title it reaches out to embrace more contemporary formulations of the field than Commonwealth models. Contains extensive annual bibliographies which are especially useful for areas such as Singapore/Malaysia, or East Africa where much of the most useful criticism exists in article form.

New Literature Review
A journal which specializes in the inter-relationship between post-colonial texts and literary theory. Often published as Special Issues on relevant areas or themes. Edited by a collective, with an editorial address at the University of Wollongong, Australia.

ACLALS Bulletin
A service journal and newsletter of the International Organizing Committee of the Association for Commonwealth Literature and Language Studies.

SPAN
A service journal and newsletter of the South Pacific Association for Commonwealth Literature and Language Studies – SPACLALS (other regional associations exist, such as the Canadian Association CACLALS; and European Association EACLALS). These are often responsible, in association with ACLALS for publishing important collections of essays from Regional Conferences. See below.)

Ariel: A Review of International English Literature
A general critical journal edited and produced at the University of Calgary, Canada. It has concentrated in recent years on post-colonial aspects of english writing.

Commonwealth
A general journal published from the Sorbonne III, Paris, and the University of Dijon.

The Literary Criterion
A general literary journal with a special interest in material pertaining to post-colonial literatures. Corresponding editor C.N. Srinath, University of Bangalore, India.

The following special issues of journals not normally devoted to this field will, nevertheless, be found useful:
Critical Enquiry, 12, 1, Autumn 1985. Special issue on race, writing, and difference.

Screen, 24, 2, March/April 1983. Special issue on Race and Colonialism in filmic texts.
Oxford Literary Review, 9, 1 & 2 1987. Special issue on colonialism.

Collections

There are a large number of useful collections of essays, most of which have emerged from the publication of the proceedings of various conferences over the last 25 years. Such publications have been a characteristic and important means of developing and promoting this area of study. It is impossible to comment in detail on the individual essays since they are both too numerous and too varied in their subject matter and quality. Though we have specified a few of the most important of these in the reading list above and in the bibliography there are many others which might well repay a reader's attention.

Press 1965   John Press (ed.). *Commonwealth: Unity and Diversity Within a Common Culture*. London: Heinemann.
Goodwin 1968   K.L. Goodwin (ed.). *National Identity*. London: Heinemann.
Rutherford 1972   Anna Rutherford (ed.). *Commonwealth*. Aarhus: Aarhus University Press.
Sellick 1972   R. Sellick (ed.). *Myth and Metaphor*. Adelaide: CRNLE Flinders University.
Maes Jelinek 1975   Hena Maes-Jelinek (ed.). *Commonwealth Literature and the Modern World*. Brussels: Didier.
Niven 1975   Alastair Niven (ed.). *The Commonwealth Writer Overseas: Themes of Exile and Expatriation*. Stirling: ACLALS.
Narasimhaiah 1978   C.D. Narasimhaiah (ed.). *Awakened Conscience: Studies in Commonwealth Literature*. New Delhi: Sterling.
Massa 1979   Daniel Massa (ed.). *Individual and Community in Commonwealth Literature*. Msida: University of Malta Press.
Gooneratne 1980   Yasmine Gooneratne. *Diverse Inheritance*. Adelaide: CRNLE Flinders University.
Nandan 1983   Satendra Nandan (ed.). *Language and Literature in Multi-Cultural Contexts*. Suva: University of the South Pacific Press.
Parameswaran 1983   U. Parameswaran (ed.). *The Commonwealth in Canada*. Calcutta: Writers Workshop.
Riemenschneider 1983   Dieter Riemenschneider (ed.). *History and Historiography of Commonwealth Literature*. Tübingen: Gunter Narr.
Olinder 1984   Britta Olinder. *A Sense of Place*. Gothenburg: University of Gothenburg Press.
Amur and Desai 1984   G.S. Amur and S.K. Desai (eds). *Essays in Comparative Literature and Linguistics*. New Delhi: Sterling.

McDermott 1984   Doireann Macdermott (ed.). *Autobiographical and Biographical Writing in the Commonwealth*. Barcelona: Sabadell.

Simpson 1985   Peter Simpson (ed.). *The Given Condition: Essays in Post-Colonial Literatures*. Span no. 21; Christchurch: SPACLALS.

Nightingale 1986   Peggy Nightingale (ed.). *A Sense of Place in the New Literatures in English*. St Lucia: University of Queensland Press.

Bock and Wertheim 1986   Hedwig Bock and Albert Wertheim (eds). *Essays on Contemporary Post-Colonial Fiction*. Munich: Huebeer.

McGaw 1987   William McGaw (ed.). *Inventing Countries: Essays in Post-Colonial Literatures*. Span 24; Wollongong; SPACLALS.

Bennett and Miller 1988   Bruce Bennett and Susan Miller (eds). *A Sense of Exile: Essays in the Literature of the Asia-Pacific Region*; CSAL; University of Western Australia.

Notes

Introduction

1 The development of English immediately before and after the First World War was also the result of the growing commercial and imperial rivalry between the great powers with the emergence of a strong Germany under Prussian influence in the late nineteenth century. English studies were designed to meet the challenge of German philology and its claims to dominance in language studies.

2 Significantly, despite America's emergence as a super-power this process of literary hegemony has not occurred there. Although many West Indian and African writers have settled in America they are not claimed as American, so much as contributors to Black writing.

3 Whilst the orthography employed may seem unfortunate, suggesting by its use of the upper and lower cases respectively that the variants are lesser, this is clearly not our intention. We prefer to see the use of the lower case as a sign of the subversion of the claims to status and privilege to which English usage clings.

1 Cutting the ground: critical models of post-colonial literatures

1 For example, in India, critics like C.D. Narasimhaiah, who supported the development of courses in American literature, were

subsequently able to argue by analogy for the introduction of indigenous Indian english texts to the tertiary curricula.

2 Although Soyinka's analysis here is based on the assertion of an African reality which is 'a product and a vindication of a separate earth and civilisation', and so is itself arguably limited by the polarizing tendency this implies, his reference to a rejection of 'Manicheisms' echoes the critique of such polarizing tendencies in the dominant European intellectual paradigms developed by later post-colonial critics such as Wilson Harris (see ch. 5). Sartre's position on Négritude is a timely reminder that post-colonial theory must be careful not to become a colonizer in its turn and must balance its rejection of monolithic cultural models against the need to be conscious always of the very distinctive features of climate, history, society, economics, and race which its discourse must acknowledge. It must not confuse the 'cross-cultural' and comparative with a new international 'universalism'.

3 Laye's work, though in French, is a very clear example of the re-placing of language on new territory and in its subversive re-orientations of subject in relation to place it echoes themes very common in post-colonial english texts.

4 As a monolithic British hegemony is faced with challenges to its centrality, and as even the notion of centrality itself is repudiated, 'literature' is seen to be no longer invested in a set of canonical practices, but rather to be generated by a creatively unstable dialectic; in Jameson's terms, 'the opposing sides of a discourse with a common code' (Jameson 1981).

5 E.D. Blodgett, for example, has pointed this out in his attack on the 'monolithic' tendencies of Canadian criticism (Blodgett 1982).

2 Re-placing language: textual strategies in post-colonial writing

1 The importance of this process has been increasingly recognized in European contexts. In the proceedings of a conference on The Linguistics of Writing at the University of Strathclyde in 1986, Colin McCabe noticed that the 'most important development of English in this century is how a whole variety of peoples subjected to the language of the imperial master have re-appropriated it for their own uses' (Fabb *et al.* 1987: 288). Significantly, though, this statement was part of an acknowledgement of the justice of objections raised at the conference by post-colonial linguists to the absence of any concern with this issue in the papers presented.

2 All settler cultures have been and are becoming increasingly multilingual, though they have not, with the exception of Canada, adopted an official bilingual or multilingual policy.

3 It is important that these categories not be seen as prescriptive. Even those societies which are officially bilingual or diglossic will probably be polydialectical to some degree. In all the categories there will be complexities and variations which actually endorse a major point of this chapter, that all english usage is located on a continuum.

4 Although the theory of the Creole continuum has not been seen by linguists as a 'post-colonial' theory, and although it is, of course, not only 'post-colonial' theorists who criticize Saussurian structuralism, there is no doubt that the view of language which emerges from continuum studies stems from the abrogation of the normative and standard in ways that are crucial to post-colonial discourse.

5 Although when using terms like 'colloquial speech' we should keep in mind the fact that such terms are themselves produced by and operate to verify the centre–margin distinction between 'standard' and 'variant' english. The 'colloquial' is most likely just as much the 'standard' for its place and time as any other variant.

6 This signification of class difference has become less true, for instance, of Melanesian *tok pisin* in Papua New Guinea since there it has become the signifier of a national culture.

4 Theory at the crossroads: indigenous theory and post-colonial reading

1 Only those ex-colonies such as Malaysia, Singapore, or Hong Kong, which have access to the massive body of Chinese cultural traditions or to the newer but still influential traditions of the Malay–Indonesian region, offer similar situations, and in both cases it must be said that so far this has happened on a much lesser scale.

2 Unfortunately, perhaps, this has sometimes led Indian critics to an excessive denigration of Indian writing in english. Comments such as the following are all too depressingly common: 'A writer like Salman Rushdie rushing to fame leaves one quite surprised; we had not thought that the book had so much in it; nor would I say that R.K. Narayan has that much in him to be made so much of' (Subramanyam 1984).

3 The difference in colonial administrative systems and educational policies resulted in an assimilationist programme in Francophone Africa which did not occur in the Anglophone colonies. This

prevented the development of pan-African theories by limiting the access of Anglophone African intellectuals to a common language and to centres such as the metropolitan universities, where such theories were largely developed.

4 For an interesting critique of this position, see Dasenbrock (1987). He argues that the 'intelligible and meaningful are not completely overlapping, synonymous terms. Indeed, the meaningfulness of multicultural works is in large measure a function of their unintelligibility for part of their audience. Multicultural literature offers us above all an experience of multiculturalism, in which not everything is likely to be wholly understood by every reader' (12). In fact language, as we argued in ch. 2 above (pp. 51–7), may in the multicultural text serve to 'install' the gap between cultures as its dominant metonymic referent.

5 Gugelberger is not, of course, an African critic but his work articulates the position of a number of younger African writers and is useful to peruse in the context of the discussion in this chapter.

6 It is the settler colonies which focus the need for a distinction between the *Indigenous* cultures, such as the Australian Aboriginal, North American Indian, and Maori, and those *indigenizing* strategies which attempt to construct in the settler culture a distinct, non-European relationship with place. Failure to make this distinction might prove to be yet another kind of colonial domination.

7 The same process occurred in Brazil in the works of Jose Alencar, as Wasserman also notes, thereby stressing its origin within a general discourse of post-coloniality and not in an exclusive condition of Anglo-American relations.

8 In an article published in *Canadian Literature* Stephen Slemon explores magic realism in two contemporary Canadian novels and discusses the ways in which it is a particularly post-colonial mode (Slemon 1987a).

5 Re-placing theory: post-colonial writing and literary theory

1 It is tempting to attribute the persistence of New Critical theory in many parts of the post-colonial world (e.g. India) to this side-effect, though this might be difficult to sustain over the whole context of post-colonial societies.

2 One must note, however, that the American interpretation of the rise of New Criticism is that it was deeply implicated in domestic and international right-wing movements.

3 The paradigmatic historical demonstration of this occurred in the

Treaty of Waitangi which the British government signed with the Maori chiefs in 1840. The sovereignty over their land which the chiefs were asked to cede, their *mana*, was translated in the Treaty as *Kawanatanga* or governance. No Maori would ever cede the sacred condition of sovereignty enclosed in the word *mana*. Thus the moment of colonial domination in New Zealand was a linguistic moment. Language maintained its power through the ability to disrupt and fracture the modalities of meaning and truth, to constitute the Maori as subject and provide the terms in which political domination was to be effected. But it maintained this power through colonial control of the means of communication of which the Treaty was an eloquent sign.

4 Though recent critics have questioned whether JanMohammed's practice in this enterprise is not vitiated by a continuing tendency to 'establish one to one relationships between text and context' which results in his study not producing 'the scenario it previews' (Parry 1987: 48).

5 Benita Parry, who opposes syncretic views of post-colonial culture ('which I take to be the resolution of colonialism's cultural manichaeaism in the harmonisation of alterities') as politically disabling, prefers JanMohammed's earlier formulations (JanMohammed 1984) which stressed the need to 'cultivate and celebrate marginality' (Parry 1987: 50). See below for a discussion of this dispute in the wider context of contemporary dissatisfaction with the politics of colonial discourse theories.

6 Studies such as Fritschi's, reflecting as they do a universal theory of orality deriving from Walter Ong, have been subjected to criticism for failing to account adequately for the differences between various oral cultures. See Schmidt (1985).

7 One qualification to this may be that the sharing of an imperial system of education and cultural patronage, issuing forth in the widespread uniformity of curricula, readers, and other cultural 'guides' used throughout Britain's empire, considerably ameliorates this distancing within the post-colonial world.

8 However one of the several points at which post-colonial theory announces its separation from poststructuralism is in the acceptance of the 'voice'. Post-colonial writing *represents* neither speech nor local reality but constructs a discourse which may intimate them. This distinction ought to be made as clearly as possible, because although writing is a new ontological event it does not cut itself off from speech. In fact, in post-colonial texts the inscription or intimation of the vernacular modality of local speech is one of the most important strategies of appropriation.

9 Although this term, coined by G.E. Moore, identifies a rather

circumscribed philosophical debate, it is a fascinating demonstration of the link between questions of value and questions of meaning. The idea of intrinsic value is logically and historically attached to the idea of determinate objective meaning, of the representation in words of an unmediated reality, and veridical perception. If intrinsic value exists, then arguably the aim of criticism is to attain the point of view of the ideal observer in order to establish that value. The evaluation of literature thus becomes a categorization according to criteria that are as inflexible as they are arbitrary. Any evaluation gives more idea about the valuing system than the inherent value of the object. But this knowledge is appropriated as a strength in a literature in which difference and absence are centrally located.

10 Interestingly, though, the possibilities for readings of this play which saw the political and cultural implications of the relationship between Caliban and Prospero predate Lamming's or Césaire's insights by more than a hundred years. J.S. Phillpot's introduction to the 1873 Rugby edition of Shakespeare notes that 'The character may have had a special bearing on the great question of a time when we were discovering new countries, subjecting unknown savages, and founding fresh colonies. If Prospero might dispossess Caliban, England might dispossess the aborigines of the colonies' (Furness Variorum Edition: 383). Significantly, this reading dates from the period when the discourse of colonialism, in its late nineteenth-century imperial form, is being vigorously constructed. Perhaps for this reason it has a visibility which it is not to have again until that structure is in process of being dismantled. (We are indebted to H.M. Felperin for this reference, which forms part of his larger study of Shakespeare criticism, in progress.) The Furness Variorum also cites the philosopher Renan's 1878 version in his play *Caliban*, in which Caliban is a representative 'of red-republicanism, or perhaps socialism', whose one remaining grace is his anti-clericalism by whose virtue he rescues Prospero from the Inquisition when he has assumed his power *à la* Napoleon following his 'revolution'. Also, for a very useful account of productions of the play from the early nineteenth century to the present day and the ways in which they reflect the changing attitudes to and awareness of the issues of colonization, see Griffiths (1983).

11 For example, Stephen Slemon even claims Swedish writer Sven Delblanc's *Speranza*, a European anti-colonial work which employs allegory counter-discursively, for post-colonial discourse. This extreme form of the assertion does not adequately address the argument that all discourses are finally situated in reading practices which are specific, constructed, and therefore subject to social and

cultural control, but it is an interesting, if provocative, extension of the claims of a discourse which, as many post-colonial critics have noted, has suffered a good deal of provocation itself in its time.

Bibliography

The bibliography includes all the works cited in the text, and some additional useful publications.

Achebe 1963a Chinua Achebe. *No Longer at Ease*. London: Heinemann.

Achebe 1963b Chinua Achebe. 'Africa and her writers'. *Massachusetts Review* 1963, in Achebe 1975.

Achebe 1964 Chinua Achebe. 'The role of a writer in a new nation'. *Nigeria Magazine*, no. 81.

Achebe 1965 Chinua Achebe. 'The novelist as teacher', *New Statesman* 29 January 1965, in Achebe 1975.

Achebe 1975 Chinua Achebe. *Morning Yet on Creation Day*. New York: Doubleday.

Achebe 1978 Chinua Achebe. 'An image of Africa'. *Research in African Literatures*, 9.1 (Spring).

Afolayan 1971 'Language and sources of Amos Tutuola' in Heywood 1971.

Alexis 1956 J.S. Alexis. 'Of the marvellous realism of the Haitians'. *Presence Africaine*, nos. 8–10.

Alleyne 1963 M.C. Alleyne. 'Communication and politics in Jamaica'. *Caribbean Studies*, 3, no. 2.

Allis 1982 Jeanette Allis. 'A case for regional criticism of West Indian literature'. *Caribbean Quarterly*, 28, 1 & 2.

Althusser 1970 Louis Althusser. 'Ideology and ideological state apparatuses (notes towards an investigation)' in *Lenin. Philosophy and Other Essays*. Trans. Ben Brewster. London: New Left Books. 1971.

Amuta 1983 Chidi Amuta. 'Criticism, ideology and society: the instance of Nigerian literature'. *Ufahuma*, 12, 2.

Amuta 1984 Chidi Amuta. 'Ideology and form in the contemporary Nigerian novel'. *Commonwealth: Essays and Studies*, 7, 1.

Amuta 1989 Chidi Amuta. *The Theory of African Literature: Implications for Practical Criticism*. London: Zed Books.

Anantha Murthy 1986 Interview with G. Griffiths recorded at Dhvanyāloka Institute, Mysore.

Aniebo 1978 I.N.C. Aniebo. *The Journey Within*. London: Heinemann.

Anozie 1970 Sunday O. Anozie. *Sociologie du Roman Africain*. Paris: Aubier-Montaigne.

Anozie 1981 Sunday O. Anozie. *Structural Models and African Poetics: Towards a Pragmatic View of Literature*. London: Routledge and Kegan Paul.

Anozie 1984 'Négritude, structuralism, deconstruction' in Gates 1984.

Anthony 1973 Michael Anthony. 'Sandra Street' in *Cricket in the Road*. London: Heinemann.

Appiah 1984 'Strictures on structures: the prospects for a structuralist poetics of African fiction' in Gates 1984.

Armah 1976 Ayi Kwei Armah. 'Larconry: or fiction as criticism of fiction', *Asemka*, no. 4.

Ashcroft 1978 W.D. Ashcroft. 'The function of criticism in a pluralist world', *New Literature Review*, no. 3.

Ashcroft 1987 W.D. Ashcroft. 'Language issues facing Commonwealth writers: a reply to D'Costa', *Journal of Commonwealth Literature*, 22, no. 1.

Ashcroft 1988 W.D. Ashcroft. 'Is that the Congo?: language as metonymy in post-colonial writing', *Literature and National Cultures*. Ed. Brian Edwards. Geelong, Victoria: Centre for Studies in Literary Education, Deakin University.

Atwood 1972 Margaret Atwood. *Survival: A Thematic Guide to Canadian Literature*. Toronto: Anansi.

Awoonor 1971 Kofi Awoonor. *This Earth My Brother: An Allegorical Tale of Africa*. New York: Doubleday.

Awoonor 1973 Kofi Awoonor. 'Voyager and the Earth'. *New Letters*, 40, no. 1 (Autumn).

Awoonor 1975 Kofi Awoonor. *The Breast of the Earth: A Survey of the History, Culture and Literature of Africa South of the Sahara*. Garden City: Doubleday.

Bailey 1966 Beryl L. Bailey. *Jamaican Creole Syntax*. Cambridge: Cambridge University Press.

Baker 1976 H.A. Baker. *Reading Black: Essays in the Criticism of African, Caribbean and Black American Literature*. Ithaca: Cornell University Press.

Bakhhin, M. 1981 *The Dialogic Imagination*; ed. M. Holquist, trans. C. Emerson and M. Holquist. Austin: University of Texas Press.

Barker *et al.* 1985 Francis Barker *et al.* (eds). *Europe and its Others*. Colchester: University of Essex.

Barnes 1969 John Barnes (ed.). *The Writer in Australia: 1856–1964*. Melbourne: Oxford University Press.

Barthold 1981 Bonnie Barthold. *Black Time: Fiction of Africa, the Caribbean and the United States*. New Haven: Yale University Press.

Batsleer 1985 Janet Batsleer *et al. Rewriting English*. London: Methuen.

Beier 1980 Ulli Beier (ed.). *Voices of Independence: New Black Writing from Papua New Guinea*. St Lucia: University of Queensland Press.

Bennett 1982 Meredith Bennett. 'The poet as language maker: Sri Chinmoy', *New Literature Review*, no. 10.

Benterrak *et al.* 1984 Krim Benterrak, Stephen Muecke, and Paddy Roe. *Reading the Country: Introduction to Nomadology*. Fremantle, W.A.: Fremantle Arts Press.

Bhabha 1983 Homi K. Bhabha. 'The Other question . . .', *Screen*, 24, 6 (Nov.–Dec.).

Bhabha 1984a Homi K. Bhabha. 'Representation and the colonial text: a critical exploration of some forms of mimeticism', in *The Theory of Reading*. Ed. Frank Gloversmith. Brighton: Harvester.

Bhabha 1984b Homi K. Bhabha. 'Of mimicry and man: the ambivalence of colonial discourse', *October*, 28 (Spring).

Bhabha 1985 Homi K. Bhabha. 'Signs taken for wonders: questions of ambivalence and authority under a tree outside Delhi. May 1817', *Critical Inquiry*, 12, 1 (Autumn).

Bickerton 1973 Derek Bickerton. 'The nature of a Creole continuum', *Language*, 49, no. 3.

Bloch 1983 Maurice Bloch. *Marxism and Anthropology*. Oxford: Oxford University Press.

Blodgett 1982 E.D. Blodgett. *Configuration: Essays on Canadian Literatures*. Downsview, Ontario: ECW Press.

Blodgett 1986 E.D. Blodgett. 'European theory and Canadian criticism', in *Zeitschrift der Gesellschaft für Kanada Studien*, 6, no. 2.

Brahms 1982 Flemming Brahms. 'Entering our own ignorance – subject–object relations in Commonwealth literature'. *World Literature Written in English*, 21, no. 2 (Summer).

Brathwaite 1967–8 E.K. Brathwaite. 'Jazz and the West Indian novel', *Bim*, 44, 275–84; 45, 39–51; 46.

Brathwaite 1971 E.K. Brathwaite. *The Development of Creole Society 1770–1820*. London: Oxford University Press.

Brathwaite 1973 E.K. Brathwaite. *The Arrivants: A New World Trilogy* (Anansi). London: Oxford U. P.

Brathwaite 1974 E.K. Brathwaite. 'Timehri' in Coombes (ed.) 1974.

Brathwaite 1976 E.K. Brathwaite. 'The love axe: developing a Caribbean aesthetic', in Baker 1976; *Bim*, 61–3, 1977–8.

Brathwaite 1977 E.K. Brathwaite. 'Caliban, Ariel, and unprospero in the conflict of Creolisation: a study of the slave revolt in Jamaica in 1831–32', *Comparative Perspectives on Slavery in New World Plantation Societies*. Eds. Vera Ruben and Arthur Turden. New York: New York Academy of Sciences.

Brathwaite 1982 E.K. Brathwaite. *Sun Poem*. London: Oxford University Press.

Brathwaite 1984 E.K. Brathwaite. *History of the Voice*. London: New Beacon.

Brewster 1989 Anne Brewster. *Towards a Semiotic of Post-Colonial Discourse*. Singapore: National University Press.

Brown 1978 L.W. Brown. *West Indian Poetry*. New York: Twayne.

Brown 1978 Russell M. Brown. 'Critic, culture, text: beyond thematics', *Essays in Canadian Writing*, no. 11 (Summer).

Brydon 1981 Diana Brydon. 'Landscape and authenticity', *Dalhousie Review*, 61, 2 (Summer).

Brydon 1984a Diana Brydon. 'Rewriting *The Tempest*', *World Literature Written in English*, 23, 1 (Winter).

Brydon 1984b Diana Brydon. 'The thematic ancestor': Joseph Conrad, Patrick White and Margaret Atwood', *World Literature Written in English*, 24, no. 2 (Autumn).

Campbell Praed 1981 Mrs Campbell Praed. *Policy and Passion*. London: Richard Bentley & Son.

Césaire 1945 Aimé Césaire. *Cahier d'un retour du pays natale*. Paris: Présence Africaine, 1971.

Césaire 1969 Aimé Césaire *Une tempête: d'apres 'La Tempête' de Shakespeare – Adaptation pour un théâtre nègre*. Paris: Editions du Seuil, 1974.

Chiapelli 1976 Fredi Chiapelli (ed.).

First Images of America: the Impact of the New World on the Old. Berkeley: University of California Press.

Chinmoy 1978 Sri Chinmoy. *From the Source to the Source.* New York. Cited in Bennett 1982.

Chinweizu, Jemie, and Madubuike 1975a Chinweizu, Onwuchekwa Jemie, and Ihechukwu Madubuike. 'Towards the decolonisation of African literature', *Transition*, no. 48.

Chinweizu. Jemie, and Madubuike 1979 Chinweizu, Onwuchekwa Jemie and Ihechuckwu Madubuike. 'Controversy. The Leeds Ibadan connection: the scandal of modern African literature', Okike 13, 1979.

Chinweizu. Jemie and Madubuike 1983 Chinweizu, Onwuchekwa Jemie and Ihechuckwu Madubuike. *The Decolonisation of African Literature*, vol. 1. Washington: Howard University Press.

Chomsky 1965 Noam Chomsky. *Aspects of the Theory of Syntax.* Cambridge, Mass.: MIT Press.

Clarke 1874 Marcus Clarke. *For the Term of his Natural Life.* Sydney: Angus and Robertson, 1974.

Colmer 1977 Rosemary Colmer. 'Kofi Awoonor: critical prescriptions and creative practice', paper delivered at SPACLALS Conference, University of Queensland: Brisbane, May 1977.

Coombes 1974 Orde Coombes (ed.). *Is Massa Day Dead? Black Moods in the Caribbean.* New York: Doubleday.

Curnow 1960 Allen Curnow. *The Penguin Book of New Zealand Verse.* Harmondsworth: Penguin.

Dabydeen 1985a David Dabydeen. *The Black Presence in English Literature.* Manchester: Manchester University Press.

Dabydeen 1985b David Dabydeen.

Hogarth's Blacks: Images of Blacks in Eighteenth Century English Art. Mundelstrup: Dangaroo.

Dasenbrock 1987 Reed Way Dasenbrock 'Intelligibility and meaningfulness in multicultural literature in English', *PMLA*, 102, 1 (January).

Dash 1973 J. Michael Dash. 'Marvellous realism – the way out of Négritude', *Caribbean Studies*, 13.

Dauber 1977 Kenneth Dauber. 'Criticisms of American literature', *Diacritics* 7 (March).

Davey 1983 Frank Davey. *Surviving the Paraphrase: Eleven Essays on Canadian Literature.* Winnipeg: Turnstone Press.

D'Costa 1983 Jean D'Costa. 'The West Indian novelist and language: a search for a literary medium', *Studies in Caribbean Language.* Ed. Carrington Society for Caribbean Linguistics, St Augustine. Trinidad: University of the West Indies.

D'Costa 1984 Jean D'Costa. 'Expression and communication: literary challenges to the Caribbean polydialectical writers', *Journal of Commonwealth Literature*, 19, no. 1.

DeCamp 1971 David DeCamp. 'Towards a generative analysis of a post-Creole speech continuum' in Dell Hymes (ed.) *Pidginisation and Creolisation of Languages.* Cambridge: Cambridge University Press.

de Lisser 1913 Herbert G. de Lisser. *Jane's Career.* London: Collins. 1971.

de Man 1969 Paul de Man. 'The Rhetoric of Temporality' in *Interpretation. Theory and Practice.* Ed. Charles S. Singleton. Baltimore: Johns Hopkins University Press.

de Man 1979 Paul de Man. *Allegories of Reading.* New Haven, Conn.: Yale University Press.

Derrida 1967a Jacques Derrida. *Of*

Grammatology. Trans. Gayatri Chakravorty Spivak. Baltimore: Johns Hopkins University Press. 1976.

Derrida 1967b Jacques Derrida. *Writing and Difference*. Trans. Alan Bass. London: Routledge and Kegan Paul. 1978.

Desani 1948 G. V. Desani. *All About H. Hatterr*. Harmondsworth: Penguin. 1982.

Devisse 1976 J. Devisse *et al*. *The Image of the Black in Western Art*. New York: Morrow. (In French as *L'Image du noir dans l'art occidental*. Fribourg: Office du Livre, 1976).

Docker 1974 John Docker. *Australian Cultural Elites* Sydney: Angus & Robertson.

Docker 1978 John Docker. 'The neo-colonial assumption in the University Teaching of English' in Tiffin 1978.

Docker 1984 John Docker. *In a Critical Condition*. Ringwood Vic.: Penguin.

Dollimore 1986 J. Dollimore. 'The dominant and the deviant: a violent dialectic', *Critical Quarterly*, 28, nos. 1 & 2 (Spring/Summer).

Dorsinville 1974 Max Dorsinville. *Caliban Without Prospero*. Erin, Ont.: Press Porcepic.

Dorsinville 1983 Max Dorsinville. *Le Pays Natal: Essais sur les littératures du Tiersmonde et du Québec*. Dakar: Les Nouvelles Editions Africaines.

Duerden 1975 D. Duerden, *African Art and Literature: The Invisible Present*. London: Heinemann.

Duras 1973 Marguerite Duras, Interview in Suzanne Horer and Jeanne Socquet (eds.) in *La Création étouffée*. Paris: Horay. Quoted in Green and Kahn (1987) p. 100.

During 1985 Simon During. 'Postmodernism or postcolonialism?', *Landfall*, 39, no. 3 (September).

Durix 1987 Jean-Pierre Durix. *The*

Writer Written. The Artist and Creation in the New Literatures in English. Westport: Greenwood.

Dutton 1984 Geoffrey Dutton. *Snow on the Saltbush: The Australian Literary Experience*. Ringwood: Viking.

Eagleton 1986 Mary Eagleton (ed.). *Feminist Literary Theory: A Reader*. London: Basil Blackwell.

Elliott 1967 Brian Elliott *The Landscape of Australian poetry*, Melbourne/Canberra. Cheshire.

Elliott 1979 Brian Elliott (ed.). *The Jindyworobaks*. St Lucia, Qld: University of Queensland Press.

Emerson 1836 Ralph Waldo Emerson. 'Nature' in Stephen E. Whicher (ed.). *Selections from Ralph Waldo Emerson*. Boston: Houghton Mifflin. 1956.

Eri 1970 Vincent Eri. *The Crocodile*. Harmondsworth: Penguin, 1973.

Fabb *et al*. 1987 N. Fabb *et al*. *The Linguistics of Writing: Arguments Between Language and Literature*. Manchester: Manchester University Press.

Fanon 1959 Frantz Fanon. *Studies in a Dying Colonialism*. Trans. H. Chevalier. Harmondsworth: Penguin, 1970.

Fanon 1961 Frantz Fanon. *The Wretched of the Earth*. Harmondsworth: Penguin.

Fanon 1967 Frantz Fanon. *Black Skin. White Masks*. New York: Grove Press.

Fiedler 1960 Leslie Fiedler. *Love and Death in the American Novel*. New York: Dell.

Fiedler 1968 Leslie Fiedler. *The Return of the Vanishing American*. London: Cape.

Fiedler 1973 Leslie Fiedler. *The Stranger in Shakespeare*. London: Croom Helm.

Findley 1984 Timothy Findley. *Not Wanted on the Voyage*. Markham, Ontario: Penguin.

Foucault 1966 Michel Foucault. *The Order of Things: An Archaeology of the Human Sciences*. Trans. A.M. Sheridan. London: Tavistock.

Foucault 1969 Michel Foucault. *The Archaeology of Knowledge*. Trans. A.M. Sheridan Smith. London: Tavistock, 1972.

Foucault 1977a Michel Foucault, *Language. Counter-Memory. Practice.* Trans. Donald Bouchard and Sherry Simon. Oxford: Basil Blackwell.

Foucault 1977b Michel Foucault. 'The political function of the intellectual', *Radical Philosophy*, 17, 12–14. Also in C. Gordon (ed.) *Power/Knowledge: Selected Interviews and Other Writings*. Brighton: Harvester.

Foucault 1982 Michel Foucault. 'Afterword: the subject and power' in Hubert L. Dreyfus and Paul Rabinow, *Michel Foucault: Beyond Structuralism and Hermeneutics*. Brighton: Harvester.

Frame 1962 Janet Frame. *The Edge Of The Alphabet*. New York: Braziller.

Frey 1979 Charles Frey. ' "The Tempest" and the New World', *Shakespeare Quarterly*, 30, 1 (Winter).

Fritschi 1983 Gerhard Fritschi. *Africa and Gutenberg: Exploring Oral Structures in the Modern African Novel.* European University Studies, series 27: Asian and African Studies, vol. 9. New York & Berne: Peter Lang.

Frye 1971 Northrop Frye. *The Bush Garden*. Toronto: Anansi.

Furman 1985 Nellie Furman. 'The politics of language: beyond the gender principle' in Greene and Kahn, 1985.

Furphy 1903 Tom Collins (Joseph Furphy). *Such Is Life*. Sydney: Angus and Robertson, 1944.

Fussell 1965 Edwin Fussell. *Frontier: American Literature and the American West*. Princeton: Princeton University Press.

Gakwandi 1977 S.A. Gakwandi. *The Novel and Contemporary Experience in Africa*. London: Heinemann.

Gardiner 1987 Allan Gardiner. 'J.M. Coetzee's *Dusklands*: colonial encounters of the Robinsonian kind', *World Literature Written in English*, 27, 2.

Gates 1984 Henry Louis Gates Jr. (ed.). *Black Literature and Literary Theory*. London & New York: Methuen.

George 1986 K.M. George (ed.). *Comparative Indian Literature*, 2 vols. Trichur and Madras: Kerala Sahitya Akademi and Macmillan.

Godelier 1977 M. Godelier. *Perspectives in Marxist Anthropology*. Cambridge: Cambridge University Press.

Godelier 1978 M. Godelier. 'The concept of the "Asiatic mode of production" and Marxist models of social evolution' in Seddon 1978.

Goldie 1984 Terry Goldie. 'An Aboriginal present: Australian and Canadian literature in the 1920s', *World Literature Written in English*, 23, 1 (Winter).

Gooneratne 1986 Yasmine Gooneratne. 'Historical "truths" and literary "fictions"', paper delivered at IAUPE Conference: York, September 1986.

Gooneratne 1988 Yasmine Gooneratne. ' "You can't put lies in a book": the historical context of Australian biography' in *Meridian*, 7, 1, May.

Green 1961 H.M. Green. *A History of Australian Literature*, 2 vols., Sydney: Angus and Robertson.

Greenblatt 1976 S.J. Greenblatt. 'Learning to curse: aspects of linguistic colonialism in the sixteenth century' in Chiapelli 1976.

Greene and Kahn 1985 Gayle Greene and Coppélia Kahn (eds). *Making a Difference: Feminist Literary Criticism*. London: Methuen (New Accents).

Griffiths 1978 Gareth Griffiths. *A Double Exile: African and West Indian Writing Between Two Cultures*. London: Marion Boyars.

Griffiths 1987a Gareth Griffiths. 'Imitation, abrogation and appropriation: the production of the post-colonial text', *Kunapipi* 9, 1.

Griffiths 1987b Gareth Griffiths. 'Chinua Achebe: when did you last see your father?' *World Literature Written in English*, 27, 1 (Spring).

Griffiths 1983 Trevor R. Griffiths. '"This Island's mine": Caliban and colonialism', *Yearbook of English Studies*, 13.

Gugelberger 1985 Georg M. Gugelberger (ed.). *Marxism and African Literature*. London: James Currey.

Gunew 1985 Sneja Gunew. 'Distinguishing the textual politics of the marginal voice', *Southern Review*, 18, no. 2 (July).

Gurr and Calder 1974 Andrew Gurr and Angus Calder (eds). *Writers in East Africa*. Nairobi: East African Literature Bureau.

Gurr 1981 Andrew Gurr. *Writers in Exile: The Identity of Home in Modern Literature*. Brighton: Harvester.

Harrex 1977 S.C. Harrex. *The Fire and the Offering: The English Language Novel in India, 1935–1970*, 2 vols Calcutta: Writers Workshop.

Harris 1960 Wilson Harris. *Palace of the Peacock*. London: Faber & Faber.

Harris 1967 Wilson Harris. *Tradition. The Writer and Society*. London, Port of Spain: New Beacon.

Harris 1970a Wilson Harris. *History, Fable and Myth in the Caribbean and Guianas*. Georgetown, Guyana: National History and Arts Council and Ministry of Information.

Harris 1970b Wilson Harris. *Ascent to Omai*. London: Faber & Faber.

Harris 1973 Wilson Harris. 'A talk on the subjective imagination', *New Letters*, 40, 1 (October). (Also in Harris 1981.)

Harris 1981 Wilson Harris. *Explorations: A Selection of Talks and Articles 1966–1981*. Ed. Hena Maes-Jelinek. Aarhus: Dangaroo.

Harris 1983 Wilson Harris. *The Womb of Space: The Cross-Cultural Imagination*. Westport, Connecticut: Greenwood.

Harris 1985 Wilson Harris. 'Adversarial contexts and creativity', *New Left Review*, 154 (Nov.–Dec.).

Harris 1986 Wilson Harris. *Carnival*. London: Faber & Faber.

Harris 1987 Wilson Harris. *The Infinite Rehearsal*. London: Faber & Faber.

Healy 1978 J.J. Healy. *The Treatment of the Aborigine in Australian Literature*. St Lucia: University of Queensland Press.

Hearne 1974 John Hearne. 'The wide Sargasso Sea: a West Indian reflection', *Cornhill Magazine*, 180, (Summer).

Heidegger 1927 Martin Heidegger. *Being and Time*. Trans. John Macquarrie and Edward Robinson, New York and Evanston: Harper & Row.

Herbert 1938 Xavier Herbert. *Capricornia*. Sydney: Publicist Pub. Co., and Angus and Robertson.

Hergenhan 1988 L. Hergenhan (ed.). *The Penguin History of Australian Literature*. Ringwood: Penguin.

Heywood 1971 Christopher Heywood. *Perspectives on African Literature*. London: Heinemann.

Hodge 1970 Merle Hodge. *Crick Crack Monkey*. London: Deutsch.

Holst-Petersen and Rutherford 1976 K. Holst-Petersen and A. Rutherford. *Enigma of Values: an Introduction to Wilson Harris*. Aarhus: Dangaroo.

Holst-Petersen and Rutherford 1985 K. Holst-Petersen and A. Rutherford (eds.). *A Double Colonization: Colonial & Post-Colonial Women's Writing*. Aarhus: Dangaroo.

Howe 1874 Joseph Howe. *Poems and Essays*. Montreal: Lovell.

Hulme 1986 Peter Hulme. *Colonial Encounters*. London: Methuen.

Hyland 1984 Peter Hyland. 'Singapore: poet, critic, audience', *World Literature Written in English*, 23, 1 (Winter).

Hyland 1986 Peter Hyland *Discharging the Canon*. Singapore U.P.

Ihimaera 1973 Witi Ihimaera. *Tangi*. Auckland: Heinemann.

Ingamells 1938 Rex Ingamells. 'Conditional culture' in Barnes 1969.

Irele 1975 Abiola Irele. 'Tradition and the Yoruba writer: D.O. Fagunwa, Amos Tutuola and Wole Soyinka', *Odu*, 2.

rele 1981 Abiola Irele. *The African Experience in Literature and Ideology*. London: Heinemann.

Irigaray 1985a Luce Irigaray. *Speculum of the Other Woman*. Ithaca, New York: Cornell University Press.

Irigaray 1985b Luce Irigaray. *This Sex Which is not One*. Ithaca, New York: Cornell University Press.

Ismond 1971 Pat Ismond. 'Walcott versus Brathwaite', *Caribbean Quarterly*, 17, nos 3 & 4 (September–December).

Iyengar 1962 K.R. Srinivasa Iyengar. *Indian Writing in English*. New Delhi: Sterling, 1984.

Jakobson and Halle 1956 Roman Jakobson and Morris Halle. *Fundamentals of Language*. S-Gravenhage: Mouton.

Jameson 1971 Fredric Jameson. *Marxism and Form: Twentieth Century Dialectical Theories of Literature*. Princeton: Princeton University Press.

Jameson 1981 Fredric Jameson. *The Political Unconscious: Narrative as a Socially Symbolic Act*. London: Methuen.

JanMohammed 1983 Abdul Jan-Mohammed. *Manichean Aesthetics: The Politics of Literature in Colonial Africa*. Amherst: University of Mass.

JanMohammed 1984 Abdul Jan-Mohammed. 'Humanism and minority literature: towards a definition of a counter-hegemonic discourse', *Boundary*, 2, 12,3–13,1 (Spring/Fall).

JanMohammed 1985 Abdul Jan-Mohammed. 'The economy of Manichean allegory: the function of racial difference in colonial literature', *Critical Inquiry*, 12, 1 (Autumn).

Jeyifo 1979 Biodun Jeyifo. 'Patterns and trends in committed African drama', *Positive Review*, 1, 2.

Jeyifo 1980 Biodun Jeyifo. *The Truthful Lie: Towards a Radical Sociology of African Literature*. London: New Beacon.

Jones 1965 Eldred Durosimo Jones. *Othello's Countrymen: The African in English Renaissance Drama*. London: Oxford University Press.

Jones 1965 Joseph Jones. *Terranglia: The Case for English as World-Literature*. New York: Twayne.

Jones 1976 Joseph Jones. *Radical Cousins: Nineteenth Century American and Australian Writers*. St Lucia: University of Queensland Press.

Jones 1985 Ann Rosalind Jones. 'Inscribing femininity: French theories of the feminine' in Greene and Kahn 1985.

Jussawalla 1985 Adil Jussawalla.

Family Quarrels: Towards a Criticism of Indian Writing in English. Berne: Peter Lang.

Kantak 1972 V.Y. Kantak. 'The language of Indian fiction in English' in Naik, Desai, and Amur 1972.

Kaplan 1985 Sydney Janet Kaplan. 'Varieties of feminist criticism' in Greene and Kahn 1985.

Kendall 1870 Henry Kendall. *Leaves From Australian Forests: Poetical Works of Henry Kendall*. Sydney: Lloyd O'Neil. 1970.

Khubchandani 1981 Lachman Khubchandani. *English in India: A Sociolinguistic Perspective*. London: Centre for Commonwealth Studies.

Kiernan 1982 Brian Kiernan (ed.). *The Essential Henry Lawson*. Melbourne: Currey O'Neil.

Kirkby 1982 Joan Kirkby. *The American Model: Influence and Independence in Australian Poetry*. Sydney: Hale and Iremonger.

Kirkby 1985 Joan Kirkby. 'The American Prospero', *Southern Review*, 18, 1 (March).

Klinck 1965 Carl F. Klinck. *Literary History of Canada: Canadian Literature in English*, 3 vols, Toronto/London: University of Toronto Press.

Kramer 1981 L. Kramer (ed.). *The Oxford History of Australian Literature*. Melbourne: Oxford University Press.

Krishnamoorthy 1984 K. Krishnamoorthy. 'The all-time relevance of Bharata's literary canons' in Narasimhaiah and Srinath 1984.

Krishnamoorthy 1986 K. Krishnamoorthy. 'Makings of the Indian novel', *The Literary Criterion*, 21, nos 1 & 2.

Krishna Rayan 1984 Krishna Rayan. 'The case for the Indian poetic based on the dhvani theory' in Narasimhaiah and Srinath 1984.

Kroetsch 1974 Robert Kroetsch. 'Unhiding the hidden: recent

Canadian fiction', *Journal of Canadian Fiction*, 3.

Labov 1969 William Labov. *The Social Stratification of English in New York City*. Washington DC: Centre for Applied Linguistics.

Lamming 1954 George Lamming. *The Emigrants*. London: Michael Joseph.

Lamming 1960 George Lamming. *The Pleasures of Exile*. London: Michael Joseph.

Lamming 1970 George Lamming. *In the Castle of My Skin*. London: Longmans.

Larson 1971 C.R. Larson. *The Emergence of African Fiction*. Bloomington: Indiana University Press.

Larson 1973 C.R. Larson. 'Heroic Ethnocentrism: the idea of universality in literature', *The American Scholar*, 42, 3.

Lashley 1984 Cliff Lashley. 'Towards a critical framework for Jamaican literature: a reading of the fiction of Victor Stafford Reid and other Jamaican writers'. Unpublished Ph.D. dissertation. St Augustine, Trinidad: University of the West Indies.

Lawrence 1916 D.H. Lawrence. *The Rainbow*. London: Heinemann.

Lawson 1980 Alan Lawson. 'Acknowledging colonialism: revisions of the Australian tradition' in A.F. Madden and W.M. Morris-Jones (eds) *Australia and Britain: Studies in a Changing Relationship*. London/Sydney: Cass/Sydney University Press.

Lawson 1983 Alan Lawson. 'Patterns, preferences and preoccupations: the discovery of nationality in Canadian and Australian literatures' in P. Crabb (ed.) *Theory and Practice in Comparative Studies: Canada, Australia and New Zealand*. Sydney: ANSACZ.

Lee 1974 Dennis Lee. 'Cadence,

country, silence: writing in colonial space', *Boundary 2*,3, 1 (Fall).

Lee 1977 Dennis Lee. *Savage Fields*. Toronto: Ananse.

Le Page and DeCamp 1960 Robert Le Page and David DeCamp. *Jamaican Creole*. London: Macmillan.

Le Page 1969 Robert Le Page. 'Dialect in West Indian literature', *JCL*, no. 7.

Lindfors 1975 Bernth Lindfors (ed.). *Critical Perspectives on Nigerian Literature*. London: Heinemann.

Lyotard 1979 Jean-François Lyotard. *The Postmodern Condition – A Report on Knowledge*. Trans. Geoff Bennington and Brian Massumi. Manchester: Manchester University Press.

McCutcheon 1969 David McCutcheon. *Indian Writing in English: Critical Essays*. Calcutta: Writer's Workshop.

McDonald 1984 A.G. McDonald, 'Men in fetters: *For the Term of his Natural Life* and *Die the Long Day*', *World Literature Written in English*, 21, 1.

McDougall and Whitlock 1987 Russell McDougall and Gillian Whitlock. *Australian/Canadian Literatures in English: Comparative Perspectives*. North Ryde: Methuen.

McGregor 1985 Gaile McGregor. *The Wacousta Syndrome: Explorations in the Canadian Landscape*. Toronto: University of Toronto Press.

Mahood 1977 M.M. Mahood. *The Colonial Encounter*. London: Rex Collings.

Mandel 1971 Eli Mandel (ed.). *Contexts of Canadian Criticism*. Chicago: Chicago University Press.

Mannoni 1950 O. Mannoni. *Prospero and Caliban: The Psychology of Colonization*. New York: Praeger 1964 (first published in French as *Psychologie de la Colonisation*).

Marx 1964 Leo Marx. *The Machine in the Garden: Technology and the Pastoral Ideal in America*. New York: Oxford University Press.

Massa 1979 Daniel Massa. (ed.) *Individual and Community in Commonwealth Literature*. Msida: University of Malta Press.

Matthews 1962 John P. Matthews. *Tradition in Exile*. Toronto: University of Toronto Press.

Matthews 1979 John P. Matthews. 'Lifeboats for the Titanic: patterns of identity in Commonwealth literature', *ACLALS Bulletin*, 5th series, 2.

Maxwell 1965 D.E.S. Maxwell. 'Landscape and Theme' in Press 1965.

Mazrui 1967 Ali A. Mazrui. 'Abstract verse and African tradition', *Zuka*, 1 (September).

Mehta 1968 P.P. Mehta. *Indo-Anglian Fiction: An Assessment*. Bareilly: Prakash Book Depot.

Melville 1857 Herman Melville. *The Confidence Man*. New York: Signet. 1964.

Memmi 1965 Albert Memmi. *The Coloniser and the Colonised*. New York: Orion Press.

Moi 1987 Toril Moi. *Sexual/Textual Politics: Feminist Literary Theory*. London: Methuen (New Accents).

Mokashi-Punekar 1978 Shankkar Mokashi-Punekar. *Theoretical and Practical Studies in English*. Dharwad: Karnatak University.

Monkman 1981 Leslie Monkman. *A Native Heritage: Images of the Indian in English Canadian Literature*. Toronto: University of Toronto Press.

Moore 1969 Gerald Moore. *The Chosen Tongue: English Writing in the Tropical World*. London: Longmans.

Moore 1971 Tom Inglis Moore. *Social Patterns in Australian Literature*. Sydney: Angus and Robertson.

Morris 1973 Mervyn Morris (ed.).

'Introduction' to Vic Reid's *New Day* (Reid 1949).

Mukherjee 1971 Meenakshi Mukherjee. *The Twice-born Fiction*. New Delhi and London: Heinemann.

Mukherjee 1977 Meenakshi Mukherjee. *Considerations*. Bombay: Allied Publishers.

Mukherjee 1981 Sujit Mukherjee. *Some Positions on a Literary History of India*. Mysore:

Mukherjee 1985 Meenakshi Mukherjee. *Realism and Reality: the Novel and Society in India*. Oxford and New Delhi: Oxford U.P.

Murphy 1987 Murphy. 'Review of Jean-Francois Lyotard's *The Postmodern Condition – A Report on Knowledge*', *The Literary Criterion*, vol. 22, no. 1.

Murray 1965 Les A. Murray. *The Ilex Tree*. Canberra: Australian National University Press.

Murray 1969 Les A. Murray. 'Wilderness' in *The Weatherboard Cathedral*. Sydney: Angus and Robertson.

Murray 1986 Les A. Murray (ed.). *New Oxford Book of Australian Poetry*. London: Oxford University Press.

Naik, Desai, and Amur 1972 M.K. Naik, S.K. Desai, and G.S. Amur. *Critical Essays on Indian Writing in English*. Dharwar: Karnatak University.

Naik 1979 M.K. Naik. *Aspects of Indian Writing in English*. Madras: Macmillan.

Naik 1981 M.K. Naik. *A History of Indian Writing in English*. New Delhi: Sahitya Akademi.

Naik 1983 M.K. Naik. *Dimensions of Indian-English Literature*. New Delhi: Sterling.

Naipaul 1957 V.S. Naipaul. *The Mystic Masseur*. Harmondsworth: Penguin. 1985.

Naipaul 1967 V.S. Naipaul. *The Mimic Men*. London: Andre Deutsch (the Russell edition 1974).

Naipaul 1971 V.S. Naipaul. *In A Free State*. London: Andre Deutsch.

Naipaul 1975 V.S. Naipaul. *Guerrillas*. London: Deutsch.

Narasimhaiah 1969 C.D. Narasimhaiah. *The Swan and the Eagle*. Simla: Indian Institute of Advanced Study.

Narasimhaiah 1977 C.D. Narasimhaiah. *Moving Frontiers of English Studies in India*. New Delhi: S. Chaud.

Narasimhaiah 1978 C.D. Narasimhaiah (ed.). *Awakened Conscience*. New Delhi: Sterling.

Narasimhaiah and Srinath 1984 C.D. Narasimhaiah and C.N. Srinath (eds) *A Common Poetic for Indian Literatures*. Mysore: Dhvanyāloka Publications.

Narayan 1967 R.K. Narayan. *The Vendor of Sweets*. Harmondsworth: Penguin.

Nazareth 1972 Peter Nazareth. *Literature and Society in Modern Africa*. Nairobi: East African Literature Bureau.

Nemser 1971 W. Nemser. 'Systems of foreign language learners' *IRAL (International Review of Applied Linguistics)* vol. 9, 2 (May).

Neuman and Wilson 1982 Shirley Neuman and Robert Wilson. *Labyrinths of Voice: Conversations with Robert Kroetsch*. Edmonton: NeWest.

New 1972 W.H. New. *Articulating West: Essays on Purpose and Form in Modern Canadian Literature*. Toronto: New Press.

New 1975 W.H. New. *Among Worlds*. Erin, Ontario: Press Porcepic.

New 1978 W.H. New, 'New language, new world' in Narasimhaiah 1978.

New 1987 W.H. New. *Dreams of Speech and Violence: The Art of the*

Short Story in Canada and New Zealand. Toronto: University of Toronto Press.

New 1989 W.H. New. *A History of Canadian Literature*. London: Macmillan.

Ngara 1982 Emmanuel Ngara. *Stylistic Criticism and the African Novel*. London: Heinemann.

Ngara 1985 Emmanuel Ngara. *Art and Ideology in the African Novel; a Study of the Influence of Marxism on African Writing*. London: Heinemann.

Ngugi 1967 Ngugi wa Thiong'o. *A Grain of Wheat*. London: Heinemann.

Ngugi 1972 Ngugi wa Thiong'o. *Homecoming: Essays on African and Caribbean Literature, Culture and Politics*. London: Heinemann.

Ngugi 1981 Ngugi wa Thiong'o. *Writers in Politics*. London: Heinemann.

Ngugi 1983 Ngugi wa Thiong'o. *Barrel of a Pen – Resistance to Repression in Neo-Colonial Kenya*. Trenton, New Jersey: African World Press.

Ngugi 1986 Ngugi wa Thiong'o. *Decolonising the Mind: the Politics of Language in African Literature*. London: Currey.

Nkosi 1986 Lewis Nkosi. *Mating Birds*. New York: St Martin's.

Obiechina 1975 Emmanuel Obiechina. *Culture, Tradition and Society in the West African Novel*. Cambridge: Cambridge U.P.

Ogungbesan 1976 K. Ogungbesan. 'Literature and cultural values in Nigeria', *West Africa Journal of Modern Languages*, 2.

Ogungbesan 1979 K. Ogungbesan. *New West African Literature*. London: Heinemann.

Okara 1964 Gabriel Okara. *The Voice*. African Writers Series: London, Nairobi, Ibadan, Lusaka: Heinemann, 1970.

Okeke-Ezigbo 1982 'The role of the Nigerian writer in a Carthaginian society', *Okike*, 21.

Olsen 1978 Tillie Olsen. *Silences*. New York: Delacorte Press/Seymour Lawrence. (London: Virago, 1980).

Omotoso 1975 Kole Omotoso. 'Form and Content in Ideologically Committed Societies', *Afriscope*, 5, 12.

Onoge 1984 Omofume Onoge. 'Towards a Marxist sociology of African literature', *Isala*, 2.

Ooi 1984 Ooi Boo Eng. 'Malaysia and Singapore', *JCL*, 19, 2.

Osofisan 1984 Femi Osofisan. 'The artist as sociologist' *West Africa*, 27 (August).

Owens 1976 Joseph Owens. *Dread: The Rastafarians of Jamaica*. London: Heinemann.

Owens 1983 Craig Owens. 'The discourse of Others: feminists and postmodernism' in Hal Foster (ed.). *The Anti-Aesthetic: Essays on Postmodern Culture*. Port Toursont: Bay Press.

Palmer 1979 Eustace Palmer. *The Growth of the African Novel*. London: Heinemann.

Palmer 1905 Vance Palmer. 'An Australian national art', *Steele Rudd Magazine* (January), reprinted in Barnes 1969.

Palmer 1954 Vance Palmer. *The Legend of the Nineties*. Sydney: Angus and Robertson.

Paniker 1982 Ayyappa Paniker. 'A dialogue with Cleanth Brooks' in Narasimhaiah and Srinath 1982.

Paniker 1986 Ayyappa Paniker. 'The oral narrative tradition in Malayalam', *The Literary Criterion*, 21, nos 1 & 2.

Parry 1987 Benita Parry. 'Problems in current theories of colonial discourse', *Oxford Literary Review*, 9, nos 1 & 2.

Parthasarathy 1977 'Homecoming' in *Rough Passage*. New Delhi. Cited in Chiratan Kulshrestha, *Contemporary Indian English Verse: an Evaluation*. New Delhi: Arnold-Heinemann.

Patankar 1984 R.B. Patankar. 'The three alternatives' in Narasimhaiah and Srinath 1984.

Pêcheux 1975 Michel Pêcheux. *Language. Semantics and Ideology*. Trans. Harbans Nagpal. New York: St Martins, 1982.

Phillips 1958 Arthur Phillips. 'The cultural cringe' in *The Australian Tradition: Studies in a Colonial Culture*. Melbourne: Cheshire.

Poe 1837 Edgar Allen Poe. *Narrative of Arthur Gordon Pym of Nantucket*. Harmondsworth: Penguin.

Powe 1984 B.W. Powe. *A Climate Charged: Essays on Canadian Writers*. Oakville, Ontario: Mosaic.

Press 1965 John Press (ed.). *Commonwealth: Unity and Diversity within a Common Culture*. London: Heinemann.

Prichard 1929 K.S. Prichard. *Coonardoo*. London: Jonathan Cape.

Ramanujan 1985 A.K. Ramanujan. *Poems of Love and War from the Eight Anthologies and the Ten Songs of the Classical Tamil*. Trans. A.K. Ramanujan. New York: Columbia University Press.

Rao 1938 Raja Rao. *Kanthapura*. New York: New Directions.

Reddy 1979 G.A. Reddy. *Indian Writing in English and its Audience*. Bareilly: Prakash Book Depot.

Reid 1949 V.S. Reid. *New Day*. London: Heinemann.

Reinecke and Tokimasa 1934 John E. Reinekke and A. Tokimasa. 'The English dialect of Hawaii', *American Speech*, no. 9.

Reising 1987 Russell Reising. *The Unusable Past: Theory and the Study of American Literature*. New York

and London: Methuen (New Accents).

Rey 1971 P.P. Rey. *Colonialisme, Néo-Colonialisme et Transition au Capitalisme*. Paris.

Richardson 1973 Major John Richardson. *Wacouste: A Tale of the Pontiac Conspiracy*. Toronto: McClelland & Stewart.

Ricou 1973 Laurence Ricou. *Vertical Man/Horizontal World*. Vancouver: University of British Columbia Press.

Riemenschneider 1983 Dieter Riemenschneider ed. *The History and Historiography of Commonwealth Literature*. Tübingen: Gunter Narr.

Riemenschneider 1984 Dieter Riemenschneider. 'Ngugi wa Thiong'o and the question of language and literature in Kenya', *World Literature Written in English*, 24, 1 (Summer).

Ringe 1966 Donald A. Ringe. *Charles Brockden Brown*. Boston: Twayne.

Roderick 1972 Colin Roderick (ed.). *Henry Lawson: Short Stories and Sketches 1888–1922*. Vol. 1 of *Collected Prose*. Sydney: Angus and Robertson.

Rubadiri 1967 David Rubadiri. *No Bride Price*. Nairobi: East Africa Publishing House.

Ruegg 1979 Maria Ruegg. 'Metaphor and metonymy: the logic of structuralist rhetoric', *Glyph*, 6.

Rushdie 1981 Salman Rushdie. *Midnight's Children*. London: Picador, 1982.

Rushdie 1985 Interview with Salman Rushdie in *Kunapipi*, 7, no. 1.

Ruthven 1968 K.K. Ruthven. 'Yeats, Lawrence and the Savage God', *Critical Quarterly*, 10, nos 1 & 2 (Spring/Summer).

Said 1978 Edward Said. *Orientalism*. New York: Pantheon.

Said 1984 Edward Said. *The World,*

the Text and the Critic. London: Faber.

Said 1985 Edward Said. 'Orientalism reconsidered', Cultural Critique. 1 (Fall).

Sartre 1943 Jean-Paul Sartre. Being and Nothingness: An Essay on Phenomenological Ontology. Trans. Hazel Barnes. London: Methuen.

Saussure 1916 Ferdinand Saussure. Course in General Linguistics. Trans. and ed. C. Bally and A. Schehaye. New York: Philosophical Library 1959.

Schmidt 1985 Nancy J. Schmidt. 'Review of Gerhard Fritschi, Africa and Gutenberg: Exploring Oral Structures in the Modern African Novel', Research in African Literatures, 16, 4 (Winter).

Seddon 1978 David Seddon (ed.), Relations of Production: Marxist Approaches to Economic Anthropology. London: Cass.

Selinker 1972 Larry Selinker. 'Interlanguage' IRAL (International Review of Applied Linguistics), 10, 2 (May).

Selvon 1975 Sam Selvon. Moses Ascending. London: Davis-Pointer.

Senghor 1977 Selected Poems of Leopold Sedar Senghor. Abiola Irele (ed.) New York: Cambridge University Press.

Serle 1973 Geoffrey Serle. From Deserts the Prophets Come: The Creative Spirit in Australia 1788-1972. Melbourne: Heinemann.

Shadle 1981 Mark Shadle. 'Polyrhythms of love and violence in No Bride Price: music of African spheres', Pacific Moana Quarterly (Special African Issue ed. Peter Nazareth).

Shaw 1985 Gregory Shaw. 'Art and dialectic in the work of Wilson Harris', New Left Review, 153 (Sept.–Oct.).

Shoemaker 1989 Adam Shoemaker.

Black Words White Page: Aboriginal Literature 1929-1988. St Lucia, Qld.: University of Queensland Press.

Singh 1984 Kirpal Singh. 'An approach to Singapore writing in English', Ariel, 15, 2 (April).

Sinha 1979 Krishna Nanda Sinha. Indian Writing in English. New Delhi: Heritage.

Sinnett 1856 Frederick Sinnett. 'The fiction fields of Australia' The Journal of Australia 1856. Reprinted in Barnes 1969.

Slemon 1986 Stephen Slemon. 'Revisioning allegory. Wilson Harris' Carnival' Kunapipi, 8, no. 2.

Slemon 1987a Stephen Slemon. 'Cultural alterity and colonial discourse', Southern Review, 21 (March).

Slemon 1987b Stephen Slemon. 'Monuments of empire: allegory/counter - discourse / post - colonial writing', Kunapipi, 9, 3, pp. 1–16.

Slemon 1988a Stephen Slemon. 'Magic realism as post-colonial discourse', Canadian Literature, 116 (Spring).

Slemon 1988b Stephen Slemon. 'Carnival and the canon', Ariel 19, 3, July.

Sowande 1979 Bode Sowande. Farewell to Babylon and Other Plays. London: Longmans.

Soyinka 1965 Wole Soyinka. The Interpreters. London: Andre Deutsch.

Soyinka 1968 Wole Soyinka. 'The writer in an African state'. Transition, 31.

Soyinka 1975 Wole Soyinka. 'Neo-Tarzanism: the poetics of pseudo-tradition' Transition, no. 48.

Soyinka 1976 Wole Soyinka. Myth, Literature and the African World. Cambridge: Cambridge University Press.

Soyinka 1986 Wole Soyinka. 'This past must address its present'.

Nobel Prize Lecture, *PMLA*, 102, 5 (October).

Spivak 1981 G. C. Spivak. 'French feminism in an international frame'. *Yale French Studies*, vol. 62.

Spivak 1985a G.C. Spivak. 'The Rani of Simur' in Francis Barker et al. (eds) *Europe and its Others*, vol. 1. Colchester: University of Essex Press.

Spivak 1985b G.C. Spivak. 'Three women's texts and a critique of imperialism'. *Critical Inquiry*, no. 12, 1 (Autumn).

Spivak 1985c G.C. Spivak. 'Can the subaltern speak? Speculations on widow sacrifice', *Wedge*, 7/8 (Winter/Spring).

Spivak 1987 G.C. Spivak. *In Other Worlds: Essays in Cultural Politics*. London: Methuen.

Stonum 1981 Gary Lee Stonum. 'Undoing American history', *Diacritics*, 11 (September).

Stow 1962 Randolph Stow. *Outrider. Poems, 1956–62*. London: Mac-Donald.

Stow 1979 Randolph Stow. *Visitants*. London: Picador.

Subramanyam 1984 'Some notes based on the Indian and western traditions' in Narasimhaiah and Srinath 1984.

Taiwo 1976 Oladele Taiwo. *Culture and the Nigerian Novel*. London: Macmillan.

Tallman 1971 'Wolf in the snow' in Mandel 1971.

Tejani 1979 'Modern African literature and the legacy of cultural colonialism', *World Literature Written in English*, no. 18.

Terdiman 1985 Richard Terdiman. *Discourse/Counter-Discourse: The Theory and Practice of Symbolic Resistance in Nineteenth-Century France*. Ithaca and London: Cornell University Press.

Terray 1975 E. Terray. 'Class and class consciousness in an Abron kingdom of Guyana' in Bloch 1985.

Thieme 1984 John Thieme. 'Beyond history: Margaret Atwood's *Surfacing* and Robert Kroetsch's *Badlands*' in Shirley Chew (ed.). *Re-visions of Canadian Literature*. Leeds: Institute of Bibliography & Textual Studies.

Tiffin 1978 Chris Tiffin (ed.). *South Pacific Images*. St Lucia. Qld.: SPACLALS.

Tiffin 1983 Helen Tiffin. 'Commonwealth literature: comparison and judgement' in Riemenschneider, 1984.

Tiffin 1984 Helen Tiffin. 'Commonwealth literature and comparative methodology', *World Literature Written in English*, 23, 1 (Winter).

Tiffin 1987 Helen Tiffin. 'Comparative literature and post-colonial counter-discourse', *Kunapipi*, 9, 3.

Todorov 1974 Tzvetan Todorov. *The Conquest of America: The Question of the Other*. Trans. Richard Howard. New York: Harper and Row 1982.

Tutuola 1952 Amos Tutuola. *The Palm-Wine Drinkard*. London: Faber & Faber.

Twain 1885 Samuel Clemens. (Mark Twain) *The Adventures of Huckleberry Finn*. New York and London: Holt Rinehart Winston 1967.

Verghese 1971 C. Paul Verghese. *Problems of the Indian Creative Writer in English*. Bombay: Somaiya.

Viswanathan 1987 Gauri Viswanathan. 'The beginnings of English literary study in British India', *Oxford Literary Review*, 9, nos 1 & 2.

Walcott 1974a Derek Walcott. 'The Caribbean: culture or mimicry?', *Journal of Inter-American Studies*, 16, 1.

Walcott 1974b Derek Walcott. 'The Muse of History' in Coombes (ed.) 1974.

Walcott 1979 Derek Walcott. *The Star-Apple Kingdom*. New York: Farrar, Straus and Giroux. 1979.

Walker 1983 Alice Walker. *In Search of Our Mothers' Gardens: Womanist Prose*, New York: Harcourt Brace Jovanovitch. (London: The Women's Press, 1984).

Walsh 1970 William Walsh. *A Manifold Voice: Studies in Commonwealth Literature*. London: Chatto & Windus.

Walsh 1973 William Walsh. *Commonwealth Literature*. London: Oxford University Press.

Ward 1958 Russell Ward. *The Australian Legend*. Melbourne: Oxford U.P.

Wasserman 1984 Renata Wasserman. 'Re-inventing the New World: Cooper and Alencar', *Comparative Literature*, 36, no. 2 (Spring).

Watters 1961 R.E. Watters. 'Original relations: a genographic approach to the literatures of Canada and Australia', *Canadian Literature*, no. 7 (Winter).

Webb 1969 Francis Webb. *Collected Poems*. Sydney: Angus and Robertson.

Wedde 1985a Ian Wedde (ed.). *The Penguin Book of New Zealand Verse*. Auckland and London: Penguin.

Wedde 1985b Ian Wedde. 'Checking out the foundations: editing the "Penguin Book of New Zealand Verse"', *Meanjin*, 44, 3 (Sept.).

White 1957 Patrick White. *Voss*. London: Eyre & Spottiswoode.

White 1973 Hayden White. *Metahistory*. Baltimore: Johns Hopkins.

Wiebe 1973 Rudy Wiebe. *The Temptations of Big Bear*. Toronto: McClelland and Stewart.

Wieland 1988 James Wieland. *The Ensphering Mind*. Washington, Three Continents.

Wilkes 1981 G.A. Wilkes. *The Stockyard and the Croquet Lawn*. Melbourne: Edward Arnold.

Williams 1969 Denis Williams. *Image and Idea in the Arts of Guyana*. Georgetown, Guyana: (Edgar Mittelholzer Memorial Lectures. National History and Arts Council, Ministry of Information).

Williams 1973 Haydn Williams. *Studies in Modern Indian Fiction*. Calcutta: Writer's Workshop.

Williams 1976 Haydn Williams. *Indo-Anglian Literature 1800–1970; a Survey*. Madras: Orient Longman.

Willis 1985 Susan Willis. 'Black women writers: taking a critical perspective' in Greene and Kahn 1985.

Wright 1966 Judith Wright. 'Australia's double aspect', *Preoccupations in Australian Poetry*. Melbourne: Oxford University Press.

Zabus 1985 Chantal Zabus. 'A Calibanic tempest in Anglophone and Francophone new world writing', *Canadian Literature*, 104 (Spring).

Zimmerman 1985 Bonnie Zimmerman. 'What has never been: an overview of lesbian feminist criticism' in Greene and Kahn 1985.

Index